RELIGION IN AMERICA TO 1865

Religion in America to 1865

BRYAN F. LeBEAU

NEW YORK UNIVERSITY PRESS
Washington Square, New York

To Matthew Le Beau with much love

Library of Congress Cataloging-in-Publication Data
LeBeau, Bryan F.
Religion in America to 1865/Bryan LeBeau
    p. cm.
Includes bibliographical references and index.
ISBN 0-8147-5163-6 (alk. paper) – ISBN 0-8147-5164-4 (pbk : alk. paper)
    1. United States–Religion–18th century 2. United States–Religion–19th Century
1 Title.
BL2525 .L434 2000
200'.973'0903–dc21   99-056488

First published in the U.S.A. in 2000 by
NEW YORK UNIVERSITY PRESS
Washington Square
New York NY 10003

Typeset in Monotype Fournier
by Bibliocraft, Dundee, and
printed and bound in Great Britain
by The Cromwell Press, Trowbridge, Wilts

Contents

Acknowledgements

As with most efforts of this kind, what appears in print is the product of many years and minds and the invaluable assistance of scores of people. Unfortunately, at this point I can name only those few directly related to this project. Thanks to Philip John Davies, BAAS Paperbacks General Editor, for his encouragement; to Nicola Carr, Commissioning Editor for Edinburgh University Press for her attention to the myriad of details involved in successfully launching this project; and to James Dale, Managing Desk Editor for EUP for seeing my manuscript through to publication. I very much appreciate the valuable advice offered by Joyce Goodfriend, Professor of History at the University of Denver, and Deborah Madsen, Professor of English at South Bank University, who read and commented on my proposal for this book in its early stages. As any scholar knows, research is nearly impossible – or at least it can be made very difficult – without the support of a team of professional librarians. My thanks to the Reference Department of the Reinert Alumni Library at Creighton University for that capable, generous, and always gracious assistance. Thank you, in particular, to Creighton Reference Librarian Chris Le Beau, for her continued support far beyond what any person ought to expect. And, finally, I owe a large debt of gratitude to my secretary, Marlene Lenhardt, whose dilligence in preparing and continually reworking this manusript every step of the way made all the difference.

Introduction

The principal themes in American history to 1865 are growth, diversity and adaptation, all of which contributed to the formation of a new nation from thirteen tiny separate colonies. Such were the themes of American religious history to 1865 as well. The number and diversity of religious bodies increased to levels unprecedented in the older nations of the world, as did the percentage of Americans that chose to belong to those religious bodies, all the while undergoing a process whereby churches with their roots in Europe were forced to adapt to their new environment, becoming something quite different from their ancestral faiths in Europe, if not uniquely American.

Regardless of their intent upon their arrival on the shores of North America, religious bodies had to play by a different set of rules and to modify their beliefs and behaviour in such manner as to be successful in what came to be a game of winning over the hearts and minds of a population that had a choice as to which church they chose to join. For enlightened philosophical as well as conservative religious reasons, but mostly because they had no choice – given their numbers and diversity – establishment gave way to denominationalism and voluntarism, and, as Sidney Mead later observed, religious leaders were forced to change their ways of attracting and holding adherents from coercion and persuasion.[1] The results, as we shall see, were astounding.

The Civil War remains the most traumatic event in American history, testing, as President Abraham Lincoln put it, whether the United States, or any other nation, 'conceived in liberty, and dedicated to the proposition that all men are created equal, can long endure'.[2] Such was the case among American churches. Slavery and related issues not only tore the nation apart, pitting American against American, but also divided the nation's religious bodies. Much as the American nation would be forever changed but nevertheless survive and even grow stronger from the war, however, so too did American churches.

I have told the story of American religion to 1865 in the context of a more or less straight line, or chronological, history of the United States. The approach affords me the opportunity to make the necessary connections between American religious and secular history: the role of religion in the American Revolution, in nineteenth-century reform, in the Civil War, etc. I begin in Chapter 1 with one group and one element of history that until comparatively recently has either been omitted from, or marginalized in, the story of American, and American religious, history – Native American religion

Foreshadowing the situation among Euro-American religious bodies in the United States by 1865, hundreds of different Native American groups and religions existed in what would become the United States at the time of colonization. I explore both their diversity and common elements. I organize my remarks on diversity by separating Native Americans into primarily hunter-gatherers and more sedentary agricultural groups, and then point to those religious beliefs and rituals that tied them together. I also explore the impact of European contact, settlement and religious missions – Spanish, French, British and even American, Protestant and Catholic – on Native American religion. Native American religions, much like Native Americans themselves, would nearly disappear in the face of waves of Euro-American population, but they would survive. Much as would happen to religions of European origins in America, adherents would be forced into foreign environments to which they had to adapt, both physically and culturally. In some cases, significantly new beliefs would result.

In Chapter 1 I also provide an introduction to Spanish and French colonization in those parts of North America that would become the United States. In Chapter 2 I turn to British colonization. In complete contrast to Spanish and French efforts, the thirteen colonies of British North America were founded almost entirely by Protestants. In religious terms British colonization was an extension of the English Reformation, both in settlement of the colonies by Protestants and in the dominance among those Protestant colonists of those who continued to dissent from the Church of England and its Elizabethan Settlement. Once again I point to the diversity of religions that came to exist in the colonies by the end of the colonial period and the seemingly inescapable acceptance of religious tolerance and even religious freedom just to keep the peace.

In the closing pages of Chapter 2, I discuss the First Great Awakening and its impact on American religious development – its continuing the process by which religions with roots in the Old World adapted to the New. In Chapter 3 I explore the Awakening's impact on the generation of the American Revolution, relating New Light theology, millennial thought and even evangelical rhetoric on morals and ethical behaviour to growing disenchantment with what an increasing number of Americans saw as British immorality and corruption. God's visible power in the Great Awakening convinced many religious leaders and those born again: that the pace of the teleological history, in which most believed, was accelerating; that the Second Coming, or at least God's millennium on Earth, was close at hand; and that the millennium might well begin in America, a land settled by God's chosen people, with independence from the country God had abandoned.

I also consider the less well-known, but important, 'bishop question', a perceived persistent threat to colonial religious autonomy that increasingly undermined trust in British rule, and whatever religious issues appear to have been factors in causing perhaps one-third of American colonists not to support the revolutionary movement. Dissenters from the Church of England, who by the mid-eighteenth century constituted a majority of the colonial population, feared that the appointment of an Anglican bishop in the colonies would lead to a more complete establishment of the Church of England and repression of dissenting bodies. As we shall see, pointing to religious factors in the Tory cause is less clear.

American religion was as much shaped by the American Revolution as it helped shape the revolutionary movement. America's peculiar brand of post-millennialism thrived on the rhetoric and reality of the independence movement and political philosophical expressions such as the Declaration of Independence. For various reasons, the American Revolution ushered in a period of significant change in the 'line up' of religious bodies as well – some denominations going into rapid decline, others growing exponentially in the new environment. Under the influence of the Enlightenment, a public religion developed for the new nation, while the centuries-old traditions of church establishment and restraints on freedom of religious expression were discarded.

Religion, more specifically religious bodies, was buffeted by a revolution whose intellectual battlefield exposed the tenuousness of popular Christianity and reinforced the vigorous secularity of its political principles. Nevertheless, it emerged with renewed vigour in the 1780s. In Chapter 4, I describe that phenomenon. I begin by reviewing the historical process by which disestablishment and free exercise of religion were gradually realized at the national and state levels. I point out that First Amendment provisions for disestablishment were not binding on the states, and that separation of church and state therefore became a local struggle. I also briefly consider evidence for original intent in religious constitutional matters.

New England Theology, or the New Divinity Movement, and the Second Great Awakening are included in Chapter 4. Primary emphasis is placed, however, on the Great Awakening in the West – truly the big story of the early nineteenth century. The series of frontier revivals that constituted that event were not only among the most colourful moments in American religious history, but they also brought religion to a rapidly expanding frontier in terms that the comparatively uneducated and uncivilized frontiersmen could understand and appreciate. Techniques used by ministers in camp meetings may have horrified their eastern brethren, but they proved effective and eventually brought grudging acceptance everywhere, transforming the way ministers brought religion to the American people.

Charles Grandison Finney became the leading prophet of the Second Great Awakening. He developed a new concept of professional mass evangelicalism that, when merged with other political and social forces in early nineteenth-century America, commonly referred to as the Age of Jackson or of the Common Man, brought about the democratization of Christianity in America. In the forefront of this democratization process were denominations either unranked or non-existent only a few decades earlier: Methodists, Baptists and Disciples of Christ, the first two becoming by 1865 the largest denominations in America.

Charles Finney developed the concept of 'disinterested benevolence', by which he argued that conversion was not an entirely private, or solitary, affair. He insisted that as people were brought to God, they were obliged to act virtuously – to help bring others, individually and collectively, to God. Finney's doctrine of perfectionism underscored rampant optimism and post-millennialism in the Early Republic, moving unprecedented numbers of Americans toward the realization of the Kingdom of God on Earth. This is the subject of Chapter 5.

I open Chapter 5 with a discussion of American Transcendentalism as a movement that reflected many of the main currents of religion and reform in the early nineteenth century. I then provide a necessarily brief overview of the unprecedented proliferation of reform efforts that came to characterize the period as much as westward expansion. Toward this end, Protestant missionary groups constituted a loosely interconnected 'benevolent empire', involving nearly all of the major religious bodies in America. Clergy were never absent from these organizations, but strikingly present in both leadership and rank-and-file capacities were middle-class laymen and women.

I conclude Chapter 5 with some discussion of the greater role American women came to play in American religion in the nineteenth century and what some historians have referred to as the feminization not only of American culture but also of American religion. Male responses to economic developments redefined gender roles in nineteenth-century America. The home became the American woman's nearly exclusive sphere within the larger context of her becoming the moral guardian of the nation. She extended her sphere of influence, however, to the church, reform efforts and cultural development.

The first half of the nineteen-century witnessed the appearance of an unusually large number of religious groups that lay outside America's religious mainstream. Some were present in the colonial period, but due to their small numbers, like Roman Catholics, incurred little outright hostility. Others, like African Americans, did not solidify their religious beliefs in any organized manner until the first half of the century, while still others, like the Mormons, were brand new. I tell the story of these 'people apart' in Chapter 6.

I begin with African Americans, for whom religion was always central but, due to their enslaved capacity, was slow to form into a consistent polity. I review the on-going debate among historians over the extent to which the character and development of African-American religion retained ties to that group's African past. I side with those who have found that African-American religion came to reflect important elements of both their African heritage and Christianity, the religion of their oppressor, producing a distinctive brand of Christianity that parallelled, but did not replicate, the religion of the dominant white religious culture.

In that the planting of the British colonies of North America was in many respects an extension of the Reformation, Roman Catholics were always suspect. If they avoided outright hostility, it was only because they were so few as not to pose any significant challenge to the Protestant Establishment. All that changed in the nineteenth century and Irish and German immigrants built the American Catholic Church into one of the nation's largest denominations. Protestants reacted to this unexpected and unwelcome course of events with alarm and outright hostility.

The Church of Jesus Christ of Latter-day Saints was in many respects distinctly American. Not only was it born in America, but it was also a product of the same frontier revivalism that reshaped American religious thought. Nevertheless, it was sufficiently different, and insistent on its differences, to cause alarm. Controversy surrounded the Latter-day Saints from the very start, if only for its belief in polygamy. For decades they were forced to move further west, seeking their Zion in the Utah Territory, but even in the wilds they could not escape the long arms of mainstream Protestant America. Ultimately, they were forced to concede on a sufficient number of points, including polygamy, so as to be tolerated, if not completely, accepted.

The point is made in Chapter 6, that Roman Catholicism, Mormonism, African-American religion and many other marginal religions of the nineteenth century were transformed by Protestant America. At the same time, however, the creative and innovative ideas they posed helped transform the new nation by forcing it to re-examine those religious beliefs it deemed acceptable and to begin a process whereby the limits of that common body of belief have been continually expanded and been made more inclusive.

Religion in America to 1865 ends with an examination of the role of religion in the Civil War. Both the nation and its churches were torn asunder, and, although both would survive and even grow stronger, they would be forever changed by the experience. Chapter 7 addresses this important subject. It begins with a discussion of the role of religion in the Antislavery Movement and the response of Southern religious leaders to criticism by Northern evangelicals to their 'peculiar institution'. I then examine the divisive influence of slavery on the nation's churches, leading to the creation of separate institutions, if not before then soon after secession. The remaining pages are devoted to the role of the churches in the Civil War and the reformulation of religious thought and polity in the war's aftermath.

This history concludes with a brief examination, in the form of an epilogue, of religion in the American cultural market-place, one of the most significant developments in American religious history, with roots in the nineteenth century. By the mid-nineteenth century religion was well on its way to becoming a marketable cultural commodity. Religion was up for sale, some would argue, and, although they at first resisted it, in time religious leaders, clergy and lay, came to terms with this new development and even embraced it. They borrowed and even invented commercial practices in order to compete for the souls of the nation, with quite amazing results, that nonetheless leave interesting and troubling questions concerning the fate of religion in America thereafter.

Religion in America to 1865 is a brief and necessarily selective history. Choices as to what would be included had to be made; much had to be left out or referred to only in passing. It nevertheless offers the reader an introduction to a fascinating subject — the role of religion in American history. Hopefully it will entice its readers to read on and to use the recommended readings at the end of each chapter to pursue the subject in all its particulars in more detail.

Notes

1. Sidney E. Mead (1956), 'From coercion to persuasion: Another look at the rise of religious liberty and the emergence of denominationalism', *Church History*, 25 (December): 317–37.
2. *Gettysburg Address* (19 November 1863).

CHAPTER I

Native American Religion

For most Americans, their history begins with the English settlement of North America, with barely a reference to Spanish and French efforts in the area, and not much more attention paid to those who occupied the land before any Europeans arrived. This foreshortened history has come under fire in recent decades, for good reason. Thus we begin with the Native Americans.[1]

'Savages we call them', wrote Benjamin Franklin of Native Americans, 'because their manners differ from ours, which we think the perfection of civility'.[2] Much the same can be said of American attitudes toward Indian religion during the period with which this book is concerned. Religion, however, has always been central to the Native American experience, to its identity and to its vitality. Some continue to describe it as primitive, but in that the word primitive implies a belief system devoid of deep feelings and subtle thought it is inappropriate. Historically, Native American religion has been marked by rich symbolism and profound thought concerning the most basic concerns of man: the creation of the world, the origin of human life, and the nature of the supernatural and of the afterlife.[3] In this chapter, we shall explore the symbolism and thought of Native American religion through the middle of the nineteenth century.

We are immediately confronted with three problems. First, we have the problem of sources. Whereas most of the major world religions have literary traditions, Native American religion has been handed down as oral tradition. Such oral accounts have little sense of time, especially linear, upon which historians depend. Further, though quite lovely in their telling, and true at one level, metaphorical and symbolic language abounds and past and present are collapsed into a single continuum.[4] Similarly fraught with danger in their use are the records of the first European and American observers of Indian culture. Explorers, traders and missionaries witnessed first-hand many aspects of Indian life, but their accounts are limited by their cultural biases.[5]

Second, our title 'Native American religion' is a misnomer and perhaps might better have been put: 'Native American religions'. Native American religion was, and still is, as diverse as the Euro-American religions with which it came into contact. In brief, there were as many Indian religions as there were Indian tribes.[6] The phrase Native American religion, then, is a fiction, but it is a convenient fiction, which we will employ. We will discuss both the diversity that separates and the commonalties that unite Native American religions.

Third, we face the challenge of describing a phenomenon that is ever changing. What we often describe as traditional behaviour is really the product of extensive alteration over many centuries. This was true for Native Americans in the Pre-Contact Period, between the migration of their north-east Asiatic ancestors beginning perhaps 30,000 or more years ago to 1492, during which hundreds of distinct Native American cultures emerged. And it was true in the period after 1492, when Indian tribes were forced into foreign environments to which they had to adapt, culturally as well as physically, encountered hitherto unknown tribes with different religious beliefs that influenced their own, and faced the oftentimes forced acculturation that followed confrontations with European and American agents of culture and religion.[7]

Common Characteristics of Native American Religion(s)

Anthropologists have identified at least 150 different Native American cultures in North America north of the Rio Grande, and, as Catherine Albanese has written: 'For Native Americans, culture was tradition was religion'. Euro-Americans may have insisted that the truths of their religion were universal, that Christianity transcended culture, but Native Americans believed that each society or group of people had its own sacred stories and rituals.[8] Nevertheless, it is possible to identify common characteristics among Native American religions.

Four prominent features linked the diverse expressions of North American Indian religion: a similar world-view, a shared notion of cosmic harmony, emphasis on directly experiencing powers and visions, and a common view of the cycle of life and death. Native Americans generally believed that human existence was designed by the creator divinities at the time of the 'first beginnings'. Myths agreed that in those days all beings were more or less human, but that a change took place that turned many primeval beings into animals and birds – thus the close affinity that remained between people and animals, as well as the animistic concept of spirits as animals and animals as spiritual.[9]

The Native American notion of cosmic harmony emphasized the unitary system of the universe made up of humans, animals, trees and plants – nature as a whole – and the supernatural. The roots of this idea may be traced to Indian hunting origins, thereby explaining its continued prominence in later hunter-gatherer tribes, but it was equally at home among agricultural Indians. Simply put, all living beings had their supernatural guardians. Each animal had its guardian, usually a mysterious spirit larger than ordinary members of the species. In the case of humans, a Supreme Being played the superior but not exclusive role.[10]

Native Americans emphasized the direct experience of powers and visions. Among the Great Plains Indians this was commonly represented in the vision quest. The vision quest may have originated as a puberty rite, wherein young men were required to seek the assistance of a guardian spirit to withstand the trials of existence and luck in hunting, warfare and love. Parents or elders sent young men into the forest or wilderness to fast, suffer from the cold, and be subject to the attacks of wild animals, from which might result a vision of the spirit that henceforth would become their guardian spirit. The vision quest was transformed, however, on the Plains into a ritual for grown men, wherein hunters or warriors repeatedly withdrew into the wilderness to seek guardian spirits, each good for a different purpose.[11]

And, finally, Native Americans, in contrast to those living in Western culture, conceived of time as cyclical, rather than linear. Rather than seeing time as having a beginning and an end, American Indians understood time as an eternally recurring cycle of years and events. So too each person made a cycle of time from birth to death, death marking both the end of the old and the beginning of a new life, either on this earth, reincarnated into another human or some animal form, or in a transcendent hereafter.[12]

Native Americans possessed a strong sense of continuity between the self and outside realities, and between themselves and the things they held sacred. Both in space and time, Native Americans saw reality as more mysterious and symbolistic, and what they saw as more holy and mysterious as closely related to, if not inseparable from, their daily existence. Whereas Euro-Americans conceived of a three-level universe of God, human being, and nature, inhabiting different realms, Native Americans envisioned a world to which all were bound by ties of kinship. There were grandfathers who were Thunder Beings; there was Grandmother Spider; and there was the Corn Mother. Animals took on human form, like Coyote the Trickster, and shamans – holy people – were said to fly like birds and talk to animals.[13]

In the Western world-view, the natural world was a resource for man; as noted in Genesis 1: 28, man was 'to have dominion over . . . every living thing that moves on the earth'. The secular and the sacred were distinct, and the human relationship to the natural environment fell into the secular sphere.[14] Native Americans made no such distinction. They conceived of animal and plant guardians as sacred beings, who, at some point in the distant past, had pledged the bodies of their species as food for man, leading Native Americans to create elaborate rituals for hunting and planting, offering gifts to the spirits of the life they took and being careful not to waste any portion of that which they killed or harvested.[15]

Native Americans held sacred the inner world as well. Dreams revealed holy, hidden things that often could not be known in other ways. Tribes had rituals wherein individuals brought their dreams to tribal councils or holy men, so that their meaning could be discerned. Especially on the Plains, leaders of the hunt were chosen from among those who had had dreams deemed relevant to the hunt, while many tribes believed that in dreams the soul was free to travel to distant places to learn and to return with information, or visions, from guardian spirits.[16]

The inner world that dreams disclosed was intimately related to the outer world, and, in order to bridge the gap between the two, people were given a name that indicated their kinship with nature and that told something of their inner essence. Those names could, and often were, changed as significant deeds or events occurred. Black Hawk, for example, might become Afraid of Horses, White Rabbit, or Moves from Your Sight Little Red Star. And the colours were significant, in that each of the four directions had its colour, and each colour its quality: the red of the north might signify wisdom, the white of the south innocence, the black of the west deep thought or introspection, and the yellow of the east inner light.[17]

Belief in shape-shifting was common. Trickster figures such as the Coyote could assume any form they chose, even in the very midst of their adventures. Thus they were seen as beings of creative power, who had helped put the present world in order, as well as disorder, and who often disturbed the regular working of society. Shape-shifting tricksters could shift from sly cunning creatures, who could outwit their opponents, to the fool, who, according to one tale, fought himself because his right arm and left arm did not know that they belonged to each other. They were without boundaries, able to become whatever inspiration and circumstance decreed, and belief in such transformations reminded Native Americans that the world was, after all, one substance.[18]

Native Americans lived their lives in accordance not only with the four directions, as noted above, but also with sacred numbers – four, for the directions of the compass, for example, and seven which added a vertical dimension to the four, namely the zenith, nadir and centre – and with shapes, most notably the circle. Circles were sacred for Native Americans because they reflected shapes they saw in nature, both in space and time. To be in harmony with nature meant to live as part of the circle, or the medicine wheel of the world. It meant living securely in what they saw as the middle of that circular world from which they did not venture toward the edges, or frontier.[19]

Also similar were Native American accounts of their origins as humans or on earth. Most tribes pictured their primordial ancestors as having ascended from the darkness under the earth. A hero, often accompanied by a god, liberated them, freeing them to emerge from the darkness into the light. Those who came to Earth ascended a tree (alternately a rope, vine or mountain) in the order of which they would assume their place in society, chiefs and shamans first. That tree, with its roots in the underworld and crown in the upper, was represented by such ritual structures as the sun dance post or sacred pole.[20]

Native Americans generally ascribed the origin and existence of good and evil to dual creation, or to the product of two creative spirits – often twins – almost always related but in conflict. They commonly credited the good spirit with having fashioned a positive and beneficent world for human beings. They saw the evil one as having introduced into the world elements that would thereafter frustrate them and make their lives more difficult, like disease and pestilence. Similar accounts told of the heroes, or gods, who gave men such indispensable gifts as fire, the ability to hunt and skill in planting.[21]

Similarities existed in Native American attitudes toward death and the afterlife. Some tribes espoused theories of reincarnation, wherein the deceased person might return to earth in a different form, commonly an animal. At the same time, their three-level view of the universe led Indians to believe that the deceased departed for either the level above, where they might enjoy a happy life of plenty and contentment, or the level below the earth, of darkness, which did not necessarily involve torture but that was deprived of warmth and satisfaction. Good people would be rewarded in the afterlife, and the bad not, thereby providing a sense of the world as a moral place which favoured good and opposed evil.[22]

And, finally, most Native Americans believed in ghosts, or the spirits of the recently departed existing for an interim period between earth and their final dwelling places. They commonly performed ceremonies to appease such spirits, especially for the first year following a person's death. Visits from the deceased in their survivor's dreams were common, however, thereby relaying important messages about decisions that needed to be made and warning of problems that lay ahead.[23]

Examples of Diversity in Native American Religions

Although the lines are often unclear, for the sake of convenience, Native American tribes can be divided in a number of ways: by language groups, by their being matrilineal or patrilineal or by their being hunter-gatherers or agricultural, to give just three examples. We shall follow the last approach and, in the process, describe some of the religious beliefs and practices of the Oglala Sioux, who lived on the Great Plains and developed religious beliefs representative of the hunter-gatherers, and of the Hopi, a primarily agricultural Pueblo people of the Southwest. Ake Hultkrantz has identified the following general features as characterizing each:

Hunting Pattern	Agricultural Pattern
Animal ceremonialism	Rain and fertility ceremonies
Quest for spiritual power	Priestly ritual
Male Supreme Being	Goddesses and gods
Annual ceremony of cosmic rejuvenation	Yearly round of fertility rites
Few stationary cult places	Permanent shrines and temples
Shamanism	Medicine society and ritualism
Life after death beyond the horizon or in the sky	Life after death in the underworld or among the clouds[24]

The Oglala Sioux

The Oglala Sioux originated in what is now the state of Minnesota and migrated onto the Plains about 1750. They obtained horses that had strayed or been stolen from the Spanish of the Southwest, with which they developed their widely recognized skill as buffalo hunters and a more nomadic lifestyle. Sioux culture was among the most intricate on the Plains, in terms of social and ceremonial organization, and, like that of all Plains Indians, Sioux religion reflected the values of hunters, in general, and the centrality of the buffalo to their existence, in particular.

According to the traditional account of the Oglala's origin, Inktomi the Spider, a trickster figure, wooed the people in the world below with food and clothing until Tokahe and three strong companions came to the upper world to investigate its virtues for themselves. Inktomi plied the visitors with more gifts and promised them youth, and they returned to their people with glowing reports of what they had experienced. Although the old chief and an old woman warned of cold wind and the need for hunting in the upper realm, Tokahe led six families onto the Plains. The results were not so fortunate as they had hoped, and the children cried for food while Inktomi laughed. But all was not lost, because they met Old Man and Old Woman, who taught them to hunt the buffalo, clothe themselves and make tipis.[25]

Another story explained the origin of the sacred pipe among the Oglala Sioux. It began when a beautiful woman in white buckskin visited the Oglala Sioux camp, entered the sweat lodge and presented the sacred pipe to the chief. 'With this sacred pipe', she is reported to have said, 'you will walk upon the Earth; for the Earth is your Grandmother and Mother and she is sacred.' Thereafter the pipe figured in the rituals of the Oglala Sioux, a sign of their felt bond to one another and to the earth, their common source.[26]

Oglala Sioux developed rituals to mark periods of passage in life – puberty, childbirth and death, for example – but the most significant were the sweat lodge ceremony, the vision quest and the sun dance. In the sweat lodge ceremony, the leader moved sunwise as he entered the lodge. Four heated stones were placed at the bottom of a special pole representing the four directions, while two stones placed on top represented the zenith and nadir. The very top stone signified the Spotted Eagle. The doors of the lodge were sealed, prayers were said over the seven stones, and more stones were added to provide the heat necessary for ritual purification.

In contrast to the group orientation of the sweat lodge ritual, the vision quest was solitary, performed on a sacred hill away from the tribal village. It was intended to enable men to gain power through a vision in which guardian spirits revealed their relationship to the seeker and bestowed the knowledge, or power, he desired. The ritual was conducted under the guidance of a holy man and involved the smoking of a sacred pipe, preliminary purifications in the sweat lodge, fasting and prayer. Once the seeker reached the sacred hill, however, he was left alone for from one to four days, reflecting the individualistic nature of the religion of the hunters.[27]

In notable contrast to those of agricultural tribes, the sun dance was the only ritual among Plains Indians that occurred at a prescribed time of the year, namely in midsummer, after the buffalo hunt. Basically a thanksgiving ceremony in which they thanked the Supreme Being for the past year and petitioned him for a prosperous and healthy year to come, by the early nineteenth century it emphasized as well the bravery, courage and individual initiative so highly prized by hunting people.[28] Often it was an intertribal affair extended over four days, each day having its particular ritual.

The sun dance began with the construction of a lodge. Oglala Sioux selected a cottonwood tree, trimmed it to form the sacred pole at the centre of the lodge, and painted and decorated the pole with symbolic offerings, placing a buffalo head at its top. Warriors danced around the pole, running to each of the directions to flatten the ground, symbolically killing the images of a man and a buffalo at the pole. The participants, however, were literally and figuratively bound to the sacred centre. They were attached by thongs to the pole, and they danced themselves into an ecstasy of sacrifice, either gazing into the sun until sunset or dancing until the skewers dug into their flesh were pulled from their bodies.[29]

The Hopi

Anthropologists number the Hopi among the Pueblo, or 'village', Indians of the American Southwest, so named because they dwelled in adobe and stone apartment villages. River, or eastern, Pueblo peoples, the Tanoans and the Keresans, settled along the Rio Grande in what is now New Mexico; the Zuni and the Hopi lived further west in the desert in New Mexico and Arizona. Unlike the Oglala Sioux, the Hopi were predominantly agricultural, and the difference was significant. As Ake Hultkrantz put it: 'Nowhere else in native North America has the tilling of the soil been as intense as among the Pueblo Indians'. And 'not only has this distinctive agricultural practice formed the basis of their economy and sedentary lifestyle, but it has also been an integral part of their religious beliefs and aesthetic expressions'.[30]

The Hopi have lived in the same area for from 1500 to 2000 years, culturally reaching their peak from about 900 to 1300 AD. They developed planned villages composed of large terraced buildings that may have housed as many as 1000 people. They constructed irrigation canals and dams, and used hillside terracing for bringing water to an arid land. Their ceramics and weavings became increasingly intricate, and their religious ceremonialism among the most elaborate of North America, complete with priests, dancers, altars, and masked performances.[31]

Myths and ritual were central to the Hopi. Myths furnished the code of Hopi religion, rituals provided the myths. They also underscored the greater emphasis among the Hopi, as compared to the Oglala Sioux, on conformity, a cooperative spirit and a harmonious village life. Villages, permanent rather than temporary, were ceremonial centres in which the terraced apartments were grouped around plazas, the sites of outdoor ceremonies, and kivas, or sacred pit houses. Women were excluded from kivas, but Hopi social organization revolved around women. Communities were organized in matrilineal clans. Women owned their houses and household goods. Children derived their clan kinship from their mothers, and Hopi tradition expressed the prominence of feminine symbolism.[32]

In their origin myth, the Hopi emerged from the womb of Mother Earth, for which the kiva itself, essentially a large hole dug in the earth, served as a reminder. The Hopi enjoyed a good life in the world below until evil entered into their hearts, sexuality ran rampant and hatred and quarrelling grew apace. In their plight the chiefs created Motsni, who flew through an opening to the upper world, found the site of present day Oraibi and encountered Masauwuu, or Skeleton. When he heard Motsni's tale, Masauwuu explained that he was living in poverty, but that he welcomed the people to join him. So the Hopi climbed plant ladders to the world above, where, aided by Spider Woman, they fashioned a symbol that turned into the moon and another that became the sun. The people began to make their way, and with the gift of corn the Hopi were given an identity.[33]

Iatiku, the Spider Woman, also referred to as the Corn Mother, gave the Hopi corn to sustain them. Corn was her heart, it was believed, and it supplied strength for human survival as if it were milk from her breasts. Iatiku commanded reverence because of her omniscience; she knew beforehand what others would do. And, as an early designer of the world and companion of the dead, Iatiku remained at the sipapu awaiting the day when she would welcome the Hopi back from their earthly life, thereby contributing substantially to a view of the cosmos as stable and benign.[34]

The agricultural basis of Hopi culture is best seen in the cycle of rituals that formed a ceremonial year in the Hopi villages. While the Oglala Sioux possessed only one calendric ritual, every Hopi ritual depended on the cycle of the seasons. Harmony with nature was paramount, and that was expressed in their ritual harmony with the changing seasons. If the buffalo was the motivating force behind Oglala Sioux rituals, the calendric rites of the Hopi made clear their dependence on the sun, earth and rain, all of which were needed to make crops grow in their desert environment.[35]

Father Sun was the life-giving god, responsible for delivering humankind from the world below. Mother Earth, often seen as a sexual partner of Father Sun, was a personification of the earth and its growth. The underworld was often seen as her womb, and the Pueblo people prayed to her, especially in winter, to bring forth the bounteousness of spring.[36] Many of the Hopi gods were capable of bringing precious rain. Some lived in the distant ocean and nearby streams and springs. A few travelled as clouds and patches of fog and were responsible for lightning and thunder.[37] So too the Kachinas brought rain when they left their abodes in the nearby mountains. All were seen as providing the gift of fertility through their life-giving rains.

The major division in the ceremonial year was between the Kachina rituals from December through July and the non-Kachina rituals from August through November. Kachinas were not considered gods, but spirits of the dead, animals, plants and even inanimate objects. They were said to be intermediaries between humans and the gods, who, during the second half of the year, dwelled in the San Francisco peaks on the outer edge of Hopi country and visited the Hopi villages during the first half of the year, when the Kachina rituals were held. Over 250 in number, the Kachinas were never worshipped but rather looked upon as friends. They were endowed with a variety of human qualities, and new ones continually appeared as old ones were forgotten. Their personalities ranged from benevolent and kindly to fearful punishers of offenders in Hopi society.[38]

Kachinas were male dancers, who, during Kachina ceremonies, wore masks and impersonated particular spiritual Kachinas, their relationship with whom, it was believed, they inherited. They danced themselves into a state in which they lost all sense of separate self and became the Kachinas they impersonated, achieving the transformation that Native Americans believed was occurring all around them, and crossing the frontier that divided ordinary reality from the extraordinary. The Kachina dancers gave carved dolls, also called Kachinas, to Hopi children during the ceremonies, whereby they hoped to teach them about Kachina beings. Made in traditional and highly stylized patterns from cottonwood root, the Kachina dolls were not toys, but neither were they sacred objects. Rather, they were objects intended to be placed in the home to remind everyone, especially the children, of the Kachinas.[39]

Kachina rituals included: the Soyal, before the winter solstice, when the sun ceased its journey southward; the Powamu, or bean dance, in February; and the Niman, or home dance, in July. In the culminating rituals of the Soyal, a cornhusk, which symbolized fertility, was brought to every person in the village so that all might breathe on it, sending a message to the spirit beings. After a ceremony in which sexual intercourse was ritually simulated by the male corn collector to encourage a corresponding fertility in nature, seed corn was gathered from the villagers and blessed. The Kachina Muyingwa, who embodied vegetation, danced, and prayer sticks were distributed to every house so that their presence throughout the year would provide a continuing plea to the spirit beings for fertility.[40]

Preparations for the Powamu included a secret planting of beans in the kivas, where, kept warm and moist, the plants began to grow. Kachinas thereafter distributed the bean plants throughout the village as gifts to the people and promises of what was to come. Early in spring came the ceremony to honour the Great Serpent Palulukong, said to confer fertility on crops and also on people. In a dramatic sequence, his voice simulated in the ritual, puppets with huge serpent heads made from corn represented him and knocked over rows of corn plants to represent the future harvest. Niman, at summer solstice, marked the time when the Kachinas were said to leave the villages. By then the first corn had come, and the Kachinas danced as a group for the Hopi as the people expressed their gratitude.[41]

Calendric rituals continued after the disappearance of the Kachinas. During alternate years, in August, Flute and Snake-Antelope ceremonies were held with the hope that they would bring rain. The Flute ceremony featured distinctive music and a procession to the sacred Flute Spring to procure water to be offered in prayers for rain. The Snake and Antelope societies performed a ritual dance with snakes and then released the snakes into the desert to carry the Hopi prayers for rain. The Hopi hoped to bring back the Snake people, according to tradition once driven in anger from one of their villages, once again seeking a reconciliation with nature so that nature, restored to harmony, would give nourishment.[42]

In September and October women's societies performed three ceremonies. Since women were seen as passive beings who received the male seed and carried it to term, their prominence in ceremonies at this time was especially important. Much as they were to be open and ready to receive the seed so that human society would grow and blossom, the earth was to be prepared for planting time, which would soon come again, the womb of nature nourishing the beginnings of life.[43]

In November came the Wuwuchim, the last of the non-Kachina ceremonies and the first of the three winter ceremonies. Wuwuchim was the initiation ritual of the Hopi, when the sipapu was kept open so that the spirits of the dead could take part. Symbolizing death and rebirth, a new fire was lit, roads to the four directions closed, hair ritually washed, and the Hopi account of emergence recited. Candidates for initiation, young Hopis ready to become men, remained in the Kiva, wrapped in blankets, while they listened to the sacred account of origin and experienced in themselves the mysteries of spiritual death and rebirth. For the Hopi, just as the cycles of the seasons brought death and rebirth to the natural world, their lives underwent an inner form of dying and rebirth.[44]

In their attention to the planting cycle, Hopi religion was similar to other agricultural Native American groups, but different from their hunter-gatherer cousins, like the Oglala Sioux. For the Oglala Sioux the ideal of religious life was the intense personal vision; among the Hopi the ideal religious life involved a submersion of the individual in group ritual activity, such that all worked in unison with the rhythms of the cosmos. In contrast to the Oglala, the Hopi suppressed, rather than emphasized, the individual and the experiential side of religion. A person who acted too much on his or her own was thought to be using religious power for evil intentions and ran the risk of being accused of witchcraft.[45]

European Contact and the Impact of Christian Missions

Native American religion was never static, even in the pre-Columbian period. Change was never so swift, however, as it was when Indians came into contact with Europeans and Euro-Americans, especially Christian missionaries. One of the great motivating forces underlying Christian European expansion into the New World was the missionary spirit of Christianity. A central agent in its colonization was the Christian church, leading some to describe the process of colonization as 'colonialism in the name of Christ'. The belief that the heathen should be converted as a Christian duty was not limited to priests and ministers. Financial supporters of the earliest expeditions, ministers of state and colonial officials, sought to carry out what they regarded as a moral duty. Colonization was closely equated with the spread of civilization, the carrying of an alleged superior European and later American culture to the so-called primitive areas of the world.[46]

Missionaries were constantly frustrated by the reluctance of most Indians to be converted, the very idea of a native Christian identity being culturally problematic. Indians recognized no line of distinction between religious and cultural life; once an Indian became a Christian, he was seen as having rejected more than the religious component of his former life. He called into question the cultural values by which he had been nurtured, resulting, in the minds of many, in deracination. Because, at the same time, the convert was seldom fully accepted into white society, conversion could result in isolation from both the white and Native American worlds.[47]

Wilcomb Washburn has argued that

> despite the numbers of converts, and the apparent strength of the Christian movement among Indians, the effects of conversion were too often either peripheral, divisive, or narcotic. Christianity at best helped the Indian accept the poor place the white world offered him and helped him overcome the rage and despair he might otherwise have felt because of his inability to prosper in that world.[48]

But Richard White may have put it best when he summarized the results of Christian missions in one story with two endings. The story: 'Indians are the rock, European peoples are the sea, and history seems a constant storm.' The two outcomes: 'The sea wears down and dissolves the rock; or the sea erodes the rock but cannot finally absorb its battered remnant, which endures.'[49]

Spanish Missions

Spanish and French missions preceded, and differed in significant ways from, English and American missions, largely as the result of their particular brands of Christianity, the number of settlers and the type of society they tried to create. Francis Parkman recognized the difference a century ago when he wrote, no doubt overstating the case, that in North America: 'Spanish civilization crushed the Indian; English civilization scorned and neglected him; French civilization embraced and cherished him.'[50]

The first missionary efforts on what would become United States soil occurred in the Southeast and Southwest under Spanish auspices. The Florida governor's first choice to establish Indian missions was the Jesuits, but after several failed attempts they withdrew, leaving the field to the Franciscans. In 1595 the Franciscans launched a major effort in what is today Florida and Georgia. They made some progress, but by 1708 the widespread Franciscan mission system was all but destroyed.[51]

Roman Catholic missionary activity in the Southwest progressed under the cover of Spanish military power, which through 1541 was marked by scandalous scenes of plunder and slaughter. When, in 1541, Francisco Coronado's expedition failed to find wealth to match that of Mexico and Peru, Spanish military might withdrew from the area, leaving the field open to those who would propagate the Word of God through less violent means.[52]

In 1598 Juan de Onate moved into the heart of the Pueblo region, in what is now New Mexico, with about 400 colonists, some soldiers and a number of Franciscan missionaries. His purpose was to colonize the area, which was inhabited by between 40,000 and 50,000 Indians living in four or five dozen villages. He authorized grants of land (*encomiendas*) in the most populous eastern, and later northern, pueblos of the upper Rio Grande to Spanish settlers with the right to utilize the services of Indians living on those grants (*repartimentos*). Missionaries built churches on the edges of Indian villages, baptized Indians, and introduced new agricultural methods.[53]

The prevailing pattern of Spanish missionary activity in this area of the Southwest was the establishment of largely self-contained missions, centred around the physical church, to which the Indians of the area were attracted for food and medicine, as well as to learn to worship the missionaries' God and to practise the arts of 'civilized' man. Franciscans actively, and often harshly, sought to prohibit the continued practice of native rites – destroying Kachina figures and raiding kivas – and they forced Indians to receive instruction in Spanish, rather than their native tongue.[54]

Jesuits soon moved into Spanish holdings, however, in what would become Arizona and California. They were led by Eusebio Francisco Kino, an Italian Jesuit, who obtained an exemption for the Indians that they encountered from the forced labour or demands for tribute employed in earlier missions. Bringing cattle with him to create a food supply for his missions, as well as tolerance and love of ceremony, Kino became one of the most successful missionaries in American history.[55]

In 1680 a general Pueblo revolt against the Spanish caused a major setback for Spanish rule and missions in the area, but, its success notwithstanding, the insurrection did not lead to a revival of Pueblo culture, which continued to decline. The Spanish re-established control by 1740, and in 1768 the Jesuits were expelled from the New World, leaving the field to the Franciscans. For a brief period, 1821–46, the Southwest came under the control of the newly independent Mexico, but in 1846 the United States moved in, initiating a new period of Indian–White relations, this time Protestant as well as Catholic. Reservations were established for the various tribes, including the Hopi. Most continued to at least formally accept Catholic ritualism, but otherwise their doors were closed to new missionary efforts.[56]

The number of recorded conversions among the Indians of the Southwest was high, and many remained Catholic even after the power of Spanish Catholic missions was broken. By the early years of the nineteenth century, however, Indians of the Southwest had modified Roman Catholic rituals in ways commensurate with their traditional ways, to better serve their spiritual needs. The result was a syncretic religion marked by ceremonial calendars that were based on traditional Native American beliefs and practices, but to which were added an amalgam of Catholic ceremonies.[57]

French Missions

French missionary efforts were built on the fur trade, and, in that the fur trade required little more than the trading of goods desired by

Indians for furs, the relationship between the French and the Indians was different from that of the Spanish and the English. Military conquest was unnecessary, and even large settlements were not required. By 1660 only 2000 Frenchmen lived in New France, compared to twenty times that number of Englishmen in New England alone.[58]

While the English used force and guile to wrest land and win political submission, the French relied on persuasion. It was a policy born of weakness, but out of it came the most lastingly amicable relations between Europeans and Indians on the continent. Fur traders paved the way for this approach by freely mixing with the Indians. Given the unique imbalance of men to women settlers, many Frenchmen took Indian mistresses and wives, a mixing of blood viewed with disdain by the English. In Nova Scotia, by 1676, one authority has noted, virtually all French families had Indian blood in their veins, and, in the 1660s, Colbert, Louis XIV's architect of imperial reorganization, called for full-fledged integration in order to 'civilize' the Indians.[59]

Those who were not traders in New France were generally Jesuit priests. They established missions and martyred themselves in hostile Indian country, especially among the Hurons of the Great Lakes area, where they worked for 'the greater glory of God' by converting Indians to Catholicism. They had greater success among the tribes of the Mississippi River Valley, extending their efforts at one time to the Gulf of Mexico. Catholicism had some advantages over reformed Protestantism in the quest for converts. Whereas their Puritan neighbours, for example, denied that people could do anything to achieve salvation, but nevertheless insisted they have faith, Catholics encouraged prospective converts to seek salvation through good work, right living and faithful worship. Catholicism was much more liturgical, thereby appealing to all the senses, as well as reason. And, in New France as in New Spain, the Jesuits were more willing than their Puritan neighbours to accept that Indian beliefs in a supreme being, in the immortality of the soul, and in supernatural forces could be revised sufficiently to find acceptance from the Christian God. Whereas the Puritans insisted Indians erase their values, renounce their way of life and abandon their religious beliefs as a starting point in accepting Christianity, the Jesuits studied the Indian structure of belief and attempted to change it slowly rather than replace it.[60]

English and American Missions

The English did not successfully plant colonies in the Western Hemisphere until 1607, 115 years after Columbus's arrival. They arrived with a split image of Native Americans. On the one hand, reflecting Christopher Columbus's earliest observations, some Englishmen expected Indians to be a gentle people, receptive to Christian 'civilizing' efforts.[61] Arthur Barlow, of the failed Roanoke colony, echoed Columbus's sentiments, but that impression was replaced over time by an image of the Native American as savage and hostile, a people cursed by God by their having been denied the presence and teaching of Christ. A flood of pamphlets in the second half of the sixteenth century described the natives as brutal, loathsome and even cannibalistic, leaving little room for optimism concerning their reception of European civilization.[62]

Concern for the conversion of Native Americans was mentioned and pursued in at least a modest manner early on in the British colonies. As per the King's charter to the Virginia Company of London for the settlement of Virginia, the company was to concern itself with bringing the Christian religion to such people 'as live in darkness and miserable ignorance of the true knowledge and worship of God'. Similar provisions would be included in later charters, but from the start, as John Smith observed, such goals were always a distinct second to that of making a profit. Historian Reginald Horseman would state the problem more directly: 'From the time the first English settlers arrived . . . the fundamental struggle with the aboriginal inhabitants was over the possession of land'.[63]

One early missionary gave up in disgust after three years, despairing: 'Heathen they are and heathen they will remain.' This did not discourage the English from pursuing a policy of intimidation, but they were largely rebuffed by a resilient Indian culture, including religious traditions. One company plan to appropriate money to educate young Indians in Virginia homes and special schools, separating the children from their families by force if necessary, failed by 1622. As more Virginians pushed inland to carve out tobacco plantations, what had been an abrasive and sometimes violent relationship became disastrous. Disease (e.g. smallpox, diphtheria and scarlet fever) proved a devastating, if unintended, weapon, but war played a significant part in the destruction of the Indians as well. When an Indian attack in 1622 wiped out almost one-third of the white population, Virginians resorted to a ruthless policy in which colonists would no longer be obliged to 'civilize' the Indians. They would simply be kept apart.[64]

The British policy of separation was quickly adopted elsewhere in the British colonies. As a social and political movement, Puritanism intended to reverse the march of disorder and wickedness in English society by creating a new, model, regenerated social order, a 'city on a hill', as John Winthrop put it. In order to reform their society, moreover, they assumed responsibility, moral stewardship, over those around them. They, the elect, were not only to save themselves, but they were also to assume the burden of reforming their Indian neighbours. If they were not receptive to Puritan efforts, they might have to be coerced and controlled, directed and dominated.[65]

The charter of the Massachusetts Bay Company called for the conversion of the Indians to Christianity. The 'principal end of this plantation', it read, was to 'win and incite the natives of [the] country to the knowledge and obedience of the only true God and savior of mankind and the Christian faith'. The colonies seal depicted an Indian pleading: 'Come over and help us', but no missionary activity was to be initiated for thirteen years. By then the rapidly increasing number of settlers and thirst for land only hastened the Puritan impulse to follow the Virginia model of removing Indians to the interior.[66]

As Roy H. Pearce has explained, the Indians stood as a vivid reminder of what the English knew they must not become. Their nature was the counterimage of civilized man, and Puritans could achieve control of themselves only if they could control and civilize that counterimage. Toward that end, the Puritans attempted to bring the Indians under civil government, making them strictly accountable to the ordinances that governed white behaviour. The most successful English missionary was John Eliot, who, with aid from the Society for the Propagation of the Gospel in New England, built the Indian College at Harvard, Massachusetts, and established a printing press, that published his Algonquian translation of the Bible.[67]

Eliot, known as the 'Apostle to the Indians', like most New England missionaries, concentrated his efforts on Indian tribes whose numbers had been deeply diminished by epidemics and war, who had already lost much of their land, and who had become economically dependent on the colonists. His most dramatic accomplishment was the creation of 'praying Indian' towns, like Natick, Massachusetts, which prior to King Philip's War in 1675 numbered fourteen and contained over 1000 inhabitants. 'Praying Indians' learned English in books of agriculture, adopted English hairstyles, dress and customs, and were nurtured on the Bible and other devotional works, translated into their language, resulting in between 2300 and 4000 conversions.[68]

Attempts to convert Native Americans continued in the eighteenth century, but expectations shifted from bringing entire tribes into the fold to small group and even individual conversions. The Great Awakening of the 1740s provided examples of pious converts, one of the most famous being Samson Occom, a Mohegan born in 1723 near New London, Connecticut. He found 'salvation through Jesus Christ' at age seventeen and, after studying with Eleazar Wheelock, played a leading role in obtaining support in England for the Indian Charity School that would become Dartmouth College. By the American Revolution, James Axtell has estimated, there were at various times in New England 22 Indian churches, 91 praying towns or reservations, 72 white missionaries, and 133 native preachers and teachers. Nevertheless, he admits, such numbers do little to enhance the otherwise lacklustre performance by Puritan missionaries.[69]

Space precludes our discussing British missions to the Indians in all thirteen colonies, but, in general, few were much more successful than those in Massachusetts and Virginia, and all fell victim to the same process of Native American decline, decimation and dispossession. The colony of Pennsylvania bears mention, here, for its brief, but genuine attempt to deal fairly with the Indians. So too does the colony of Georgia, because of its proprietor's comparatively better relations with the Indians. The United Brethren, or Moravians, were among the most active missionaries of eighteenth-century British America. But British missions were met with increasing resistance as they moved inland. Interior tribes, such as the Iroquois, Creeks and Cherokees, were not impressed with most institutions of British life, including religion, and they saw no reason to replace what they had with them.[70]

Adding to the resistance among northern Indian tribes was the preaching of Neolin, a charismatic Delaware prophet. As would several subsequent prophets, Neolin preached that Native Americans should return to the state they were in before the whites arrived, or face extinction. In Neolin's vision, the Master of Life told his people that salvation lay in returning to their ancient customs, forswearing rum and other elements of white culture, and in population control through abstinence. His disciples carried Neolin's message throughout the western territories, attracting large numbers of Indians, including the Ottawa leader, Pontiac. Pontiac made Neolin's doctrine the spiritual underpinning of the failed uprising he led against the English in 1763.[71]

Attitudes toward Native Americans had not changed on the eve of independence. The Declaration of Independence charged George III with trying to loose on the frontier 'the merciless Indian savages, whose known rule of warfare is an undistinguished destruction of all ages, sexes, and conditions'. During the American Revolution most Indian tribes remained loyal to the British, whom they hoped (no doubt encouraged by British agents) would defend them and their land from the onrush of settlers. The result did not bode well for Indian inhabitants of the new nation, and clashes between tribes on the frontier and citizens of the new nation continued unabated until they were forced to sign the Treaty of Greenville in 1795.[72]

Protestant missionary activity burgeoned in the 1790s, stimulated by the Second Great Awakening and the creation of several religious organizations committed to the idea that civilization must go hand in hand with Christianization if either was to succeed. 'In the school and in the field, as well as in the kitchen', one missionary wrote, 'our aim was to teach the Indians to live like white people'.[73]

New missionary efforts at 'civilizing' the Indians had to work within the context of the equally new American nation's policy of Indian removal. Although justified on humanitarian grounds, as well as on the need for American expansion – to protect Native Americans as well as to provide land for a rapidly increasing population – the Indian removal policy provoked resentment, resistance and some armed conflict.[74]

The Cherokees of the Old Southwest were among the groups most resistant to removal. In 1808, having acquired the benefits of 'civilization', and expressing a preference for severalty and citizenship, they formally requested exclusion from the new policy. Jefferson rejected their appeal. Between 1808 and 1832 scores of treaties were negotiated providing for the removal of nearly all remaining tribes located east of the Mississippi, but still the Cherokee resisted, peaceably. A messiah, incongruously named Whitepath, appeared, appealing to the Cherokee to reverse their direction and to return to their more traditional ways, but the movement was squelched by those who chose to continue the course.[75]

In 1832 the Cherokee case was successfully argued before the United States Supreme Court in *Worcester* v. *Georgia*, but Chief Justice John

Marshall's majority opinion that federal, not state, law prevailed was ignored. President Jackson's remark, 'John Marshall has made his decision, now let him enforce it', may be apocryphal, but it accurately reflects Jackson's refusal to use executive power to implement the Court's defence of the Cherokees. Cherokee removal, known as 'the trail of tears', resulted in the deaths of more than 4000 Cherokees.[76]

Federal plans for 'civilizing' the Indians centred on the Civilization Fund, an annual sum first appropriated by Congress in 1819, but supplemented over the years by various missionary groups. Missionaries established schools, including boarding schools, which grew to include model farms and training in mechanical skills as well as religious instruction. The first head of the Bureau of Indian Affairs was so impressed that he predicted that through such efforts, within one generation, the Indians would be 'civilized', but attendance records were poor and parental disinterest marked. Indian students found it impossible to cope with their old world, from which they felt estranged, after having been educated for the new world, entrance into which they were denied.[77]

Movement of whites into those areas of the West set aside for American Indians precipitated what has been called 'the warriors last stand', roughly dated as occurring between 1840 and 1890. Gold was discovered in California setting off an unprecedented human migration, while the availability of fertile lands in the West beckoned still other pioneers to cross and eventually settle in lands the Indians believed belonged to them by virtue of the treaties they signed with the Federal Government. American citizens insisted that 'manifest destiny' justified their choosing not to honour such humanly contrived limitations on Divine Will and the divinely inspired progress of civilization. 'Final stands' by various Indian tribes were therefore inevitable, but futile and brutal, culminating in the Battle of Wounded Knee in 1890.[78]

In 1831, the Nez Perces sent delegations to St Louis seeking religious instruction. Missionaries of various denominations responded by relocating to the Northwest, the best known of which were the Methodist Jason Lee, Marcus and Narcissa Whitman and Henry Spauldings, all Presbyterians, and the Jesuit Catholic Pierre Jean de Smet. These early missionaries had some success in persuading various Indian tribes to combine the ways of their ancestors with Christian teachings, but they struggled in vain to protect the Indians from the onrush of white settlers. Indian wars began, precipitated by the murder of the Whitmans by a group of Cayuses in 1847, and by 1860 nearly all tribes of the Northwest were confined to reservations.[79]

In 1865 Congress created a joint committee to inquire into the condition of the Indian tribes, and 'especially into the manner in which they are treated by civil and military authorities of the United States'. Taking its unlikely name from the senator who chaired the Committee, James Doolittle, the Committee reported that, except for the tribes in the Indian Territory, the Indian population was rapidly declining as the result of disease, intemperance, war and the pressure of white settlement. Although the Committee recommended a reorganization of the Indian service, and provided the impetus for the creation of a reservation system, the importance of the Committee lay not in immediate legislation but in its effort as the Christian conscience of reform-minded humanitarians in the East.[80]

Congress established the Board of Indian Commissioners in response to demands for a non-partisan organization to oversee the administration of Indian affairs. Staffed by distinguished reformers, the board was frequently at odds with the Interior Department and thus largely ineffective in becoming a voice for Native Americans. They prompted several attempts at reform, but until 1887, which lies beyond the scope of this book, federal policy remained focused on concentrating Indians on reservations and providing them with 'Christianized civilization'.[81]

Summary

As Catherine Albanese has written:

> The story of American Indian religion is a microcosm of the religious encounters that would confront each of the immigrant peoples to America. All would come with the ways of their ancestors; all would intend to preserve them. Yet each people was among many . . . and the presence of other ways led to changes in traditional religions.[82]

Change was particularly marked in the period after 1492, during which time Indian culture encountered, and was nearly overwhelmed by, European and Euro-American culture, especially at the hands of Christian missionaries. In the past fifteen to twenty years, historians of Protestant and Catholic missions have cast doubt on the quantity and quality of native conversions. To be sure, such revisionism was a necessary corrective to earlier missionary propaganda, but as James Axtell has warned, much of the revisionist history of the 1970s and

1980s has proven to be incorrect and political as well. The truth, he and others have argued, lies somewhere in the middle. The European conquest of America was nearly total, but as Richard White noted earlier, battered remnants of Indian culture – including Indian religion – have endured.[83]

Notes

1. Although Native American is now preferred, the word Indian is more commonly used historically. Both will be used herein, the latter to be consistent with historical references and to avoid confusion with those more popularly labelled American.
2. Gary B. Nash (1992), *Red, White, and Black: The Peoples of Early North America*, 3rd edn (Englewood Cliffs, NJ: Prentice Hall), p. 3.
3. Ake Hultkrantz (1987), *Native Religions of North America* (San Francisco: Harper and Row), p. 10; Harold E. Driver (1969), *Indians of North America*, 2nd edn (Chicago: University of Chicago Press), p. 396.
4. Howard L. Harrod (1995), *Becoming and Remaining a People: Native Americans on the Northern Plains* (Tucson: University of Arizona Press), p. 15.
5. Harrod, *Becoming and Remaining a People*, p. xvi; Gregory H. Nobles (1997), *American Frontiers: Cultural Encounters and Continental Conquest* (New York: Hill and Wang), p. 29.
6. Hultkrantz, *Native Religions of North America*, p. 16; Robert F. Berkhofer (1978), *The White Man's Indian: Images of the American Indian from Columbus to the Present* (New York: Alfred A. Knopf), p. 3.
7. Alvin M. Josephy (ed.) (1992), *America in 1492: The World of the Indian Peoples before the Arrival of Columbus* (New York: Alfred A. Knopf), p. 280; Nash, *Red, White, and Black*, p. 9; Alvin M. Josephy (1970), *The Indian Heritage of America* (New York: Alfred A. Knopf), pp. 23–4.
8. Catherine Albanese (1992), *America: Religions and Religion* (Belmont, CA: Wadsworth Publishing), pp. 25–6.
9. Hultkrantz, *Native Religions of North America*, pp. 21–2.
10. Ibid., pp. 27–8.
11. Ibid., p. 31.
12. Ibid., p. 33.
13. Denise Lardner Carmody and John Tully Carmody (1998), *Native American Religions: An Introduction* (New York: Paulist Press), p. 8; Albanese, *America*, pp. 26–7.
14. Nash, *Red, White, and Black*, pp. 25–6.
15. Carmody and Carmody, *Native American Religions*, pp. 235–7.
16. Albanese, *America*, p. 28.
17. Ibid., p. 28.
18. Ibid., pp. 28–9.
19. Ibid., p. 30.
20. Carmody and Carmody, *Native American Religions*, pp. 219–20; Hultkrantz, *Native Religions of North America*, p. 25.
21. Carmody and Carmody, *Native American Religions*, p. 221.

22. Ibid., pp. 239, 244, 250; Ake Hultkrantz (1981), *Belief and Worship in Native North America* (Syracuse, NY: Syracuse University Press), chap. 11.
23. Hultkrantz, *Native Religions of North America*, p. 33.
24. Ibid., p. 14.
25. Albanese, *America*, pp. 31–2.
26. Ibid., p. 32.
27. Ibid., pp. 33–4.
28. Hultkrantz, *Native Religions of North America*, p. 9.
29. Albanese, *America*, p. 34; Hultkrantz, *Native Religions of North America*, pp. 66–76.
30. Hultkrantz, *Native Religions of North America*, p. 89.
31. Ibid., p. 90; Nash, *Red, White, and Black*, p. 90.
32. Albanese, *America*, pp. 37–8; Hultkrantz, *Native Religions of North America*, pp. 89–90.
33. Albanese, *America*, p. 37; Hultkrantz, *Native Religions of North America*, p. 93.
34. Henry Warner Bowden (1981), *American Indians and Christian Missions: Studies in Cultural Conflict* (Chicago: University of Chicago Press), pp. 37–8.
35. Hultkrantz, *Native Religions of North America*, p. 96.
36. Ibid., pp. 96–7.
37. Ibid., p. 97.
38. Ibid., p. 102; Albanese, *America*, p. 39.
39. Albanese, *America*, pp. 39–40.
40. Ibid., p. 41.
41. Ibid., p. 41.
42. Ibid., p. 41.
43. Ibid., pp. 41–2.
44. Ibid., p. 42.
45. Hultkrantz, *Native Religions of North America*, pp. 108, 128–31; Bowden, *American Indians and Christian Missions*, pp. 29–30.
46. Nash, *Red, White, and Black*, p. 28; James Axtell (1985), *The Invasion Within: The Contest of Cultures in Colonial North America* (New York: Oxford University Press), p. 329; Francis Jennings (1975), *The Invasion of America: Indians, Colonialism, and the Cant of Conquest* (Chapel Hill: University of North Carolina Press), pp. 4, 6, 43–4.
47. Wilcomb E. Washburn (1975), *The Indian in America* (New York: Harper and Row), pp. 111–12, 115; Axtell, *Invasion Within*, p. 330.
48. Washburn, *Indian in America*, p. 116.
49. Richard White (1991b), *The Middle Ground: Indians, Empires, and Republics in the Great Lakes Region, 1650–1815* (New York: Cambridge University Press), p. ix..
50. Nash, *Red, White, and Black*, p. 88. Due to space limitations, Dutch missionary efforts, which were comparatively few, are not included. See, Nash, *Red, White, and Black*, pp. 92–3.
51. James Hennesey (1981), *American Catholics: A History of the Roman Catholic Community in the United States* (New York: Oxford University Press), pp. 11–13.
52. Washburn, *Indian in America*, p. 117; Nash, *Red, White, and Black*, p. 112.
53. Edward H. Spicer (1962), *Cycles of Conquest: The Impact of Spain, Mexico, and the United States on the Indians of the Southwest, 1533–1960* (Tucson: University of Arizona Press), pp. 156–9; Bowden, *American Indians and Christian Missions*, pp. 9–10.
54. Washburn, *Indian in America*, p. 118.
55. Ibid., pp. 117–19; Spicer, *Cycles of Conquest*, pp. 120–6, 315; Ramon A. Gutierrez

(1991), *When Jesus Came, the Corn Mother Went Away: Marriage, Sexuality, and Power in New Mexico, 1500–1846* (Stanford: Stanford University Press), pp. 46–94.

56. Peter Nabokov (1991), *Native American Testimony: A Chronicle of Indian-White Relations from Prophecy to the Present, 1492–1992* (New York: Viking), pp. 54–6; Richard White (1991a), *'It's Your Misfortune and None of My Own': A History of the American West* (Norman: University of Oklahoma Press), pp. 11–12; Spicer, *Cycles of Conquest*, pp. 326–7.

57. Albanese, *America*, pp. 43–4.

58. Nash, *Red, White, and Black*, pp. 104–5.

59. Ibid., pp. 106–9.

60. Axtell, *Invasion Within*, pp. 272–3, 277–9; Nash, *Red, White, and Black*, pp. 107–8; Bowden, *American Indians and Christian Missions*, pp. 75–95; Peter A. Dorsey (1998), 'Going to school with savages: Authorship and authority among the Jesuits of New France', *William and Mary Quarterly*, 3rd sers, 55 (July): 399–401.

61. Berkhofer, *White Man's Indian*, p. 6.

62. Ibid., pp. 13–14; Nash, *Red, White, and Black*, pp. 37–9, 43.

63. Nash, *Red, White, and Black*, p. 45; Reginald Horsman (1967), *Expansion and American Indian Policy, 1783–1812* (East Lansing: Michigan State University Press), p. 1.

64. William T. Hagan (1961), *American Indians* (Chicago: University of Chicago Press), p. 9; Nash, *Red, White, and Black*, pp. 60–5.

65. Nash, *Red, White, and Black*, pp. 68–9.

66. Ibid., pp. 77–8; Neal Salisbury (1992), 'Religious encounters in a colonial context: New England and New France in the seventeenth century', *American Indian Quarterly*, 16 (Fall): 501; Alden T. Vaughan (1995), *New England Frontier: Puritans and Indians, 1620–1675*, 3rd edn (Norman: University of Oklahoma Press), pp. 235–6.

67. Roy Harvey Pearce (1965), *The Savages of America: A Study of the Indian and the Idea of Civilization* (Baltimore: Johns Hopkins University Press), pp. 3–24; Jennings, *Invasion Within*, p. 233; Vaughan, *New England Frontier*, pp. 244–52.

68. Salisbury, 'Religious encounters in colonial context', p. 503; John F. Freeman (1965), 'The Indian convert: Theme and variation', *Ethnohistory*, 12 (Spring): 113–28.

69. Washburn, *Indian in America*, p. 114; Colin G. Calloway (ed.) (1994), *The World Turned Upside Down: Indian Voices from Early America* (New York: Bedford Books), pp. 55–70; Axtell, *Invasion Within*, pp. 273, 276.

70. Hagan, *American Indians*, pp. 11–12, 16; Paul A. Wallace (ed.) (1958), *Thirty Thousand Miles with John Heckewelder* (Pittsburgh: University of Pittsburgh Press), pp. 3, 31, 189–200; Axtell, *Invasion Within*, p. 225.

71. Nash, *Red, White, and Black*, p. 266; Anthony F. C. Wallace (1970), *The Death and Rebirth of the Seneca* (New York: Alfred A. Knopf), p. 118.

72. Hagan, *American Indians*, pp. 31, 36, 49–50; Josephy, *Indian Heritage of America*, pp. 314–16.

73. Francis Paul Prucha (1984), *The Great Father: The United States Government and the American Indians* (Lincoln: University of Nebraska Press), I: p. 145; Robert F. Berkhofer (1965), *Salvation and the Savage: An Analysis of Protestant Missions and American Indian Response, 1787–1862* (Lexington: University of Kentucky Press), pp. 1, 10; Bowden, *American Indians and Christian Missions*, pp. 167–9.

74. Ronald H. Satz (1975), *American Indian Policy in the Jacksonian Era* (Lincoln: University of Nebraska Press), p. 2; Reginald Horsman (1970), *The Origins of Indian Removal, 1815–1824* (East Lansing: Michigan State University Press), pp. 1–5.
75. Hagan, *American Indians*, pp. 55, 66–7, 74; Horsman, *Origins of Indian Removal*, pp. 5–13.
76. Satz, *American Indian Policy in the Jacksonian Era*, p. 11, Hagan, *American Indians*, p. 11.
77. Hagan, *American Indians*, pp. 87–8, 90–1, 134–6; Satz, *American Indian Policy in the Jacksonian Era*, pp. 288, 253, 263; Prucha, *Great Father*, I: pp. 283–92.
78. Hagan, *American Indians*, pp. 97, 112, 118; Reginald Horsman (1981), *Race and Manifest Destiny: The Origins of American Racial Anglo-Saxonism* (Cambridge, MA: Harvard University Press), pp. 3–6, 189–207; White, *'It's Your Misfortune and None of My Own'* p. 73; Josephy, *Indian Heritage of America*, pp. 338–40, 331–4.
79. Josephy, *Indian Heritage of America*, pp. 326–7; Washburn, *Indian in America*, pp. 123–4; Robert Ignatius Burns (1966), *The Jesuits and the Indian Wars of the Northwest* (New Haven: Yale University Press), pp. 31–116.
80. Prucha, *Great Father*, I: pp. 485–500.
81. Hagan, *American Indians*, pp. 111–12, 121.
82. Albanese, *America*, p. 48.
83. James Axtell (1988), *After Columbus: Essays in the Ethnohistory of Colonial North America* (New York: Oxford University Press), pp. 101, 108.

Recommended Readings

Axtell, James (1988), *After Columbus: Essays in the Ethnohistory of Colonial North America*, New York: Oxford University Press.

Axtell, James (1985), *The Invasion Within: The Contest of Cultures in Colonial North America*, New York: Oxford University Press.

Berkhofer, Robert F. (1965), *Salvation and the Savage: An Analysis of Protestant Missions and American Indian Response, 1787–1862*, Lexington: University of Kentucky Press.

Berkhofer, Robert F. (1978), *The White Man's Indian: Images of the American Indian from Columbus to the Present*, New York: Alfred A. Knopf.

Bowden, Henry Warner(1981), *American Indians and Christian Missions: Studies in Cultural Conflict*, Chicago: University of Chicago Press.

Burns, Robert Ignatius (1966), *The Jesuits and the Indian Wars of the Northwest*, New Haven: Yale University Press.

Driver, Harold E. (1969), *Indians of North America*, 2nd edn, Chicago: University of Chicago Press.

Griffiths, Nicholas and Fernando Cervantes (eds). (1998), *Spiritual Encounters: Interactions between Christianity and Native Religions in Colonial America*, Lincoln: University of Nebraska Press.

Gutierrez, Ramon A. (1991), *When Jesus Came, the Corn Mother Went Away: Marriage, Sexuality, and Power in New Mexico, 1500–1846*, Stanford: Stanford University Press.

Harrod, Howard L. (1995), *Becoming and Remaining a People: Native Americans on the Northern Plains*, Tucson: University of Arizona Press.

Horsman, Reginald (1967), *Expansion and American Indian Policy, 1783–1812*, East Lansing: Michigan State University Press.

Horsman, Reginald (1970), *The Origins of Indian Removal, 1815–1824*, East Lansing: Michigan State University Press.

Horsman, Reginald (1981), *Race and Manifest Destiny: The Origins of American Racial Anglo-Saxonism*, Cambridge, MA: Harvard University Press.

Hultkrantz, Ake (1981), *Belief and Worship in Native North America*, Syracuse, NY: Syracuse University Press.

Hultkrantz, Ake (1987), *Native Religions of North America*, San Francisco: Harper and Row.

Jennings, Francis (1975), *The Invasion of America: Indians, Colonialism, and the Cant of Conquest*, Chapel Hill: University of North Carolina Press.

Josephy, Alvin M. (1970), *The Indian Heritage of America*, New York: Alfred A. Knopf.

Nash, Gary B. (1992), *Red, White, and Black: The Peoples of Early North America*, 3rd edn, Englewood Cliffs, NJ: Prentice Hall.

Nobles, Gregory H. (1997), *American Frontiers: Cultural Encounters and Continental Conquest*, New York: Hill and Wang.

Pearce, Roy Harvey. (1965), *The Savages of America: A Study of the Indian and the Idea of Civilization*, Baltimore: Johns Hopkins University Press.

Prucha, Francis Paul (1984), *The Great Father: The United States Government and the American Indians*, vols I and II, Lincoln: University of Nebraska Press.

Satz, Ronald H. (1975), *American Indian Policy in the Jacksonian Era*, Lincoln: University of Nebraska Press, 1984.

Spicer, Edward H. (1962), *Cycles of Conquest: The Impact of Spain, Mexico, and the United States on the Indians of the Southwest, 1533–1960*, Tucson: University of Arizona Press.

Vaughan, Alden T. (1995), *New England Frontier: Puritans and Indians, 1620–1675*, 3rd edn, Norman: University of Oklahoma Press.

Wallace, Anthony F. C. (1970), *The Death and Rebirth of the Seneca*, New York: Alfred A. Knopf.

Washburn, Wilcomb E. (1975), *The Indian in America*, New York: Harper and Row.

White, Richard (1991a), *'It's Your Misfortune and None of My Own': A History of the American West*, Norman: University of Oklahoma Press.

White, Richard (1991b), *The Middle Ground: Indians, Empires, and Republics in the Great Lakes Region, 1650–1815*, New York: Cambridge University Press.

CHAPTER 2

British Colonization and the Origins of American Religion

'God is English', an English clergyman told his parishioners in 1558,[1] but England did little to convince the world of that, or at least to establish the Church of England in the New World until over 100 years after Columbus arrived in the Caribbean. A British clergymen, Richard Hakluyt, deserves considerable credit for finally bringing that about.

In his *A Discourse on Western Planting* (1584), Hakluyt argued the allied causes of Protestantism and England. In speaking of spreading the word of God through colonization, he wrote: 'It remains to be thoroughly weighed and considered by what means and by whom this most godly and Christian work may be performed of enlarging the glorious gospel of Christ.' But, he continued, it should be done by those 'who have taken upon them the protection and defense of the Christian faith', namely the Kings and Queens of England, who, having been named Defenders of the Faith, 'are not only charged to maintain and patronize the faith of Christ, but also to enlarge and advance it'.[2] That charge grew out of the English Reformation, which first delayed and then made more urgent English colonization of America.

During the reign of King Henry VIII, England severed its ecclesiastical ties with Rome, but this marked only the beginning of the turbulence that rocked England for generations. When Henry died, the kingdom veered sharply toward Protestantism under Edward VI, then toward Catholicism under Mary I, before arriving at a 'settlement' under Queen Elizabeth. A measure of stability returned as the Church of England steered a middle course between Roman Catholicism and the Protestantism of either Calvin or Luther, but such a course did not please everyone. The most quarrelsome of the dissidents became known as the Puritans, who, despairing of the degree of reform effected, withdrew into their own churches, and then, in large numbers, when they came under increasing attack by the Stuart kings, from England altogether.[3]

The Virginia Colony

On 10 April 1606, King James I chartered the London Company, and almost exactly one year later the company cast anchor off the coast of Virginia, establishing a colony named for its monarch, Jamestown. Tragedy marked the first years of the settlement. Of little more than 100 settlers in May, half were dead by September, and so the pattern continued for several years in the face of Indian attacks, disease and starvation. It would be at least a dozen years before reasonable men could believe that Virginia might survive.

There was no question from the start that the Church of England would be the Established Church in Virginia. For many reasons, however, the Church in Virginia found itself incapable of duplicating the Church left behind. First, parishes were not neat parcels of land centred on the village green. They were measured in miles, not blocks, and they were sparsely settled, especially with single young men. Virginia offered little to a potential pastor but personal hardship and hostile country. His salary was set by law, but since he was paid in a fixed amount of tobacco or corn, fluctuations on the market undermined a stable income. In 1662 Roger Green bitterly complained of a clerical shortage so severe that settlers 'see their families disordered, their children untaught, the public worship and service of the great God they own neglected'.[4]

Further adding to the difficulties of the Church of England in Virginia was the absence of theological training for prospective ministers, the poor quality of those ministers attracted to the colony from England, and troubles between the clergy and the laity, the last being complicated by uncertain and uneven church discipline. Virginia had no bishop and no ecclesiastical court to examine orthodoxy or enforce discipline. That left such matters to individual congregations and the men elected to the church vestry. Under such circumstances, the rector was sometimes at the mercy of an unsympathetic vestry; the vestry was sometimes under the spell of an unworthy minister.[5]

Despite these handicaps, as the colony grew so too did the Church. There were twenty parishes in Virginia by 1650 and twice that number by the end of the century. In 1693, the College of William and Mary was chartered 'to the end that the Church of Virginia may be furnished with a seminary of ministers to the gospel'. Nevertheless, Anglicanism lost favour and following to the rapidly growing forces of dissent. After England adopted its Act of Toleration in 1689, the Church's restrictive walls crumbled, and Presbyterians, Baptists and Methodists made deep inroads. Part of the growth of the dissenting or noncomforming churches resulted from new immigration; the rest migrated from New England and the Middle Colonies. The pattern had begun that would be repeated throughout the colonies, regardless of which particular group was responsible for that colony's settlement: Where once there was one, there soon appeared many.[6]

New England

In 1620 the Pilgrims sailed for the New World. Like other Puritans, the Pilgrims contended that England's established church had not completed its reformation. Unlike other Puritans, they had given up trying to reform it from within. Having become Separatists, they fled England to escape the heavy penalties of the law – first to Amsterdam, in 1607, then to Leyden, where though they had more freedom they did not feel at home, and finally to America. With 'great hope and inward zeal', William Bradford, one of their leaders, wrote, they set out to lay 'some good foundation for propagating and advancing the gospel of the Kingdom of Christ in those remote parts of the world; yea, though they should be but even as stepping-stones unto others for the performing of so great a work'.[7]

Authorized to settle in Virginia, the Pilgrims made landfall off the coast of New England, where, with supplies short and winter near, they decided to remain. The site of Plymouth was chosen, a compact agreed to for social order, and a community begun. Bradford, soon to be governor of the Plymouth Colony, recorded his observations upon arrival: 'The season, it was winter', he wrote, and they were 'subject to cruel and fierce storms'. They had arrived in 'a hideous and desolate wilderness, full of wild beasts and wild men', and 'what could now sustain them but the Spirit of God and His grace?'.[8]

By the following spring about one-half of the settlers had died, but the colony itself did not perish. By fall the Pilgrims and Indians, who had done much to insure the Pilgrims' survival, shared a thanksgiving feast, and soon the colony was on more firm footing. Growth in Plymouth, however, was never great, and it was soon eclipsed by the far larger migration of their Puritan cousins to Massachusetts Bay. By the middle of the seventeenth century Plymouth still numbered fewer than 1000 inhabitants; Massachusetts Bay was nearly twenty times as large.

Unlike the Pilgrims, the Puritans of Massachusetts Bay had not separated from the Church of England. For them the Church of England, though having lost its way, remained their church and they bore the responsibility of reforming it. To do so, however, they would emigrate to a new land 3000 miles from England's ecclesiastical courts, where they would be free to create a true Church of England, a church purified. Their goal was 'to do more service to the Lord' by increasing 'the body of Christ where of [they were] members', and to preserve themselves and their posterity 'from the common corruptions of this evil world'. They would 'work out [their] salvation under the power and purity of [God's] holy ordinances', and become 'a city on a hill', which would serve as a model for those they left behind.[9]

In Puritan Congregationalism, the 'New England way', each local church ruled itself, joining with other churches only for counsel, admonition, and fellowship. In contrast to the Church of England's hierarchical structure, the local congregation was the highest earthly ecclesiastical authority. Only those who gave evidence of conversion were eligible for church membership, and the church was formed by means of a voluntary covenant among the converted.[10]

The Puritans, standing firmly in the tradition of John Calvin, indulged in no sentimental illusions about the nature of man. Man was a sinner, and New England Puritans acknowledged from the beginning the need for law, discipline and control. In addition to a church covenant and a covenant of grace, a civil compact was provided. Because Massachusetts was a commonwealth, all were equally subject to the active dominion of God. Because it was a Puritan commonwealth, the saints were in charge, and the entire experiment rested on the premise that church and state would be one, not in their organization, but in their common recognition of the sovereignty and omniscience of God. As Edwin Gaustad put it: 'New England was not "priest-ridden" in the sense that clergymen forced reluctant magistrates to do their bidding. The colony was "piety-driven" . . . in the sense that basic religious motives propelled the state no less than the church'.[11]

Decades ago, Perry Miller exposed what he referred to as the New England Puritans' Augustinian strain of piety.[12] More recent scholarship, however, has shown that beyond being intellectual, Puritanism was as well an upwelling of religious emotion bounded and articulated by the canons of Reformed Protestantism. This piety was established in conversion, spiritually the soul's rebirth, wherein fear of God and self-humiliation over one's unworthiness and incapacity to achieve salvation gives way to peace, joy and love for God and fellow-saints from recognition that God's grace is freely given. Such love then provides regenerates with a measure of spiritual potency to obey God's laws and reform society, which in turn was seen as a necessary step in the restoration of the church order buried under more than a millennium of Catholic corruption and human innovation.[13] To ensure religious orthodoxy and uniformity, especially among the clergy, the colonies of Massachusetts and Connecticut established Harvard College in 1636 and Yale in 1701.

Some chose to dissent from the Massachusetts dissenters' establishment. Roger Williams arrived in Boston in 1631, whereupon Governor Winthrop received him as one of the 'godly ministers'. Boston offered Williams its pulpit, but he declined because, as he later wrote, 'I durst not officiate to an unseparated people.' The people of New England must separate 'holy from unholy, penitent from impenitent, godly from ungodly'.[14] Williams accepted an offer from Plymouth, where the Pilgrims found nothing objectionable in Williams's separatism. In 1633, he moved to Salem.

In his brief ministry, Williams attacked not only church government but also civil government, arguing that magistrates should not punish Sabbath-breakers or violators of any other religious requirement. Massachusetts authorities saw Williams's religious zeal as misdirected and threatening to the peace and covenanted harmony upon which their 'errand into the wilderness' depended, but Williams responded by arguing that civil magistrates had no power to punish him or anyone else for their religious opinions. In 1635 the Massachusetts authorities brought Williams to trial, found him guilty of having 'broached and divulged new and dangerous opinions against the authority of the magistrates and churches', and ordered him to depart Massachusetts's jurisdiction. Williams moved to Narraganset Bay and what would become Providence, Rhode Island.[15]

Promising freedom of religion to all comers, Williams's colony became a haven for dissenters and the persecuted. Williams remained as zealous in his faith as ever, but he came to realize that state compulsion was not conducive to that end. Rather than arguing that the state had to be protected from ambitious religionists, as his actions might be interpreted today, he concluded that Christianity had to be protected from the state. As he explained in *The Bloody Tenent of Persecution* (1644), 'persecution for cause of conscience [was] against the

Doctrine of Jesus Christ'.[16] Religion must be voluntary, not forced; church and state must be separate. In 1663, when Rhode Island received a colonial charter, religious liberty remained a guarantee, not only for Christians but also for Jews. Ten years later, Jews, originally from the Iberian peninsula, but later from Central and Eastern Europe as well, dedicated what is now the oldest surviving synagogue in British America, the Touro Synagogue in Newport, Rhode Island.

Anne Hutchinson, too, came as an insider, having followed her clerical hero, John Cotton, from England. She heard Cotton preach, that, prior to the Fall, God gave Adam and his heirs a convenant of works. God then promised man a new covenant of grace, which Jesus Christ sealed when he gave himself to death on the cross. Cotton favoured the second covenant, Hutchinson accepted it exclusively. She opposed those who suggested that salvation could be achieved through obedience to moral law, arguing even, it was charged, that once people were under the covenant of grace, or had received God's saving grace, they were absolved from the necessity of obeying moral law. Massachusetts Puritans rejected the covenant of works, as well, but they had tacitly allowed, if not encouraged, a preparationist understanding of obedience to moral law and taught that people under the covenant of grace would necessarily lead a holy life. Her enemies called Hutchinson's heresy Antinomianism; they feared it would lead to lawlessness and anarchy.[17]

Instead of keeping her religious views to herself, Hutchinson expounded on them to increasingly large crowds of men and women in her home. She also attacked Cotton's fellow-minister, John Wilson, for having lapsed back to the covenant of works. To colonial authorities, of church and state, she had gone too far. Anne Hutchinson had preached falsely, they charged, and she had violated good practice and church order.

When tried before the Massachusetts General Court, in 1637 and 1638, Hutchinson asked what law she had broken. Officials cited the Fifth Commandment, because, while it only demanded respect for father and mother, they interpreted it to include all other authority in church and state as well. Hutchinson asked whether true children of God were obliged to obey parents, if those parents asked them to do wrong, but Winthrop chose not to debate the matter, responding: 'we do not mean to discourse with those of your sex'.[18]

Hutchinson made it clear that she followed a igher law than that laid down by religious authorities. Moreover, she insisted that individuals could communicate with the spirit of Christ and interpret biblical teachings on their own. This, Winthrop convinced the Court, was the root of all Hutchinson's mischief. Church and state could never survive such capricious assertions; they could not tolerate claims that God spoke new words apart from Scripture to Hutchinson or anyone else. Hutchinson and her followers were either banished or silenced.[19] The Reverend John Wheelwright, Hutchinson's brother-in-law, moved to New Hampshire, where he joined others in planting that colony. Hutchinson, her family and others moved to Rhode Island. Still the eye of the storm even among Rhode Islanders, following the death of her husband she moved to the Pelham Bay area of Long Island Sound where she was killed in 1643 in an Indian attack.

A less inflammatory form of discontent led the Reverend Thomas Hooker, in 1634, to petition the Massachusetts General Court for permission to leave. Hooker, finding Massachusetts too crowded and contentious, moved to what is now northern Connecticut. Three years later, the Reverend John Davenport, finding Massachusetts too compromising, led a group to the port of New Haven. Their contrasting ideological origins notwithstanding, the two colonies were joined under one colonial charter in 1665.

Other individuals and groups – including Baptists and Quakers – continued to challenge Puritan rule. Authorities attempted to close their doors to such radicals, but, in a pattern that would be repeated throughout American history, they failed and ultimately had to adjust. By 1660, Philip Gura has found, an ideological system evolved that, while it could not fully satisfy the longings of all radicals, harnessed enough of the potential energies of their ideas to garner the support of the majority of settlers. The dissenters became members of the congregational order from which Winthrop and others had worked to exclude them.[20]

Dissenters' challenges to the Puritan establishment were further defused by the political and religious settlement of the Restoration, but discontent continued to manifest itself in other ways in New England, underscoring the witch trials of 1692. Although perhaps not the direct cause, the unravelling of Puritan New England's religious experiment at the end of the century no doubt made fertile soil for witch-hunting. What David Hall has described in his analysis of popular religion as a long-standing tension between orthodox ministerial expectations and deeply embedded, centuries-old magical and occult beliefs broke down.[21]

Before the Salem witch trials ended, 19 people had been hanged and 1 man pressed to death. Others died in the process, and over 150 people from twenty-four towns and villages were jailed, some for several months. Compared to other witch-hunts in the Western world, it was but 'a small incident in the history of a great superstition', but it was the largest of its kind in the British colonies of North America. It has left its mark on the historical conscience of Americans, and, some would argue, marked the turning point from the more medieval/reformation religious world of the seventeenth century to the modern period that followed. Puritan hegemony had been broken, forever.[22]

The Middle Colonies

No other section of the American colonies is less visible in the literature than those called the Middle Colonies. It may be the case, however, as more recent scholarship suggests, that it was those colonies, in their great diversity of faiths, much more so than the more homogenous Puritan New England and Anglican South, that demonstrated that voluntarism, or denominationalism, the free exercise of religion and disestablishment were not necessarily destructive to belief in God; and that out of diversity can come unity: *e pluribus unum*. New York, New Jersey and Pennsylvania present the most striking picture of religious diversity in British America.[23]

New York began as the colony of New Netherlands, established by the Dutch West India Company in 1623 at the mouth of the Hudson River. Although established with the express purpose of bringing to Holland 'a share of the rumored riches of the New World', largely through the fur trade and with no reference to religion in the company's charter, colonial promoters proposed that ministers be sent to instruct both the settlers and the Indians 'in religion and learning'.[24] In 1629 the Dutch Reformed Church was officially established, but the directors of the company followed a liberal policy encouraging colonists of many faiths to settle there, including Jews.

In 1664 the Dutch colony came under British rule. The Dutch Reformed Church was permitted to remain, and New York's comparatively liberal policy attracted Congregationalists from New England, Presbyterians from Scotland and Ireland, Quakers from a number of locations, and Lutherans from the Palatinate. Anglican leaders were not pleased by such promiscuous mixing, but once the English Toleration Act was passed exclusion ceased to be an option. Instead the colony of New York adopted new laws to encourage the building of Anglican churches and the growth of an Anglican ministry. By the mid-eighteenth century, largely the result of the efforts of the Society for the Propagation of the Gospel, about sixty Anglican churches existed in the Middle Colonies. In 1754 Anglicans succeeded in establishing in New York City King's College, later to be renamed Columbia, but actual establishment of the Church of England was limited to the four counties around New York City.[25]

New Jersey's even more liberal policy toward dissenters attracted diverse religious groups as well. Among the largest groups added to the founding Dutch Reformed Church were Presbyterians, out of Scotland and Ireland, New England Congregationalists, who would become Presbyterians, and Quakers from England. By 1746 Presbyterians had gained sufficient strength of numbers to establish synods in Philadelphia and New York and to secure a charter for the College of New Jersey, later known as Princeton.[26] English Quakers settled in West New Jersey – for a time separated from East New Jersey – from which, the Quaker William Penn later wrote, they laid 'a foundation for after ages to understand their liberty as men and Christians, that they may not be brought in bondage but by their own consent'.[27] Penn would soon, however, set his sights elsewhere, creating his own colony of Pennsylvania.

William Penn was no stranger to intolerance. During the reign of Charles II fifteen thousand Quakers had been confined to British jails, where more than four hundred died. In 1670 he wrote a passionate defense of religious liberty, *The Great Case of Liberty of Conscience*, wherein he argued that force had no place in matters of the spirit. Much as had Roger Williams, Penn insisted that when force is used in religion – a direct reference to an established church using its position to silence dissenters – God is dishonoured, the Christian religion overthrown, reason violated and government undone.[28]

Penn launched his 'Holy Experiment' in 1681, when King Charles II, in payment for a debt, granted Penn the area that was to become the colonies of Pennsylvania and Delaware (separated from Pennsylvania in 1701). Penn intended his colony to be a model of what men of good will could be, when guided by the inner light of God's Spirit – the Quaker way. Penn's generous land policy and offer of religious

freedom attracted other religious groups as well. Tens of thousands of
Reformed, but mostly Lutheran, Germans, began arriving as early as
1683 led by Francis Daniel Pastorius, and by 1740 they equalled nearly
one-third of the entire Pennsylvania population. Scotch-Irish Presbyterians, equalling another third, began to arrive in large numbers during
the second and third decades of the eighteenth century, moving to the
frontier, where they became one of the most formidable groups of
frontiersmen in American history. There were also smaller but significant numbers of Mennonites, Catholics, Amish, German Baptist Brethren, or Dunkers, Jews and Anglicans.[29]

In that 'Penn's Woods' attracted and accommodated such diversity, Penn's Holy Experiment was a success. While Penn worked for
'a blessed government, and a virtuous, ingenious and industrious
society',[30] however, the Quakers' leadership was soon rent with dis-
putes; civil authority grew tangled and corrupt; and Quaker pacifism
was compromised by the colony's frontier conditions. In sum, Penn's
much-exalted Quaker belief in the 'holy law within', upon which the
colony was to be built, disappeared.

The Southern Colonies

In contrast to the Middle Colonies, the Southern Colonies followed
Virginia's example in attempting to maintain its Anglican establishment.
Maryland was the single exception. In 1632 King Charles I granted to
Cecil Calvert, Lord Baltimore, a charter for lands around Chesapeake
Bay, north of Virginia. Lord Baltimore was the only Roman Catholic
proprietor among American colonists. Although intended as a haven for
Catholics, Maryland – honouring both England's last Catholic monarch
and the Virgin Mother – also welcomed Protestants, but the latter
arrived in such large numbers that the founders' original intent was
repeatedly and ultimately successfully challenged. In 1649, in response
to one such challenge, Calvert sought to protect the Catholic minority
by framing a toleration act, whereby 'no persons professing to believe
in Jesus Christ should be molested in respect of their religion, or in the
free exercise thereof, or be compelled to the belief or exercise of any
other religion, against their consent'.[31]

Opposition from resident Protestants continued until, in April 1689,
they persuaded King William to make Maryland a royal colony. In 1692
the Maryland colonial assembly adopted an act 'for the service of
Almighty God and the establishment of the Protestant religion', and

the new governor administered English test oaths and oaths of office to all office-holders, with which Catholics could not comply. In 1718 the Maryland legislature disfranchised Catholics altogether.[32]

The first permanent settlement in the Carolinas was established in 1670 at Charleston. The colony attracted settlers from Barbados, Jamaica and other Caribbean islands, as well as immigrants from England, Ireland and France, and migrants from New England. Nearly all were Protestant, but a major centre of colonial Judaism arose in Charleston, as well. As in Virginia, the arrival of such dissenting groups in what was to be officially a Church of England preserve caused some alarm. Anglicans leaders viewed dissenters as interlopers, not only forgetful of colonial prerogatives and royal wishes, but also a threat to the peace and security they believed establishment and uniformity of belief guaranteed.

Quaker John Archdale made matters only worse, when he urged all in authority to give up their quarrelling over 'poor trifles and barren opinions'. In 1707 Archdale wrote: 'It is stupendous to consider how passionate and preposterous zeal not only veils but stupefies oftentimes, the rational powers.' Reasonable men should consider the qualifications of prospective settlers as settlers, not on their religious beliefs. If Carolina were to take away freedom of conscience or deprive men of their liberty and property because of their religious beliefs, Archdale continued, settlers would leave, or not be attracted to the colony in the first place. It was a telling argument, heard again and again all along the Atlantic coast, not only against the Anglican Establishment but also against the Puritans of Massachusetts and Connecticut. The result, in the Carolinas as elsewhere, was an increase in religious toleration, eventually leading, as we shall see, to religious freedom.[33]

The area that was to become North Carolina had no settlement until colonists began about 1653 to migrate from Virginia into the region around Albemarle Sound. Many were Quakers, their affiliation encouraged by George Fox's visit in 1672. By the early years of the eighteenth century over 4000 inhabited the area, but the region developed a reputation for its rough ways. Anglican missionaries were appalled at the lack of 'decency and order'. Although the colonial assembly made legal provision for Anglicanism as early as 1715, successful implementation of the law depended, as always, on the sentiment and sympathy of the people, and the people of North Carolina were unwilling or unable to establish effectively the Church of England in their midst.[34]

In 1731 Thomas Bray, founder of the Anglican Society for the Propagation of the Gospel and Society for the Promotion of Christian Knowledge, commissioned an organization 'for instructing the Negroes in the Christian religion and establishing a charitable colony for the better maintenance of the poor of this kingdom, and for other good purposes'. He attracted James Oglethorpe to his cause, and soon thereafter Oglethorpe petitioned King George III for a land grant south of South Carolina for imprisoned debtors and impoverished unemployed. In 1733 the King granted him a charter and about 100 men, women and children embarked for King George's colony.[35]

Oglethorpe made clear his intent to instruct and convert blacks in the charter's prohibition against slavery. He was forced to remove the restriction, however, in 1749. The 'poor of this kingdom' were nevertheless conspicuous among the colony's first settlers, and the 'charitable colony' welcomed Lutherans fleeing persecution in Salzburg, Moravians leaving the protection of Saxony, and Scottish Presbyterians escaping political and economic distress. Even Jews, although officially forbidden to come, arrived in 1733, whereupon Oglethorpe not only permitted them to stay but also granted them land. In 1740 George Whitefield started an orphanage in Bethesda, near Savannah.[36]

In 1758 the Georgia Assembly formally recognized the Church of England as the colony's official denomination, created eight parishes, and stipulated a salary for eight nonexistent clergymen. Like the 1715 law in North Carolina, however, this act had little force for lack of actual church buildings and ministers. Failing, as did Anglicans in the other British colonies, to have a bishop appointed, Georgia Anglicans met little more than frustration in their efforts to solidify their hold on a colony that, like most of the rest, became an attractive destination for dissenters.[37]

The First Great Awakening

The transplanting of European religion to the New World was made more difficult by the environment into which it entered. Given the unsettled, frontier-like world into which immigrants plunged – the absence of church, ministry or even community – it was easy for many to simply fall into non-practise. Given the presence of so many religious groups among those who might wish to practice, rather than one established church as had been the case in Europe, no one church could permanently claim any turf as its own. They would have to compete both with the wilderness and one another to win believers. The First Great Awakening constituted one such competition.

Initial impulses for the First Great Awakening arrived from Europe – from pietistic movements that tried to fire up casual believers, like the revivals that shook Britain during the 1730s and 1740s.[38] But something new arose in America in the 1730s, an awakening that took many shapes, forms and expressions. It is hard to prove that religious participation was low before the stirrings and greatly increased thereafter. Moreover the Awakening was really a series of loosely connected outbreaks, each of which took on the colour of its local milieu. No central person or religious organization planned or coordinated it; 'no single plot unfolded'.[39] Nevertheless, something of significance did happen during the fourth and fifth decades of the eighteenth century.

The Great Awakening can be seen as a move toward the development of modern religion in the West, in general, and American religion, in particular. At its heart was the notion of choice: colonists were obliged to choose Jesus Christ, to decide to let the Spirit of God work in their hearts, and to select one version of Christianity over another. In this regard, the Great Awakening changed the landscape of the American religious community. As Martin Marty has put it: 'Where once a single steeple towered above the town, there soon would be a steeple and a chapel, Old First Church and competitive Separatist Second Church or Third Baptist Chapel – all vying for souls.'[40] Most of the mainline Protestant churches of the modern period exist because they set out to convert people during the First and Second Great Awakenings. Those, like the Anglicans/Episcopalians, who shunned them were left behind. One figure, Jonathan Edwards, looms especially large in the history of the movement.

Jonathan Edwards, a religious thinker and evangelical preacher, towered above all others of his time. No one both participated in and studied the Awakening more thoroughly. No one interpreted the psychology of conversion or the meaning of the revival for community life better than he did. Perry Miller has credited Edwards with salvaging the central points of Puritan authority by modernizing its outmoded metaphysics with the enlightened harmonies of Isaac Newton and John Locke, thereby paving the way for the New England mind becoming the American mind.[41] Edwards's story, however, like that of most evangelicals of the Great Awakening, makes best sense when set against the background of the immediate world in which he lived, that is the

early-eighteenth-century Connecticut River Valley, that had been presided over by his grandfather Solomon Stoddard. Stoddard ministered
to the region for over fifty-seven years, earning the title 'pope' from his
detractors due to his pervasive influence.

Stoddard and Edwards inherited a problem that each would address
but in different ways, the declining number of 'visible saints' who were
to govern church and state in Puritan New England. With each passing
decade, fewer adults experienced conversion and thereby qualified for
church membership and the right to baptize their children. The problem
had only been temporarily assuaged by the Half-Way Covenant of
1662, wherein church members, who were baptized as children, grew up
in agreement with the doctrine of faith and did not lead scandalous
lives, could enter the covenant and have their children baptized. The
Covenant appears to have done nothing to arrest the declining number
of conversions!

Stoddard's solution – known as Stoddardeanism – was to move
beyond even the limits of the Half-Way Covenant to throw the gates of
full church membership open to all baptized persons. Where only one
sacrament, baptism, had been used to promote conversions, he would
add the Lord's Supper. All baptized persons could become full church
members, but only as a means toward an end – their conversion. Once
they became church members, Stoddard whipped up revivals and
preached emotionally to stir conversion, and it seemed to work, at
least for awhile.[42]

Stoddard's revivals ran their course, before his grandson joined him
in the Northampton pulpit. When Stoddard died in 1729, Edwards took
charge and promptly pronounced the residents of Northampton 'very
insensible of the things of religion'. He represented his town as corrupt,
and began preaching the terror and mercy of God. In 1733 people began
to stir, and for the next two years people crowded the aisles and pews,
converting in such numbers that ever since some observers have spoken
of the Great Awakening as having begun there and then.[43]

Edwards himself observed, that when he preached, 'the town seemed
to be full of the presence of God' and never 'so full of love, nor so full of
joy; yet so full of distress'. The balance was crucial, because the
Awakening was built on their interplay. As if the hearts of people were
pierced with a dart, Edwards wrote, their consciences stung and they
feared to meet God. Then, when they surrendered, God gave them a
sudden bright sense of newness. Terror in distress was only the first

stage of rebirth. Next came an awareness of the depth of the human predicament and the justness with which God stood ready to condemn the sinner. Finally came relief through the gift of grace.[44]

Edwards rewrote history, with the Awakening as its climax. Aware that revivals were breaking out in several other places in the colonies, Edwards established British America as an instrument of the promised Second Coming of Jesus. As if they belonged in the unfolding plot of the Bible itself, Connecticut Valley villagers and other converts were to see their lives now filled with a special sense of meaning and destiny. As Martin Marty has put it: 'In a strange way the all-powerful God himself depended on their will, their voluntary choice, to complete his work and end history.' The Bible prophesied that such changes would occur and Edwards was sure that his followers could not 'reasonably think otherwise'.[45]

Edwards spelled out his vision in *Some Thoughts Concerning the Present Revival of Religion in New England* (1742). The Old World would no longer enjoy the honour of communicating religion in its most glorious state to America, but vice versa. Edwards insisted that the America that once supplied gold and tobacco to Europe now must send spiritual good. God had hidden America from the world until Protestant reformers could attack the great antichristian Catholic apostasy. Now 'this utmost, meanest, youngest, and weakest part' of the world would change the rest of it. Those who opposed revivals or kept silent thereafter, Edwards argued, exposed themselves to the curse of God. But, opponents there would be.[46]

Among the revivalists' prime opponents was Charles Chauncy, minister of the First Church in Boston. Chauncy – leader of what came to be known as the Old Lights (or Old Siders in the Middle Colonies) – portrayed the revival as a force of infinite evil. Popery itself, he wrote, had not been 'the mother of more and greater blasphemies and abominations'. Pointing especially to excesses of evangelical fanatics like James Davenport, who even Edwards came to condemn, Chauncy charged the Awakening with filling the church with confusion and the state with disorder, pitting parishioner against parishioner, parishioner against minister, minister against minister and citizen against citizen in an uncompromising stance.[47]

Perhaps because he pushed too hard and was too uncompromising, when the fires of the Awakening cooled, Edwards's authority subsided as well. In a dispute made up of many petty issues, his council removed him from his Northampton position. For seven years he worked among the Indians at Stockbridge, Massachusetts, from which he moved on to assume the presidency of Princeton, a college born of the Great Awakening among Presbyterians in the Middle Colonies, where he died in 1758.

The Northampton revival was only one of several local revivals that broke out in the colonies during the 1730s and early 1740s, that may well have remained entirely local had it not been for the efforts of another evangelical giant, George Whitefield. Whitefield, it may be said, was responsible for whipping the flames of the local revivals into the general conflagration known as the Great Awakening. He also came to represent the most controversial aspect of the Awakening, itinerancy.

As noted earlier, Whitefield started coming to America from England to advance the cause of Georgia's Bethesda orphanage. Arriving in the late 1730s, however, he became one of the Great Awakening's most ardent proponents. Whitefield whipped people into enthusiasm for God with a voice and style that led actor David Garrick to assert enviously that Whitefield could melt an audience merely by pronouncing 'Mesopotamia'.[48] He also adopted up-to-date marketing techniques to merchandise his product: religion. Advertising his feats in print, hawking his journals, and staging confrontations to attract publicity, he gained unparalleled notice. When Benjamin Franklin heard Whitefield address crowds in Philadelphia, despite his initial scepticism, he offered to be Whitefield's publisher and made a donation for the erection of a meeting-house and the Georgia orphanage.[49]

Whitefield drew praise for his work among the unconverted, condemning lying, cursing, Sabbath-breaking and other forms of irreverence. His evangelical style and itinerancy, however, provoked opposition as well. In England and America, he was barred from some churches as an enthusiast, so he took his crowds into the streets and open fields. By Franklin's estimate, Whitefield preached to up to 30,000 people upon one occasion in Philadelphia. In doing so he further undercut the Establishment, both within his own Church of England, that generally opposed the Awakening, and in other churches that were divided on the issue. He joined with those who attacked Old Light/ Old Side, or even neutral, ministers as preaching an unknown and unfelt Christ, for allowing laxity and for not promoting the preaching of grace.[50]

Although the Great Awakening influenced nearly every colonial denomination to some extent, New England Congregationalists and their Calvinist Presbyterian cousins of the Middle Colonies were most affected. Some have found the first stirrings of the Awakening in the Middle Colonies among German radical Pietists in the 1720s. Others have pointed to the work of the German-born Dutch Reformed minister Theodorus Frelinghuysen, who in the mid-1720s created a storm in New Jersey's Raritan Valley by seeking to awaken the spiritually dead and contented. But the Awakening reached its greatest heights among Presbyterians, beginning in the 1730s and peaking during the 1740s.[51]

The Presbyterian awakeners were led by the Tennent family. William Tennent, a Scotch-Irish immigrant, operated what was popularly known as the 'Log College', near Philadelphia, which trained much needed ministers for the church. Its graduates were listed among the most fervent evangelicals. William's son Gilbert became the leader of the Awakening in Presbyterian circles, as well as one of its most divisive forces. As supporters rallied to his call in large numbers, critics faulted him for claiming that he could look at people's faces and see whether they would be saved or damned, for his causing those who listened to his preaching to cry out 'under the impression of terror and love' and, when in Nottingham, Pennsylvania, for offering one of the most heated sermons of the entire Awakening, wherein he spoke of 'the dangers of an unconverted ministry'. In 1741, one year after the Nottingham sermon, the Presbyterian Synod of Philadelphia split into two parties – Old Side and New Side, or, more formally, the Synod of Philadelphia and the Synod of New York – which were not reunited until 1785.[52]

Recent scholarship indicates that the Great Awakening only temporarily altered patterns of church adherence, which soon settled back into a pattern of more gradual but sustained growth.[53] It did, however, leave its mark on American religious history. In the short term it politicized religious tensions. Disputing the propriety of letting an unregenerate pastor keep his pulpit sanctioned similar arguments against corrupt imperial officials. Organizing churches to advance denominational goals modelled the mechanisms ultimately used to promote patriot dreams, and protestations against local infringements of religious liberty habituated colonists to advancing similar defences against Imperial threats. During the colonial period, Patricia Bonomi has written, 'the world was set in which American religious institutions have developed ever since',[54] but more on that in the next chapter.

The effects of the Great Awakening were long term, as well. If the First Great Awakening ended, revivals did not; they became permanent features of the American religious landscape. In this respect, the Great Awakening was not an interpretative fiction. It may well have been a turning point in the Christianization of the colonies, or the churching of America.

Summary

By the end of the colonial period, America stood poised to become one of the most religiously diverse countries in the world. Within that diversity, however, there was considerable unity, in that nearly all believers were Protestant and most were Reformed, or Calvinist. Anglicans, although the Established Church of mother England, claimed slightly less than 16 per cent of all religious adherents, while dissenting Congregationalists, Presbyterians and Baptists accounted for approximately 20 per cent, 19 per cent, and 17 per cent, respectively.[55]

There was, therefore, widespread agreement on certain principles. First, Protestantism was a religion of the Word, the Word of the Bible, and colonists rebuked the Catholic Church for having drifted from that mandate, toward sacramentalism. Second, most colonists believed that, without God's help through the grace of Jesus Christ, humans were powerless to effect their own salvation. They were sinners, who on their own could not do anything to win the grace of God. Nevertheless, just as God must perform a decisive act to save them, so they must live out their loyalty to him by decisive action in the world.

Third, colonial Protestant ministers, much like their European Calvinist counterparts, preached justification through faith. Justification was a legal term used to connote salvation, and faith meant the trust that human beings felt for God in Jesus. Faith was not, as in the Catholic Church, a collection of doctrinal truths to be accepted. Instead, it was a response to a divine and trustworthy person. Such faith put the emotional experience of an individual at the centre of religion, an emphasis that Protestantism renewed in the First Great Awakening.

Fourth, colonists continued the Protestant insistence on the priesthood of all believers, once again departing from the medieval church with its sacramental understanding of the role of the priest as a ritual leader who represented the community before God. Among Roman Catholics, the community offered a common act of worship. Protestants brought individualism into the communal consciousness of the church.

If each person was a priest, then each as an individual was offering worship to God.

These basic principles did not significantly distance colonial Protestants from their European counterparts. They did not remain static, however, but rather, in their New World environment evolved into beliefs that were more distinctly American. The emphasis on individualism, for example, would become increasingly important in the new nation. It spoke to the new middle class that would quickly come to dominate the population, underscoring individualism in the social and economic sectors as well. Further, these Reformation principles came to complement what British Americans saw as a call for moral action in the world. The Word of the Reformers did not call humans to be idle, but instead to witness to their beliefs by their deeds. As Catherine Albanese has put it: 'Protestantism led out of the churches and into the world'.[56]

Notes

1. Carl Bridenbaugh (1968), *Vexed and Troubled Englishmen, 1590–1642* (New York: Oxford University Press), p. 13.
2. Edwin Scott Gaustad (1966), *A Religious History of America* (New York: Harper and Row), p. 28.
3. Wallace Notestein (1962), *The English People on the Eve of Colonization, 1603–1630* (New York: Harper Torchbooks), pp. 146–71.
4. Gaustad, *Religious History of America*, pp. 40–1.
5. Ibid., p. 41.
6. Ibid., pp. 41–2, 45.
7. William Bradford (1981), *Of Plymouth Plantation, 1620–1647* (New York: Modern Library), p. 26.
8. Ibid., pp. 70–1.
9. Perry Miller and Thomas H. Johnson (eds) (1963), *The Puritans: A Sourcebook of Their Writings*, 2 vols (New York: Harper Torchbooks), I: pp. 197, 199.
10. Gaustad, *Religious History of America*, p. 50.
11. Ibid., p. 54.
12. Perry Miller (1939), *The New England Mind: The Seventeenth Century* (New York: Macmillan Company), chap. 1.
13. Charles Cohen (1986), *God's Caress: The Psychology of Puritan Religious Experience* (New York: Oxford University Press); Theodore Dwight Bozeman (1988), *To Live Ancient Lives: The Primitivist Dimension in Puritanism* (Chapel Hill: University of North Carolina Press).
14. Gaustad, *Religious History of America*, p. 64.
15. Miller and Johnson, *Puritans*, I: p. 214–15; Gaustad, *Religious History of America*, p. 65.
16. Miller and Johnson, *Puritans*, I: p. 217.
17. Edmund Morgan (1937), 'The case against Anne Hutchinson', *The New England Quarterly*, 10 (December): 635–49; Fairfax Withington and Jack Schwartz (1978),

'The political trial of Anne Hutchinson', *The New England Quarterly*, 51 (Summer): 226–40.

18. Glenda Riley (1987), *Inventing the American Woman: A Perspective on Women's History* (Arlington Heights, IL: Harlan Davidson), p. 21; Lyle Koehler (1974), 'The case of the American Jezebels: Anne Hutchinson and female agitation during the years of antinomian turmoil, 1636–1640', *The William and Mary Quarterly*, 3rd sers, 31 (January): 55–78; Lad Tobin (1990), 'A radically different voice: Gender and language in the trials of Anne Hutchinson', *Early American Literature*, 25, 3: 253–70.

19. Amanda Porterfield (1992), *Female Piety in Puritan New England: The Emergence of Religious Humanism* (New York: Oxford University Press), p. 99; Riley, *Inventing the American Woman*, p. 20. For a documentary history of Hutchinson's ordeal, see: David D. Hall (1990), *The Antinomian Controversy, 1636–1638: A Documentary History*, 2nd edn (Durham, NC: Duke University Press).

20. Philip F. Gura (1984), *A Glimpse of Sion's Glory: Puritan Radicalism in New England* (Middletown, CT: Wesleyan University Press), pp. 6, 14. See also: Janice Knight (1994), *Orthodoxy in Massachusetts: Rereading American Puritanism* (Cambridge, MA: Harvard University Press), p. 5.

21. David D. Hall (1989), *Worlds of Wonder, Days of Judgment: Popular Religious Belief in Early New England* (New York: Alfred A. Knopf).

22. John Demos (1970), 'Underlying themes in the witchcraft of seventeenth century New England', *American Historical Review*, 75 (June): 1311. See: John Demos (1982), *Entertaining Satan: Witchcraft and the Culture of Early New England* (New York: Oxford University Press) and Bryan F. LeBeau (1998), *The Story of the Salem Witch Trials* (Upper Saddle River, NJ: Prentice Hall).

23. Patricia U. Bonomi (1986), *Under the Cope of Heaven: Religion, Society, and Politics in Colonial America* (New York: Oxford University Press), pp. 72–3. See also: Douglas Jacobsen (1991), *An Unprov'd Experiment: Religious Pluralism in Colonial New Jersey* (Brooklyn: Carlson).

24. Gaustad, *Religious History of America*, p. 80.

25. Arthur Lyon Cross (1902; 1964), *The Anglican Episcopate and the American Colonies* (Hamden, CT: Archon Books), pp. 1–2, 36–53, 88–113.

26. See Leonard J. Trinterud (1949), *The Forming of an American Tradition: A Reexamination of Colonial Presbyterianism* (Freeport, NY: Books for Libraries Press) and Bryan F. LeBeau (1997), *Jonathan Dickinson and the Formative Years of American Presbyterianism* (Lexington: The University Press of Kentucky), chaps 2, 9.

27. Gaustad, *Religious History of America*, p. 91.

28. Ibid., pp. 92–3.

29. Ibid., pp. 92–9.

30. Catherine Albanese (1992), *America: Religions and Religion* (Belmont, CA: Wadsworth Publishing), p. 94.

31. Gaustad, *Religious History of America*, p. 73; John D. Krugler (1979), 'Lord Baltimore, Roman Catholics and toleration: Religious policy in Maryland during the early Catholic years, 1634–1649', *Catholic Historical Review*, 65 (Winter): 49–75; Kenneth Lasson (1989), 'Free exercise in the free state: Maryland's role in religious liberty and the First Amendment', *Journal of Church and State*, 31 (Autumn): 423–32.

32. John D. Krugler (1984), 'With promises of liberty in religion: The Catholic Lords Baltimore and toleration in seventeenth century Maryland, 1634–1692', *Maryland Historical Magazine*, 79 (Spring): 36–8; Lasson, 'Free exercise in the free state': 432–8.

33. Gaustad, *Religious History of America*, pp. 100–1.
34. Ibid., p. 103.
35. Ibid., p. 104.
36. Ibid., pp. 104–6.
37. Ibid., pp. 104–6.
38. See: W. R. Ward (1992), *The Protestant Evangelical Awakening* (Cambridge: Cambridge University Press).
39. See, for example: Bonomi, *Under the Cope of Heaven*, p. 37; William G. McLoughlin (1978), *Revivals, Awakenings, and Reform: An Essay on Religion and Social Change in America, 1607–1977* (Chicago: University of Chicago Press), pp. 52–3.
40. Martin E. Marty (1986), *Pilgrims in Their Own Land: 500 Years of Religion in America* (New York: Penguin Books), p. 109.
41. See: Bozeman, *To Live Ancient Lives* and Perry Miller (1967), *Nature's Nation* (Cambridge, MA: Harvard University Press). For a more modern corrective on Edwards, see Stephen J. Stein (1988), 'The spirit and the word: Jonathan Edwards and scriptural exegesis', in Nathan O. Hatch and Harry Stout (eds), *Jonathan Edwards and the American Experience* (New York: Oxford University Press), pp. 118–30.
42. McLoughlin, *Revivals, Awakenings, and Reform*, p. 51.
43. Marty, *Pilgrims in Their Own Land*, p. 113; Sydney E. Ahlstrom (1972), *Religious History of the American People* (New Haven: Yale University Press), p. 282.
44. Marty, *Pilgrims in Their Own Land*, p. 114; Ahlstrom, *Religious History of the American People*, p. 282.
45. Marty, *Pilgrims in Their Own Land*, p. 115.
46. Ahlstrom, *Religious History of the American People*, p. 302.
47. Marty, *Pilgrims in Their Own Land*, p. 116; Ahlstrom, *Religious History of the American People*, pp. 302–3.
48. Marty, *Pilgrims in Their Own Land*, p. 118.
49. David T. Morgan (1985), 'A most unlikely friendship: Benjamin Franklin and George Whitefield', *The Historian*, 47 (February): 208–18. See: Frank Lambert (1994), *Pedlar in Divinity: George Whitefield and the Transatlantic Revivals, 1737–1770* (Princeton: Princeton University Press).
50. Trinterud, *Forming of an American Tradition*, pp. 87–8.
51. See: Charles H. Maxson (1958), *The Great Awakening in the Middle Colonies* (Gloucester, MA: Peter Smith), and Martin E. Lodge (1964), 'The Great Awakening in the Middle Colonies', Ph.D. dissertation, (Berkeley: University of California).
52. Trinterud, *Forming of an American Tradition*, pp. 58–64; Marty, *Pilgrims in Their Own Land*, p. 125. See also: Milton J. Coalter (1986), *Gilbert Tennent, Son of Thunder: A Case Study of Continental Pietism's Impact on the First Great Awakening in the Middle Colonies* (Westport, CT: Greenwood Press).
53. Jon Butler (1990), *Awash in a Sea of Faith: Christianizing the American People* (Cambridge, MA: Harvard University Press), p. 293.
54. Bonomi, *Under the Cope of Heaven*, p. 217.
55. Roger Finke and Rodney Stark (1994), *The Churching of America, 1776–1990: Winners and Losers in Our Religious Economy* (New Brunswick, NJ: Rutgers University Press), p. 55.
56. Albanese, *America*, p. 105.

56   RELIGION IN AMERICA TO 1865

Recommended Readings

Bonomi, Patricia U. (1986), *Under the Cope of Heaven: Religion, Society, and Politics in Colonial America*, New York: Oxford University Press.

Boyer, Paul and Stephen Nissenbaum (1974), *Salem Possessed: The Social Origins of Witchcraft*, Cambridge, MA: Harvard University Press.

Bozeman, Theodore Dwight, (1988), *To Live Ancient Lives: The Primitivist Dimension in Puritanism*, Chapel Hill: University of North Carolina Press.

Bradford, William (1981), *Of Plymouth Plantation, 1620–1647*, New York: Modern Library.

Bridenbaugh, Carl (1968), *Vexed and Troubled Englishmen, 1590–1642*, New York: Oxford University Press.

Coalter, Milton J. (1986), *Gilbert Tennent, Son of Thunder: A Case Study of Continental Pietism's Impact on the First Great Awakening in the Middle Colonies*, Westport, CT: Greenwood Press.

Cohen, Charles (1986), *God's Caress: The Psychology of Puritan Religious Experience*, New York: Oxford University Press.

Cowing, Cedric B. (1971), *The Great Awakening and the American Revolution: Colonial Thought in the 18th Century*, Chicago: Rand McNally.

Demos, John (1982), *Entertaining Satan: Witchcraft and the Culture of Early New England*, New York: Oxford University Press.

Goodfriend, Joyce (1992), *Before the Melting Pot: Society and Culture in Colonial New York*, Princeton: Princeton University Press.

Gura, Philip F. (1984), *A Glimpse of Sion's Glory: Puritan Radicalism in New England*, Middletown, CT: Wesleyan University Press.

Hall, David D. (1990), *The Antinomian Controversy, 1636–1638: A Documentary History*, 2nd edn, Durham, NC: Duke University Press.

Hall, David D. (1989) *Worlds of Wonder, Days of Judgment: Popular Religious Belief in Early New England*, New York: Alfred A. Knopf.

Karlsen, Carol F. (1987), *The Devil in the Shape of a Woman: Witchcraft in Colonial New England*, New York: W. W. Norton.

Knight, Janice (1994), *Orthodoxy in Massachusetts: Rereading American Puritanism*, Cambridge, MA: Harvard University Press.

Lambert, Frank (1994), *Pedlar in Divinity: George Whitefield and the Transatlantic Revivals, 1737–1770*, Princeton: Princeton University Press.

LeBeau, Bryan F. (1997), *Jonathan Dickinson and the Formative Years of American Presbyterianism*, Lexington: The University Press of Kentucky.

LeBeau, Bryan F. (1998), *The Story of the Salem Witch Trials*, Upper Saddle River, NJ: Prentice Hall.

McLoughlin, William G. (1978), *Revivals, Awakenings, and Reform: An Essay on Religion and Social Change in America, 1607–1977*, Chicago: University of Chicago Press.

Maxson, Charles H. (1958), *The Great Awakening in the Middle Colonies*, Gloucester, MA: Peter Smith.

Miller, Perry (1933), *Orthodoxy in Massachusetts: 1630–1650*, Cambridge, MA: Harvard University Press.

Miller, Perry (1939), *The New England Mind: The Seventeenth Century*. New York: Macmillan Company, 1939.

Miller, Perry (1956), *Errand Into the Wilderness*, Cambridge, MA: Harvard University Press.

Miller, Perry (1953), *The New England Mind: From Colony to Province*, Cambridge, MA: Harvard University Press.

Miller, Perry and Thomas H. Johnson (eds) (1963), *The Puritans: A Sourcebook of Their Writings*, 2 vols, New York: Harper Torchbooks.

Morgan, Edmund S. (1958), *The Puritan Dilemma: The Story of John Winthrop*, Boston: Little, Brown and Company.

Morgan, Edmund S. (1963), *Visible Saints: The History of a Puritan Idea*, New York: New York University Press.

Morgan, Edmund S. (1967), *Roger Williams: The Church and the State*, New York: Harcourt, Brace and World.

Notestein, Wallace (1962), *The English People on the Eve of Colonization, 1603–1630*, New York: Harper Torchbooks.

Porterfield, Amanda (1992), *Female Piety in Puritan New England: The Emergence of Religious Humanism*, New York: Oxford University Press.

Trinterud, Leonard J. (1949), *The Forming of an American Tradition: A Re-examination of Colonial Presbyterianism*, Freeport, NY: Books for Libraries Press.

CHAPTER 3

Religion and the
American Revolution

The period from 1763 to 1789 brought momentous changes to Americans. They confronted, then overthrew, the only government they had known, and they established new governments and what they hoped would be a new society. As Jon Butler has suggested, Americans were not wrong to trumpet their handiwork as 'the new order of the ages'.[1]

The Era of the American Revolution held immense consequences for religion in America as well, much of which was stimulated by fears of low level church adherence on the eve of independence, of the potential for religious instability during the Revolution, and of the fate of the republic if republican virtues, necessary to its survival, were not underscored by organized religion. In retrospect these fears proved to be unfounded. Organized religion not only survived but also prospered. In the process, however, as Martin Marty has argued, the new nation underwent two more revolutions. In the first, church and state, which had been united for ages, were separated. In the second, in the minds of at least some leaders of church and state, religion became a matter of reason more than the heart.[2]

The Role of Religion in the American Revolution

The role of religion in the American Revolution failed to receive any great attention until Carl Bridenbaugh published his *Mitre and Sceptre* in 1962. He drew attention to the 'bishop question', wherein Dissenters denounced alleged Anglican plots to install a colonial bishop while colonial assemblies were fighting off taxes and the escalation of imperial authority. Other historians soon followed: Alan Heimert, in his *Religion and the American Mind from the Great Awakening to the Revolution* (1966), as well as Gary Nash, Rhys Isaac, Harry Stout, Patricia Bonomi and others. Common to these later works was a stress on the importance of evangelical style in shaping the Revolution, which in turn was tied to the Great Awakening, discussed in Chapter 2.

The Bishop Question

The bishop question was significant because it undermined trust in British politicians and their motives. It began at nearly the inception of colonization, but it grew much worse in the mid-eighteenth century, when Dissenters came to constitute a majority of Americans. They feared an Anglican bishop, because they knew how they had fared under Anglican establishment in England. As Dissenters in New England showed, given the chance, they were not necessarily opposed to an establishment of their own faith, but by the mid-eighteenth century none would have such a chance.

The Anglican–Dissenter contest over a bishop for America surfaced regularly until the 1760s, when it was joined to colonial protests against taxes and other English efforts at imperial centralization. It climaxed in protests against the Quebec Act of 1774, through which the English government recognized the Roman Catholic Church in the conquered territories of Canada. Beyond its stated purpose of offering freedom of religion to Catholics in their own homeland, the Quebec Act helped perpetuate colonists' belief in Catholicism's secret association with every attempt at tyranny in England since the 1640s, and especially with the reign of the Stuart kings.[3] It also resonated with colonial anti-Catholicism, which had been a staple of British colonial life for two centuries, and to which we will return in Chapter 6.

Religious support for the Revolution

Protestant Christianity reinforced the Whig political convictions that lay behind early revolutionary rhetoric. Whig sentiment extended throughout the colonies, where it was descended from eighteenth-century English political culture generally rather than from the more narrow sources of revivalism or New England Calvinism. Thus, religious support for the Whigs was not limited to New England or to evangelical Dissenters. The basic Whig texts – John Locke's *Second Treatise of Government* (1689), for example – were disseminated throughout the colonies, and reached more than evangelicals. Whiggism did not guarantee homogeneity, however. More than minor subtleties separated the Whiggism of Anglicans, Congregationalists and Baptists, and on the eve of the Revolution the religious implications of their Whiggism was not entirely clear.[4]

Systematic public discussion of virtue and morality came more frequently from ordained Christian clergymen than from any other single source. Clerics' emphasis on virtue, responsibility and morality helped make sense of revolutionary rhetoric about corruption and evil among English politicians and society. And, as protest escalated, some ministers discussed revolutionary politics specifically. This could occur in Sabbath sermons, but in New England it more often happened during mid-week fast days and thanksgiving sermons, as best fitted the state–church tradition. As they had done before, the ministers excoriated the unchurched, criticized the British and promoted the quest for salvation, but now they also brought Christianity directly to bear on the revolutionary crisis.[5]

John Adams singled out the Reverend Jonathan Mayhew of Boston as one of the first to promote the cause of liberty. After some participation in the Great Awakening as a youth, Mayhew parted company with its proponents and followed the path of 'reasonable Christianity' to being accused of Arminianism. Adams and his peers, however, remembered him for setting forth ideas of revolution a generation before the wave of independence.[6]

In *A Discourse Concerning Unlimited Submission and Non-Resistance to the Higher Powers* (1750), Mayhew took on the biblical text of Paul, in Romans 13, that, since God established all authorities, whoever resisted authority resisted God and must be condemned. Since Paul presumably wrote these lines while Nero was persecuting Christians, his words would have meant that believers should obey evil rulers. Mayhew, however, argued that rulers had no authority from God to do mischief. Bad rulers were ministers of Satan, not God, and Christians were obliged to disobey any laws they might promulgate that ran contrary to the word of God.[7]

In 1762 Mayhew led a ministerial attack on the rumoured appointment of an American Anglican bishop, and three years later he preached his most inflammatory sermon in opposition to the passage of the Stamp Act. Once again he used a text from Paul: 'Ye have been called unto liberty.'[8] The date was 25 August 1765, five months after the passage of the Stamp Act, and, as Martin Marty has put it, if Boston was tinder, Mayhew's sermon helped ignite it by hinting that some local people were conniving with the British. The mob had already burned in effigy Andrew Oliver, stamp collector. The day after Mayhew preached, they burned Lieutenant Governor Thomas Hutchinson's house, and Governor Bernard accused Mayhew of fomenting the disorder.[9] Mayhew died in 1766.

Ministerial support for the Revolution extended beyond New England. Despite some probable exaggeration in his report on the 'thunder and lightening' that marked the Philadelphia ministers' weekly anti-British sermons, John Adams was not alone in remarking on the local clergies' political involvement. Thomas Jefferson commented that in Anglican Virginia 'pulpit oratory ran like a shock of electricity through the whole colony'. One minister, he continued, 'did very pathetically exhort the people in his sermons to support their liberties . . . and, in the room of God save the king, he cried out: God preserve all the just rights and liberties of America'.[10]

Nevertheless, ironically, the most common denominator among pro-Revolutionary ministers was a state–church pulpit, whether it be in New England among Congregationalists, or in the southern colonies among Anglicans. Clearly, Middle Colony Presbyterians and Virginia Baptists proved to be important exceptions to this rule, but virtually all Anglican ministers in the Northern and Middle Colonies, where Anglicans often had to act the role of dissenters, became loyalists! A third of the Anglican clergy in Virginia and Maryland, where Anglicans held tax-supported pulpits, backed the Revolution, while elsewhere the correlation was even stronger.[11]

In most colonies the Revolution pitted a colonial political establishment against an expanding imperial administration, and the colonial clergy often owed more to the former than to the latter, even if the clergy involved were Anglican. The kind of politically active colonists who led the protest against British policy after 1763 usually supported the locally established church in colonies with state–church systems; the established, tax-supported minister commonly supported the Revolution. Moreover, like the colonial political elites who used local government as a base from which to launch revolutionary-era protest and rebellion, ministers in the state churches used their fast and thanksgiving day sermons in the war against British policies. In this way establishmentarian coercion, rather than Dissenting anti-authoritarian voluntarism, underwrote much of the American promotion of liberty and attack on Toryism.[12]

Also interesting to consider is Roman Catholic and Baptist support for the Revolution. Although they numbered only about 25,000, Catholic support was solid. Not only were Catholics outsiders and widely discriminated against, but also they were constantly ridiculed. Even Harvard College had its annual Dudleian Lecture, dedicated to publicly exposing Romish idolatry, wherein, in 1759, Jonathan Mayhew denounced Rome as a filthy prostitute and the mother of harlots. On Pope Day in Newport and Boston, mobs burned the pope in effigy, and, when Parliament passed the Quebec Act of 1774, anti-Catholic hatred turned to fury.[13]

Nevertheless, American Catholics supported the revolutionary cause. Catholic France provided loans, soldiers and war material, in time becoming an official ally. With the urging of General George Washington and other leaders, anti-Catholic activity, if not sentiment, ceased, and Charles Carroll, of Carrollton Manor in Maryland, and a Catholic, signed the Declaration of Independence. In 1776 the Continental Congress sent Carroll's cousin, John, later first Catholic bishop in the United States, as part of a delegation to Canada in a failed effort to lure the Canadians into an alliance against England.[14]

The more numerous Baptists defined themselves as concerned first and foremost with salvation and the life to come, but they could not avoid taking political stands as well. Never being among the established, and almost always a persecuted minority, they struck out against the 'previous oppressions and persecutions from the "Standing Order"', and by 1770 that translated into support for independence. In Massachusetts, for example, Isaac Backus not only protested religious taxes levied by the Congregational establishment on all denominations, but he also urged fellow Baptists to refuse to pay such taxes or to avail themselves of exemptions eventually offered them by the colonial legislature. Nevertheless, on 22 November 1774, Backus announced Baptist support for Massachusetts's resistance to Great Britain.[15]

And finally there were the New Lights (and New Siders) – those who, regardless of their denominational affiliation, were drawn toward independence by their evangelical fervour. The strength of the New Lights in the decades after the Great Awakening lay chiefly in their rediscovery and cultivation of an aesthetic feeling for the 'beauty of union', the communal piety of the saved. The beauty of union was the joy the awakened felt when they worshipped together, apart from Arminians, to be sure.[16]

The New Lights found happiness in holiness, in revivals, in communion with fellow saints, and in the prospect of the kingdom to come. They longed for purity – the recognition that the power of God's light was directly proportional to the number of saints gathered in one place, and that it was correspondingly diminished by the number in fellowship who were unregenerate. The quest for perfection and union gave rise to millennialism, a natural outgrowth of the revival. God's power in the Awakening suggested that the pace of history was accelerating, and that the Second Coming was close at hand.[17]

The Great Awakening raised the hopes of the evangelicals, and they shifted to the more optimistic post-millennial view: God's reign of a thousand years on earth would precede, not follow, Judgement Day. With this postponement, the New Lights could anticipate his coming with unmixed joy. Those who understood Edwards knew that the 'good society' would begin simply with God's restoration to the Elect of the powers man lost at Adam's fall. Edwards envisioned no destruction or reconstruction, but rather a massive renewal – a bigger and better revival. God would turn this world into Paradise, that is to say, into a Christian commonwealth.[18]

In that they believed the millennium would begin in America, New Light arguments were traditional and logical: that Paradise was to be found in the west; that according to scriptural prophecy, on the 'new day' the sun of righteousness would rise in the west; and that logically God would begin this great work in a new country and where his people were concentrated. It was not God's manner 'to introduce a new excellence into the churches of an old, corrupt region'.[19]

In assuming that America was the centre of God's interest in the world, the New Lights were behaving like chosen people. They were returning to the Puritan conception of 'a city on a hill'. They would produce in the New World a better society than the Old World had ever known. They hoped to build on the Awakening, using various strategies to induce 'heavenly showers', and to extend them to more people, so that the earthly kingdom – the better society – might be hastened. And one way to hasten that better society was to gain American independence from the corrupt, Old World Great Britain.[20]

Abstention and Opposition to the Revolution

It is important to note that most colonial ministers remained silent about politics during the upheavals of the 1760s and 1770s. Moravians and Quakers proved to be consistent pacifists, while Pennsylvania German Reformed and Lutheran clergy, as well as Scots-Irish clergymen serving frontier settlements, said or did little. In part, this may have resulted from their minority status and frequent tension with provincial elites who led the Revolution in Pennsylvania. But there was more to it.

They and many of their clerical colleagues in other denominations saw
the Revolution as a threat to Christianity. They agreed with the
German Reformed Coetus' statement of May 1775, which stated that
they lived 'in precarious times, the like of which . . . has never been
seen in America. The Lord knows what He has in store for us, and
especially for our beloved Church'. In 1777 the Coetus described the
revolution as a 'sad war' that had uprooted 'many a praiseworthy
observance . . . especially in regard to the keeping of the Sabbath Day
and Christian exercises in the families at home'.[21]

Most members of the Presbyterian Synod of Philadelphia – Middle
Colony Presbyterians being well represented among pro-Revolution-
aries – refrained from public comment on the impending conflict. In a
pastoral letter to its congregations in 1775, the Synod acknowledged
that 'it is well known . . . that we have not been instrumental in
inflaming the minds of the people, or urging them to acts of violence
and disorder'. Indeed its ministers could not remember when 'political
sentiments have been so long and so fully kept from the pulpit', by
which they meant sentiment supporting rebellion.[22]

The demand for obedience was as strong among colonial Presbyterians as it was among Anglicans, and the Presbyterian commitment had
been tested only shortly before the Revolution. During the so-called
Regulator Movement in North and South Carolina in the late 1760s,
backcountry Presbyterian ministers, supported by German Lutheran
and Anglican pastors, used their pulpits to denounce rebellion against
colonial governments dominated by tidewater planter elites, and cited
the traditional Pauline texts in doing so. A letter to the laity promulgated
by the Synod in 1775 both instructed the laity on loyalty to George III
and voiced support for Whig political principles. Synod members
expressed their 'attachment and respect to our sovereign King George',
but they also expressed their regard for the 'revolutionary principles by
which his august family was seated on the British throne'.[23]

The Presbyterian statement suggested why loyalism so frequently
had a dual religious foundation and extended beyond the ranks of
Church of England ministers, two-thirds of whom departed for England
after the Revolution began. First, there was the traditional emphasis on
authority and obedience in colonial preaching. As protest turned to
independence, for many ministers previously abstract fears that the
flight from authority and obedience would turn everything upside down
became a reality.[24]

A second reason centred on religious discrimination. The political elites who guided the American Revolution in so many places also had frequently mistreated religious minorities in earlier times. Scottish and Scotch-Irish Presbyterians in North and South Carolina, English Baptists in Virginia, German Lutheran and German Reformed in Pennsylvania, Anglicans in New England and others had all experienced religious discrimination that ranged from minor annoyances to governmental persecution. Most found the patriots' anti-Parliamentary protests ironic and even hypocritical. Some groups, like the Virginia Baptists, supported the Revolution anyway. But backcountry Presbyterians, German Lutherans and German Reformed settlers, and Middle and Northern Colony Anglicans, often found themselves drawn to loyalism not only out of political principles but also because of antagonisms with settlers who had earlier used the government and the law against them.[25]

The Revolution Shapes American Religion

The American Revolution shaped American religion, and it did so in complex ways. This complexity emerges even in the story of the decline and growth of various Christian denominations. The most serious erosion occurred in the Anglican congregations. In parish after parish Anglican ministers left because they openly supported the Crown, because they could not endure abuse by local patriots, or because they were no longer paid by either the Society for the Propagation of the Gospel or their vestries. Fifty Anglican priests were working in Pennsylvania, New York, and New England before the Revolution; only nine remained afterward. About 100 of the 150 priests in the southern colonies also fled to England. As a result 75 per cent of the Church of England parishes, built up so carefully in the previous half century, lost their clergymen and with them their principal leadership in sustaining public Christian worship.[26]

Between 1761 and 1776 the Philadelphia Baptist Association grew from twenty-nine congregations with 1300 adult members to forty-two congregations with 3000 members. But the Association's congregations quickly felt the sting of war. By 1781 the Association lost the membership gains and institutional growth achieved in the previous fifteen years. Its congregations declined in number to twenty-six, and its membership from 3000 to 1400 adults. Many congregations disbanded, and even surviving congregations lost a fifth of their members. Between

1776 and 1781 average church membership declined from seventy-one to fifty-five adults.[27]

Other Protestant groups advanced during the American Revolution. South Carolina's Charleston Baptist Association experienced significant growth. In 1775 it counted 9 congregations, 7 ministers and 529 members; in 1779 it counted 12 congregations, 12 ministers and 890 members; and in 1783 it counted 13 congregations, 9 ministers and 966 members. Presbyterian statistics described similar growth after, though not before or during, the Revolution. In 1774 the Synod of Philadelphia reported 139 ministers, 153 churches with ministers (some serving more than one congregation), and 180 vacant pulpits. By 1788 the Presbyterians counted 177 ministers, 215 congregations with clergymen and 206 congregations without clergy.[28]

Denominational statistics conveyed only part of the story, however. Methodism had the fewest difficulties, in part because it had the least to lose. Methodist missionaries had worked in America less than a decade, and all of them, except Francis Asbury, returned to England at John Wesley's command. Anglicans, in contrast, suffered the most because they had the most to lose, in terms of both ministers and buildings. The physical destruction loosed on Anglican churches was reminiscent of sixteenth-century English anti-Catholic depredation. In parish after parish supporters of the Revolution stripped Anglican churches of their royal coats of arms, although they usually left the buildings and other fittings intact.[29]

The Rise of Public Religion

The association of society and government with Christianity was traditional in colonial political culture. But the American Revolution strengthened the demand to associate with Christianity in several ways: by revealing the previously shallow foundations of the association; by stressing a particular form of republicanism in government and society; and by stimulating a strong sense of cultural optimism that fitted certain religious themes, particularly American millennialism.

Many aspects of the American Revolution caused concern about America's religious future. The destruction of church buildings, the interruption of denominational organizations, the occasional decline in congregations and membership, the shattering of the Anglican church and the rise of secular pride in revolutionary accomplishments, all weighed on American religious leaders. Even as the Revolution

advanced, denominational leaders often bemoaned rather than celebrated America's moral fibre.[30]

Contemporaries agreed that a successful republican society and
government depended on a virtuous people. This sentiment did not
take root in a reborn Puritanism but in more modern eighteenth-
century principles. Most equated republican longevity with widely
inculcated moral virtue. The whole of society, not merely some of its
parts, constituted the bedrock of the future. Massachusetts Colonial
Governor John Winthrop's Puritan society had been ordered by means
of hierarchical responsibilities assigned among the people, 'some high
and eminent in power and dignity; others mean and in subjection'. The
1780 Massachusetts constitution, however, rested order on a broader
foundation: 'The happiness of a people, and the good order and
preservation of civil government, essentially depend upon piety, religion, and morality.' It did not mention the 'high and eminent' or 'others
mean and in subjection'.[31]

Optimism fuelled the new republic, but much of post-revolutionary
optimism was openly secular, not religious, and reflected the Founding
Fathers' Enlightenment convictions. This was especially true of those
often called the 'old revolutionaries'. Franklin, Washington and Jefferson all professed beliefs in the supernatural; they were not willing to
risk identification as atheists. But their references to the supernatural
were vague and ethereal, and their views of religion were far different
from those of the Congregational, Baptist, Presbyterian and Episcopa-
lian clergymen who backed the Revolution. Franklin's god was a god of
ethics, not revelation. Although he remained a Church of England
vestryman, Washington was utterly disinterested in theology, and
Jefferson openly rejected sectarianism.[32] What all three Founding
Fathers sought to replace orthodox Christianity was what we today
call public religion.

The substance of American public religion was drawn from the
Enlightenment, as it was realized in America. Its most visible statement
was the Declaration of Independence, wherein 'God' refers to the God
of nature, rather than the God of Christian revelation – and who
emerges as 'the Supreme Judge of the world', to whom Americans
would appeal 'for the rectitude of [their] intentions', and as 'Divine
Providence', in whom they would rely for protection. The words were
Jefferson's, but Benjamin Franklin was the first of his generation to call
for public religion and fashion its design. Not surprisingly, what he

proposed reflected his preference for an Age of Reason over an Age of Faith, of mind over the heart, of reason over revelation, of morals over miracles, and of public virtue over private salvation.[33]

Franklin issued his first call for public religion in his *Proposals Relating to the Education of Youth in Philadelphia*, which he published in 1749. Therein, he defended 'the necessity of a public religion', arguing that such a faith would be useful to the public. It would be advantageous in promoting a religious character among private persons, and it would counter 'the mischiefs of superstition', which he found in most denominations. Franklin's American public religion was not, however, to be anti-Christian; indeed he insisted that it would show 'the excellency of the Christian religion above all others ancient or modern'.[34]

The seed that Franklin planted in 1749 grew over the next three decades, leading to the Declaration of Independence, but not without mixed reactions. To many religious leaders it was infidelity, deism or a new heathenism. To philosophers it was a homegrown American version of the Enlightenment. Proponents saw it as the 'religion of the Republic', an entity Americans would later identify variously as civil faith, public piety or civil religion.[35]

Franklin and the other founders of American public religion did not intend the end of individual denominations, but rather the cessation of sectarianism. They hoped to erect a tent over the various religious groups by means of a commonly agreed upon universal creed. It would be essentially Protestant Christian, as were nearly all Americans at the time, but, by leaving to denominations theological specifics, public religion would serve a common morality.[36]

American Millennialism

American religious leaders attempted to absorb and redirect secular optimism. If claims measured God's approval, the clergy put the new nation in good stead. Providential rhetoric fixed God's sovereignty over the Revolution. Some clergymen even described the struggle in Manichean terms – the cause of heaven against the cause of hell – while many returned to the seventeenth-century motif of Americans as a chosen people.[37]

Millennialist rhetoric also expanded. Millennialism thrived on dramatic events such as the American Revolution. Providential rhetoric revealed God's approval of the Revolution, but millennialist rhetoric located it in sacred time. Thinking that Christ's second coming would occur in a specific historical setting, Ebenezer Baldwin, a Connecticut clergyman, thought that the American Revolution was 'preparing the way for this glorious event'. Samuel West, a New Hampshire minister, described the Revolution as fulfilling Isaiah's millennialist predictions. Some clergymen went further and suggested that the Revolution was a precursor to the beginning of the millennium and, perhaps, the 'sixth vial' described in Revelation, which would destroy the Antichrist when it was emptied and usher in Christ's reign.[38]

Yet the very ubiquity of such predictions produced a bewildering variety of styles. No single millennialist vision emerged in the era of the American Revolution. As Ruth Bloch has noted, proponents variously predicted the coming of true liberty and freedom, a rise in piety, American territorial expansion and even freedom from hunger. Many propagandists hedged their predictions, just as their predecessors had done in the 1740s and 1750s. The few who provided definite dates for specific events usually developed different chronologies, and, when Americans experienced political, social and economic setbacks, some turned to darker visions of the world and the new nation's place in it.[39]

Apocalyptic thinking nevertheless declined in the revolutionary period. With the success of the Revolution, millennialism suited the American temperament better than apocalypticism, and in this regard the Revolution profoundly shifted the colonial millennialist tradition. The Revolution was an event whose character and outcome seemed to have signalled the beginning of Christ's thousand-year reign, thus making the apocalypse either history or irrelevant.[40]

Millennialism had important political implications, as well. Millennialist rhetoric secured the allegiance of an unwilling and often perplexed society. It demanded lay adherence in a society where the people were now sovereign. When New Englanders sought a unicameral legislature and an elected executive on the ground that 'the voice of the people is the voice of God', the rhetoric largely benefited the advancement of Christianity: a legislature that spoke for God should also listen to those who articulated Christian theology, morals and ethics.[41]

The Campaign Against Irreligion

The millennialist incorporation of secular optimism in the revolutionary period was parallelled by equally adamant campaigns against irreligion in its intellectual disguises of scepticism, atheism and deism. Before the Revolution, clergymen had often endured derogatory remarks steeped in the doubts of the Enlightenment. The Revolution removed one source of this activity by stripping away the imperial elite of governors, magistrates and other officials who frequently supported such Enlightenment scepticism. But scepticism survived nonetheless. Its most prominent representatives – Franklin, Jefferson, Madison and Washington – seemed the apotheosis of the Enlightenment, and their support for it revealed a tolerance of scepticism many saw as altogether dangerous in a new republic.

Deism became a chief object of attack in the war against irreligion. It had the attraction of being relatively new yet suspiciously commonplace among the new nation's political and social leaders. The word itself dated only from the seventeenth century and had achieved a place in common vocabulary only in the early eighteenth century. Most important, deism offered extraordinary opportunities to its critics to demonstrate the need for real religion, meaning orthodox Christianity, in the new republic. To its critics, deism was the epitome of hypocrisy. It masqueraded as religion but was thoroughly irreligious. Deists admitted the justice of religious claims, but they attempted to make religion irrelevant to contemporary life. The deists' god was dead, critics charged. At best, signs of his existence could be found only in the distant past.[42]

As Americans turned from war making to nation making, clergymen turned to deism to explain their post-revolutionary failures and crises. Deism served as a new and dangerous label under which a broad list of evils, old and new, could be assembled. Thomas Paine's *Age of Reason*, published in 1794, was denounced far more than it was read. In 1798 Jedidiah Morse described why the deism Paine promoted should be so feared: 'The existence of a God is boldly denied. Atheism and materialism are systematically professed. Reason and nature are deified and adored. The Christian religion, and its divine and blessed author, are not only disbelieved, rejected and condemned, but even abhorred.'[43]

Thomas Jefferson's try for the presidency in 1800 brought out a second anti-deist campaign. It was particularly important because it focused on the potentially intimate relationship between a president's personal religious views and the fate of the American republic. Jefferson's religious views were complex. He was a deist, but he also expressed a quiet regard for Christ and Christian ethics. He rejected

Christ's divinity and criticized religious coercion with a vigour that made some suspicious of his real religious views, despite the fact that evangelicals had long supported him for his efforts on behalf of religious freedom. Federalists linked Jefferson to anticlericalism and atheism in the notorious French Revolution, and many ministers denounced Jefferson from their pulpits, decrying the fate of the nation in the hands of a deist, an obvious agent of the Devil.[44]

The Further Separation of Church and State

The final area in which the American Revolution affected American religion was in its move toward disestablishment, if, prior to 1789, only at the state level. (Church and state at the national level will be discussed in Chapter 4). By 1763 pluralism and denominationalism had taken their toll. If the thirteen colonies that were poised to become the United States of America had belonged to England for over 150 years, the Church of England had been established in only five of those colonies (Maryland, Virginia, North and South Carolina and Georgia), all in the South, and in parts of New York. Three New England colonies (Massachusetts, Connecticut and New Hampshire) had established Congregationalism, while the rest had no establishment at all.

How this state of affairs came about has already been considered in Chapter 2. The peculiar nature of that establishment that survived, however, merits some further consideration. In sum, all eight of those colonies wherein an establishment existed began breaking with European precedent by providing legal recognition and support for more than one church or denomination. As a general rule, those colonies taxed everyone for the support of religion, but allowed most people's taxes to be remitted to the church of their choice. Establishment was coming to mean non-preferential establishment, or the financial support of religion – Protestant Christianity really – by public taxation.[45] Massachusetts will serve as a case in point.

Massachusetts, the major and archetypal Puritan colony, did not provide for the establishment of the Congregational Church by name after 1692. In that year, its original colonial charter having been revoked and replaced by a less exclusive one bearing the influence of England's recently adopted Religious Toleration Act, the General Court (the Massachusetts legislature) provided for an establishment of religion on a town-by-town basis. It required every town to maintain an 'able, learned and orthodox' minister, to be chosen by the voters of the town and supported by a tax levied on all taxpayers. As a matter of law it was theoretically possible for several different denominations to benefit from the establishment.[46]

Because Congregationalists were the overwhelming majority in nearly every Massachusetts town, they stood to reap the benefits of establishment, with only a few exceptions. The act of 1692 exempted Boston because voluntary contributions there had successfully maintained the Congregational churches, making the compulsion of law unnecessary. The town of Swansea was dominated by Baptists. By 1693 it had two Baptist churches, and they became the official town churches, supported by public taxation. That, in turn, provoked an equally unusual response. Swansea Congregationalists sued in the county court under the pretext that the town, in establishing Baptist churches, had not provided for an 'orthodox learned minister', in violation of the act of 1692. In 1708 the court ruled that religious taxes raised in Swansea must be divided equally between the two denominations, thereby setting the precedent in that colony for dual establishment.[47]

In a few towns, where Baptists and Quakers together constituted a majority, both successfully challenged the law. In those cases, however, they refused to pay the tax at all, arguing that the state had no jurisdiction over religion, which should be left to the voluntary support of believers. When they were granted exemptions, both challenged the law colonywide. Quakers argued their case before authorities in London on the grounds that the Massachusetts establishment violated the Toleration Act of 1689, and, in a partial victory for Dissenters, England's Privy Council ruled that Congregationalists could not impose ministerial taxes in towns where they did not constitute a majority.[48]

From 1727 until the end of the colonial period (and beyond as we shall see), the Congregational Church was forced to retreat until the other denominations were on an equal footing with it. In 1727 Anglicans won the right of having their religious taxes turned over for the support of their own churches. In 1728 Massachusetts exempted Quakers and Baptists from all taxes for the payment of ministerial salaries; then in 1731 and 1735 each denomination received an exemption from sharing the taxes for building new town churches, and so on.[49]

The American Revolution lent momentum to the movement toward disestablishment of religion in the states. The five colonies that had no establishment continued to avoid it as states. Joining their ranks was North Carolina, provisions in the Pennsylvania state constitution of

1776 being typical of that group: no person, it read, 'ought or of right can be compelled to attend any religious worship, or erect or support any place of worship, or maintain any ministry, contrary to, or against, his own free will and consent'.[50]

Colonies that continued their church establishment as states made concessions to the growing sentiment against any establishment by moving toward multiple or nonpreferential establishment. By and large, establishment of religion in those states, rather than being restricted in meaning to a state church, became instead a means by which to provide public support for several churches, with exclusive preference for none.[51] Massachusetts, once again, and Virginia, because of its major players, will serve as examples.

The Massachusetts' Constitution of 1780 ordered the legislature to authorize its towns 'to make suitable provision, at their own expense, for the institution of the public worship of God, and for the support and maintenance of public Protestant teachers of piety, religion, and morality'. It also empowered the legislature to make church attendance compulsory. Towns were to have the right of electing their ministers, however, and each taxpayer could designate the Protestant church of his choice to receive his church tax money, thereby creating a multiple establishment. Another clause provided that none of the above-mentioned Protestant churches would ever be made subordinate to any other by law.[52]

In one regard the Massachusetts Constitution of 1780 constituted a step backward from the liberalizing tendencies of the previous fifty years. It did not continue exceptions made in the colonial period for Baptists and Quakers, who because of their conscientious objections had enjoyed an exemption from religious taxes. They were forced to pay for the support of their own worship.[53]

The Virginia Constitution of 1776 avoided the issue of an establishment of religion, although it guaranteed the 'free exercise of religion', thanks to the efforts of James Madison. Madison failed, however, to win acceptance for his proposal which would have ended any union of church and state. Baptists and Presbyterians protested the decision but the dominant tidewater conservative element in the legislature remained convinced that republican government and society could not flourish without a religious establishment. As 1776 ended the legislature repealed almost every statute that supported the establishment of the Church of England. Dissenters, for example, were to be exempt from church taxes.

But under the law, and in administration of certain sacraments, particularly marriage rites, the Anglican establishment remained.[54]

In 1779 two conflicting bills were introduced in the legislature. Thomas Jefferson's *Bill for Religious Freedom* provided in part 'that no man shall be compelled to frequent or support any religious worship, place, or ministry whatsoever'. *A Bill Concerning Religion* proposed a general assessment, or tax, declared the Christian religion to be the 'established religion' of Virginia, and provided articles of faith to which church members must subscribe in order to be incorporated as an established church and share in the church tax proceeds.[55] Neither bill could muster a majority for the next five years.

In 1784 Patrick Henry introduced a new general assessment bill, entitled *A Bill Establishing a Provision for Teachers of the Christian Religion*. It retained the substance of the earlier measure, but added the more liberal statement that all Christian denominations were equal before the law, none preferred over others. Eliminated were reference to established religion and proposed articles of faith.[56] James Madison rallied opposition to the bill, questioning the need for any form of establishment, and a final vote was postponed until the next session.

Henry's bill became a major issue in the intervening election, in response to which Madison published his famous *Memorial and Remembrance against Religious Assessments*. Madison argued that religion is a private, voluntary affair not subject to government in any way. A general assessment, he noted, was in fact an establishment of religion, and any establishment violated the free exercise of religion and threatened public liberty. To Madison, Christianity did not need government support; nor did government need the support of religion. Establishments produced bigotry and persecution, defiled religion, corrupted government, and ended in spiritual and political tyranny.[57]

Others opposed general assessment, including Presbyterians, Baptists, and Quakers. A petition from the Presbyterian churches of Virginia echoed the sentiments of Baptists and Quakers in arguing that Christianity was most effective when left alone under God, 'free from the intrusive hand of the civil magistrate'. Religion and morality, the Presbyterians asserted, 'can be promoted only by the internal conviction of the mind and its voluntary choice which such establishments cannot effect'.[58]

The Virginia legislature let Henry's general assessment bill die, and passed instead Jefferson's bill on disestablishment, reconstituted by

James Madison in his *Statute of Religious Freedom*. Madison's statute declared in its preface that to compel anyone to support religious opinions he did not share was tyrannical, and 'that even forcing him to support this or that teacher of his own religious persuasion, is depriving him of the comfortable liberty' of giving his money as he pleased. The enabling provision stated 'that no man shall be compelled to frequent or support any religious worship, place, or ministry whatsoever'. The significance of the statute, Leonard Levy has written, 'is not just that it broadened freedom of worship or of opinion in matters of religion but that it separated church and state in the context of protecting religious liberty'.[59]

Summary

Religion played a major role in the American independence movement. The war shook existing churches to their core, but most churches recovered from the American Revolution with remarkable alacrity. The churches, though buffeted by a revolution whose battlefield exposed the tenuousness of popular Christian adherence and reinforced the vigorous secularity of its political principles, emerged with renewed vigour in the 1780s. Public, or civil, religion found its voice in America, as did a peculiar brand of national millennialism. All thirteen states that came to constitute the United States moved closer to the separation of church and state and free exercise of religion. In the next half century American denominations would begin to master the new American environment by initiating a religious creativity that renewed spiritual reflection and perfected institutional power, all to serve Christian ends.

Notes

1. Jon Butler (1990), *Awash in a Sea of Faith: Christianizing the American People* (Cambridge, MA: Harvard University Press), p. 194.
2. Martin E. Marty (1986), *Pilgrims in Their Own Land: 500 Years of Religion in America* (New York: Penguin Books), p. 131.
3. Carl Bridenbaugh (1962), *Mitre and Sceptre: Transatlantic Faiths, Ideas, Personalities, and Politics, 1689–1775* (New York: Oxford University Press). See also: Arthur Lyon Cross (1902; 1964), *The Anglican Episcopate and the American Colonies* (Hamden, CT: Archon Books).
4. Butler, *Awash in a Sea of Faith*, p. 199.
5. Ibid., pp. 200–1.
6. Marty, *Pilgrims in Their Own Land*, pp. 134–5.
7. Ibid., p. 135.
8. Gal. 5: 13.

9. Marty, *Pilgrims in Their Own Land*, pp. 136–7.
10. Harry S. Stout (1986), *The New England Soul: Preaching and Religious Culture in Colonial New England* (New York: Oxford University Press), chap. 14; Patricia U. Bonomi (1986), *Under the Cope of Heaven: Religion, Society, and Politics in Colonial America* (New York: Oxford University Press), pp. 209–10.
11. Stout, *New England Soul*, chap. 14; Butler, *Awash in a Sea of Faith*, p. 202.
12. Stout, *New England Soul*, chap. 14; Butler, *Awash in a Sea of Faith*, p. 202.
13. Marty, *Pilgrims in Their Own Land*, pp. 140–2.
14. Ibid., pp. 143–5.
15. Ibid., pp. 150–4.
16. Cedric B. Cowing (1971), *The Great Awakening and the American Revolution: Colonial Thought in the 18th Century* (Chicago: Rand McNally), p. 201.
17. Ibid., p. 202.
18. Ibid., p. 202.
19. Ibid., pp. 202–3.
20. Ibid., p. 203.
21. Butler, *Awash in a Sea of Faith*, pp. 202–3.
22. Butler, *Awash in a Sea of Faith*, p. 203.
23. Mark Noll (1977), *Christians in the American Revolution* (Grand Rapids, MI: Christian University Press), pp. 65–8; Nathan O. Hatch (1977), *The Sacred Cause of Liberty: Republican Thought and the Millennium in Revolutionary New England* (New Haven: Yale University Press), pp. 22, 61; Butler, *Awash in a Sea of Faith*, p. 203.
24. Wallace Brown (1969), *The Good Americans: The Loyalists in the American Revolution* (New York: Morrow), pp. 56–8, 243–4, 253–4.
25. Bernard Bailyn (1967), *Ideological Origins of the American Revolution* (Cambridge, MA: Harvard University Press), p. 312; John F. Woolverton (1984), *Colonial Anglicanism in North America* (Detroit, MI: Wayne State University Press), pp. 227–33.
26. Woolverton, *Colonial Anglicanism in North America*, pp. 228–33.
27. Butler, *Awash in a Sea of Faith*, p. 207.
28. Ibid., p. 207.
29. Ibid., p. 207.
30. Gordon Wood (1969), *The Creation of the American Republic, 1776–1787* (Chapel Hill: University of North Carolina Press), pp. 114–18, 344–89; J. R. Pole (1972), *Foundations of American Independence*, 1763–1815 (Indianapolis, IN: Bobbs-Merrill), pp. 80–1.
31. Wood, *Creation of the American Republic*, p. 427.
32. Mark A. Noll, Nathan O. Hatch and George M. Marsden (1983), *The Search for Christian America* (Westchester, IL: Crossway Books), pp. 74–6; Paul Boller (1963), *George Washington and Religion* (Dallas: Southern Methodist University Press); Marty, *Pilgrims in Their Own Land*, pp. 160–1.
33. Marty, *Pilgrims in Their Own Land*, p. 155.
34. Ibid., pp. 155–6.
35. Ibid., pp. 155–6.
36. Ibid., pp. 156–7.
37. Ruth H. Bloch (1985), *Visionary Republic: Millennial Themes in American Thought, 1756–1800* (New York: Cambridge University Press), chap. 3.

38. Bloch, *Visionary Republic*, pp. 59, 79–80; James West Davidson 1977, *The Logic of Millennial Thought: Eighteenth-Century New England* (New Haven: Yale University Press), pp. 248–50.
39. Bloch, *Visionary Republic*, pp. 105–10.
40. Butler, *Awash in a Sea of Faith*, p. 217.
41. Bloch, *Visionary Republic*, p. 80; Wood, *Creation of the American Republic*, pp. 344–89.
42. Henry F. May (1976), *The Enlightenment in America* (New York: Oxford University Press), pp. 20–3, 116–32.
43. Butler, *Awash in a Sea of Faith*, p. 219.
44. Fawn Brodie (1974), *Thomas Jefferson: An Intimate History* (New York: W.W. Norton), pp. 431–2.
45. Leonard W. Levy (1986), *The Establishment Clause: Religion and the First Amendment* (New York: Macmillan Publishing Company), pp. 8–9.
46. Levy, *Establishment Clause*, p. 15.
47. Levy, *Establishment Clause*, pp. 15–16; William G. McLoughlin (1971), *New England Dissent 1630–1833: The Baptists and the Separation of Church and State* (Cambridge, MA: Harvard University Press), I: pp. 136–48, 160.
48. McLoughlin, *New England Dissent*, I: pp. 165–99.
49. Ibid., I: pp. 217, 225–43.
50. Levy, *Establishment Clause*, p. 25.
51. Levy, *Establishment Clause*, p. 26.
52. Levy, *Establishment Clause*, p. 27; Thomas J. Curry (1986), *The First Freedoms: Church and State in America to the Passage of the First Amendment* (New York: Oxford University Press), pp. 163–4.
53. McLoughlin, *New England Dissent*, II: p. 1092.
54. Thomas E. Buckley (1977), *Church and State in Revolutionary Virginia, 1776–1787* (Charlottesville: University of Virginia Press), p. 19; Levy, *Establishment Clause*, pp. 52–3; Curry, *First Freedoms*, pp. 135–6.
55. Buckley, *Church and State in Revolutionary Virginia*, pp. 47–62; Curry, *First Freedoms*, pp. 139–41.
56. Buckley, *Church and State in Revolutionary Virginia*, pp. 189–91.
57. Levy, *Establishment Clause*, p. 55; Curry, *First Freedoms*, p. 143.
58. Levy, *Establishment Clause*, pp. 56–7; Curry, *First Freedoms*, p. 144.
59. Levy, *Establishment Clause*, p. 60; Curry, *First Freedoms*, p. 146.

Recommended Readings

Bailyn, Bernard (1967), *Ideological Origins of the American Revolution*, Cambridge, MA: Harvard University Press.
Bloch, Ruth H. (1985), *Visionary Republic: Millennial Themes in American Thought, 1756–1800*, New York: Cambridge University Press.
Boller, Paul (1963), *George Washington and Religion*, Dallas: Southern Methodist University Press.
Bonomi, Patricia U. (1986), *Under the Cope of Heaven: Religion, Society, and Politics in Colonial America*, New York: Oxford University Press.
Bridenbaugh, Carl (1962), *Mitre and Sceptre: Transatlantic Faiths, Ideas, Personalities, and Politics, 1689–1775*, New York: Oxford University Press.

Brown, Wallace (1969), *The Good Americans: The Loyalists in the American Revolution*, New York: Morrow.

Buckley, Thomas E. (1977), *Church and State in Revolutionary Virginia, 1776–1787*, Charlottesville: University of Virginia Press.

Butler, Jon (1990), *Awash in a Sea of Faith: Christianizing the American People*, Cambridge, MA: Harvard University Press.

Cowing, Cedric B. (1971), *The Great Awakening and the American Revolution: Colonial Thought in the 18th Century*, Chicago: Rand McNally.

Cross, Arthur Lyon (1902), *The Anglican Episcopate and the American Colonies*, Hamden, CT: Archon Books.

Curry, Thomas J. (1986), *The First Freedoms: Church and State in America to the Passage of the First Amendment*, New York: Oxford University Press.

Davidson, James West (1977), *The Logic of Millennial Thought: Eighteenth-Century New England*, New Haven: Yale University Press.

Gaustad, Edwin S. (1996), *Sworn on the Altar of God: A Religious Biography of Thomas Jefferson*, Grand Rapids, MI: W. B. Eerdmans.

Hatch, Nathan O. (1977), *The Sacred Cause of Liberty: Republican Thought and the Millennium in Revolutionary New England*, New Haven: Yale University Press .

Heimert, Alan E. (1966), *Religion and the American Mind from the Great Awakening to the Revolution*, Cambridge, MA: Harvard University Press.

Hoffman, Ronald, and Peter J. Albert (eds) (1994), *Religion in a Revolutionary Age*, Charlottesville: University of Virginia Press.

Isaac, Rhys (1982), *The Transformation of Virginia, 1740–1790*, Chapel Hill: University of North Carolina Press.

Levy, Leonard W. (1986), *The Establishment Clause: Religion and the First Amendment*, New York: MacMillan Publishing Company.

May, Henry F. (1976), *The Enlightenment in America*, New York: Oxford University Press.

Nash, Gary (1979), *The Urban Crucible: Social Change, Political Consciousness, and the Origins of the American Revolution*, Cambridge, MA: Harvard University Press.

Noll, Mark (1977), *Christians in the American Revolution*, Grand Rapids, MI: Christian University Press.

Noll, Mark, Nathan O. Hatch and George M. Marsden (1983), *The Search for Christian America*, Westchester, IL: Crossway Books.

Pole, J. R. (1972), *Foundations of American Independence, 1763–1815*, Indianapolis, IN: Bobbs-Merrill.

Sanford, Charles B. (1984), *The Religious Life of Thomas Jefferson*, Charlottesville: University Press of Virginia.

Stout, Harry S. (1986), *The New England Soul: Preaching and Religious Culture in Colonial New England*, New York: Oxford University Press.

Wood, Gordon (1969), *The Creation of the American Republic, 1776–1787*, Chapel Hill: University of North Carolina Press.

Woolverton, John F. (1984), *Colonial Anglicanism in North America*, Detroit, MI: Wayne State University Press.

CHAPTER 4

Religion and the Early Republic

In 1787, in the constitution by which the new nation would operate, the United States of America committed itself to securing 'the blessings of liberty to ourselves and our posterity'. Among the liberties to which the new republic committed itself was freedom of religion, and that freedom was spelled out four years later in the First Amendment to the US Constitution: 'Congress shall make no law respecting an establishment of religion, or prohibiting the free exercise thereof.'

The early republic witnessed a second series of religious revivals, the Second Great Awakening, and an unprecedented democratization of religion. As Nathan Hatch has written: 'The wave of popular religious movements that broke upon the United States in the half century after independence did more to Christianize American society than anything before or since.'[1] The overall rate of religious adherence, the percentage of the entire population that belonged to a church, doubled from 17 per cent to 34 per cent, while the denominational landscape changed dramatically. In 1776 Congregationalists claimed 20.4 per cent of all religious adherents; by 1850 they encompassed only 4 per cent. Episcopalians dropped from 15.7 per cent to 3.5 per cent and Presbyterians from 19 per cent to 11.6 per cent. Baptists, however, grew from 16.9 per cent to 20.5 per cent of all adherents, while Methodists exploded from 2.5 per cent to 34.2 per cent![2]

Disestablishment and Free Exercise of Religion at the National Level

The Founding Fathers, in establishing a new nation, struggled with the question of whether the United States should, or even could, be organized around a single religious creed drawn from one or several churches. The Declaration of Independence and the Articles of Confederation, by which the nation was governed from 1781 to 1789, made reference to God but did not delegate any authority in religious matters

to the federal government. The Northwest Ordinance of 1787, however, established a bill of rights for the Northwest Territory intended to
extend 'the fundamental principles of civil and religious liberty', upon
which the states to be created therein, their laws and constitutions, were
to be created. Article I declared: 'No person, demeaning himself in a
peaceable and orderly manner, shall ever be molested on account of his
mode of worship, or religious sentiments, in the said territory.' Nevertheless recognizing the importance of religion to the new nation, the
authors added in Article III: 'Religion, morality, and knowledge being
necessary to good government and the happiness of mankind, schools
and the means of education shall be encouraged.'[3]

The Constitutional Convention of 1787 paid only slight attention to
the subject of religion. The Constitution contains no reference to God,
or even to religion, except for a prohibition of religious tests as a
qualification for federal office-holders. They would be bound 'by oath
or affirmation' to support the Constitution, 'but no religious test shall
ever be required as a qualification to any office or public trust under the
United States' (Article VI). The federal test oath clause was primarily
the work of Charles Pinckney of South Carolina, and it was adopted
with little debate. Luther Martin was one of the few to even comment
on it:

> [The test oath clause] was adopted by a great majority of the conven-
> tion, and without much debate; however, there were some members
> so unfashionable as to think, that a belief of the existence of a Deity
> and of a state of future rewards and punishments would be some
> security for the good conduct of our rulers, and that, in a Christian
> country, it would be at least decent to hold out some distinction
> between the professors of Christianity and downright infidelity or
> paganism.[4]

During the state ratification debates Connecticut Federalist Oliver
Ellsworth defended the federal ban on religious tests as a means toward
securing 'the important right of religious liberty'. A religious test oath,
he explained, was 'the parent of hypocrisy, and the offspring of error
and the spirit of persecution'. Isaac Bachus, a Baptist and anti-Federalist
delegate to the Massachusetts convention, decided to support the
Constitution in part because of its prohibiting religious oaths. Imposing
such oaths, Backus reasoned, violated a principle evident by reason and
Scripture, 'that religion is ever a matter between God and individuals'.[5]

The delegates to the Constitutional Convention did not adopt a bill of rights. That omission did not reflect any opposition on their part to personal liberties, or to religious freedom. They simply regarded such measures as superfluous. They reasoned that the new national government possessed only expressly enumerated powers, and no power had been granted to legislate on any such subject that would be the concern of a bill of rights. Because no such power existed, none could be exercised, and therefore all provisions against that possibility were unnecessary. As Edmund Randolph of Virginia put it, 'no power is given expressly to Congress over religion', and Congress could exercise only those powers 'constitutionally given' it.[6]

When Congress submitted the Constitution to the states for ratification, it met with a firestorm of criticism that nearly brought about its premature demise. Opponents of ratification feared that the centralizing tendencies of a consolidated national government would extinguish the rights of the states and individuals, unless protected by a bill of rights. Thomas Jefferson, then in France, wrote in support of a bill of rights that would protect freedom of religion, while Richard Henry Lee explained that while contemporary America suffered little religious turmoil, a constitution made for the ages should proclaim the right to 'the free exercise of religion'.[7]

In the end, six of the thirteen original states added to their votes for ratification of the Constitution recommendations for amendments, some of which would secure specific fundamental personal liberties, including freedom of religion. In response to those recommendations, on 8 June 1789, as one of the Congress's first orders of business, Representative James Madison proposed for the House a series of amendments to the Constitution. The section on religion read: 'The civil rights of none shall be abridged on account of religious belief or worship, nor shall any national religion be established, nor shall the full and equal rights of conscience be in any manner, or on any pretext, infringed.'[8]

The term 'national' proved troublesome. To some it meant that the federal government could not establish, or prefer, one denomination over another. To others it precluded any preference for any number, or even all, denominations. Madison did not explain what he meant, but instead agreed to the following rewording of his proposed amendment: 'No religion shall be established by law, nor shall the equal rights of conscience be infringed.' On this, Madison was more explicit. When the proposed amendment was debated by the House, he reported that he understood the words to mean that Congress would be prohibited from establishing 'a religion, and enforce the legal observation of it by law'. Neither should Congress be allowed, he continued, 'to compel men to worship God in any manner contrary to their conscience'. The House version finally sent to the Senate read: 'Congress shall make no law establishing religion or prohibiting the free exercise thereof, nor shall the rights of conscience be infringed.'[9]

The Senate entered into a similar debate between those who favoured a more narrow versus a broader construction of the proposed amendment, taking up and then rejecting various rewordings of the House's proposal: (1) 'Congress shall not make any law establishing one religious sect or society in preference to others'; (2) 'Congress shall not make any law infringing the rights of conscience, or establishing any religious sect or society'; and (3) 'Congress shall make no law establishing any particular denomination of religion in preference to another.' The failure of these and other motions suggests that the Senate too rejected any attempt at narrowing the amendment's intent, preferring a ban on federal involvement in religion of any kind, even in a non-preferential manner. Nevertheless, its proposed amendment differed from the House's: 'Congress shall make no law establishing articles of faith or a mode of worship, or prohibiting the free exercise of religion.'[10]

When the House rejected the Senate's version of the proposed amendment, the measure went to a joint conference, where the following wording was adopted: 'Congress shall make no law respecting an establishment of religion, or prohibiting the free exercise thereof.' The United States Supreme Court did not offer its interpretation of those words until 1947, when, in *Everson* v. *Board of Education*, it ruled:

> The 'establishment of religion' clause of the First Amendment means at least this: Neither a state nor the Federal Government can set up a church. Neither can pass laws which aid one religion, aid all religions, or prefer one religion over another.[11]

Much clearer is that those who framed the First Amendment meant its language, like that of the rest of the Bill of Rights, to apply only to the national government. The United States Supreme Court in *Permoli* v. *Municipality No.* 1 of New Orleans (1845) pointed out that the First Amendment explicitly levies a ban on Congress. In 1789 James Madison proposed an amendment to the Constitution prohibiting the states from violating 'the equal rights of conscience'. Had that amendment been adopted, the federal government could easily have construed it to prohibit the states from maintaining establishments of religion.[12] A rule of constitutional interpretation known as the incorporation doctrine posits that the Fourteenth Amendment, ratified in 1868, incorporates the rights protected by the First Amendment, including religion. But it was not until 1940 that the Supreme Court incorporated the free exercise of religion clause into the Fourteenth Amendment and 1947 before it did the same for the establishment clause. Until then, in matters of religion at least, the states stood apart from the guarantees of the First Amendment and proceeded according to their own constitutions and bills of rights.

Disestablishment and Free Exercise of Religion at the State Level

At the formation of the new nation seven states retained a church establishment. None was affected by the First Amendment to the United States Constitution, except perhaps by the influence of its words. Nevertheless, by 1833 all state establishments collapsed. Massachusetts was the last to relinquish its establishment and therefore will provide an example of how disestablishment finally came about, moving from a multiple establishment to a non-preferential establishment, before finally giving up establishment altogether.

A Massachusetts state supreme court decision of 1811 reaffirmed its 1785 ruling against the constitutional right of unincorporated religious societies to secure the rebate of their members' taxes. That decision could have had the effect of enhancing significantly the Congregational advantage over the less numerous unincorporated non-Congregational churches. It was initiated by a Universalist minister, who had sued the parish of Falmouth (in what is now Maine) for the monies paid by members of his unincorporated congregation, only to have the supreme judicial court sustain the claim of the parish that the state constitution authorized only the ministers of incorporated religious societies to obtain tax rebates.[13] Rather than silencing the opposition, however, it only encouraged them.

Outraged opponents of the decision, whose churches were rapidly increasing in number, orchestrated a public campaign for relief and fashioned an alliance with the Republican party to defeat the Federalists, who backed the courts, in the elections of 1811. The result was the

Religious Freedom Act of 1811 which authorized any religious society, whether incorporated or not, to receive the taxes of its members. After 1811, the basic law of the state confirmed and expanded its commitment to a multiple establishment of religion among Protestant denominations.[14]

By 1820, when Massachusetts held a new constitutional convention, the mushrooming growth of non-Congregationalists and a schism within Congregationalism foreshadowed the unviability of even this multiple church–state relationship. At the convention Congregationalists staved off radical changes in the relevant sections of the old constitution. Delegates recommended modest changes, such as use of 'Christian' instead of 'Protestant', a concession to the growing Roman Catholic population, abolition of the requirement of compulsory public worship, already a dead letter, and constitutional recognition of the Religious Freedom Act of 1811, but they would add nothing to the existing rights of unincorporated religious societies. Resentful voters overwhelmingly withheld ratification, but a decision by the state's high court in early 1821 produced unforeseen results that nevertheless transformed the church–state relationship.[15]

Baker v. *Fales* (1821) became notorious as 'the Dedham case', by which a state court assisted Unitarians in 'plundering' the old Congregational churches. Unitarianism was largely born of schism within Congregational ranks – between Unitarians and Trinitarians – the First Congregational Church in Dedham being typical, in that regard. A majority of the parish had become Unitarian, as a result of which the more orthodox church members seceded. Both groups claimed title to the church, but the state's high court held unanimously that those members that remained constituted the church and retained the rights and property belonging to it.[16]

Nearly ten years after the Dedham decision, the state's supreme court decided the Brookfield case, *Stebbins* v. *Jennings* (1830). During the preceding decade there had been at least thirty Congregational schisms. In most of the cases the seceders were Trinitarians, and in all cases the seceders lost the properties of the churches involved. In 1830, with a new chief justice at the head of the court, the entire issue was re-argued, and Chief Justice Lemuel Shaw reaffirmed the principle of the Dedham decision.[17]

Massachusetts Congregationalists finally understood that establishment – which they had created and supported for so long – could work against them. Shortly after the Brookfield decision, they abandoned their historic position and joined with Baptists, Quakers and even Unitarians in opposition to any establishment of religion. On 11 November 1833, Massachusetts voters, by a ten-to-one majority, ratified an amendment to the state constitution mandating disestablishment.[18] Massachusetts may have been the last state to end its establishment, but the process by which it occurred had been replicated, by and large, in nearly all of those states that had preceded it in that decision.

A Summary View of the Founding Fathers on Church and State

It is impossible to reduce the various views of the Founding Fathers on church and state to one position. It is possible, however, to group them into three categories: enlightened separationists, political centrists, and pietistic separationists. All three were committed to the ideal of religious liberty, but they approached the issue from different perspectives.

Both enlightened and pietistic separationists worked to separate church and state in an institutional sense. Those deeply influenced by the Enlightenment, such as Thomas Paine and Thomas Jefferson, adhered to anticlerical views and focused on insulating government from religious domination. Madison shared this view, but tempered it with a concern for protecting the purity of religious belief and practice as well. Those Founders espousing pietistic separation, Isaac Backus for example, inherited the emphasis of Roger Williams and William Penn on protecting religion from the corrupting effect of governmental interference, while political centrists such as George Washington and John Adams approached the issue of church and state in more pragmatic terms. Less concerned than the separationists with the specific means of attaining religious liberty, they regarded religion as an essential source of personal and social morality and, when in office, repeatedly recognized its importance in the nation's public life.[19] All agreed that the Republic could not survive without religion's moral influence. Consequently, they did not envision a secular society, but rather one receptive to voluntary religious expression, and that has made all the difference in the course of American religious history.

The New England Theology

As noted in Chapter 3, the roots of liberal Christianity can be found in the colonial period, especially colonial New England. The central doctrinal characteristic of the movement was God's role as architect and governor of the universe, but without the wrath associated with Him by Puritan Calvinists. Benevolence became the deity's chief character-istic, and people were no longer consigned to heaven or hell irrespective of their actual beliefs or wilful deeds. Man became a free agent. God's grace continued to be necessary for salvation, but liberals showed much greater confidence in man's ability to effect his own salvation.[20]

In 1787 King's Chapel in Boston became the first Unitarian Church in America. For two decades it stood alone, but both the number of Unitarians and their authority grew. With the election of John Thorton Kirkland, President of Harvard, in 1810, the College became a bastion of liberal Unitarian theology. By 1820 William Ellery Channing, Minister of the Federal Street Church in Boston, became the leading Unitarian theologian. In 1825 he helped organize the American Uni-tarian Association, which brought 125 churches under its banner.[21]

Still active in New England during the early republic were Old Calvinists, who continued to honour the traditional doctrine and polity of New England as it had gradually adjusted to changing circumstances. Like the liberals, they renounced the excesses of revivalism. But in contrast to liberals, they did not repudiate the Puritan conviction that regeneration was essential to the Christian life, nor did they cease to hope that the Holy Spirit would descend with special favour on whole communities and nations. The Old Calvinists had among them several prominent figures, like Jedediah Morse, Minister in Charlestown, Massachusetts, David Tappan, Professor of Divinity at Harvard, Joseph Willard, President of Harvard, and Thomas Clap, President of Yale. Nevertheless, as a whole, the moderates were undistinguished in strictly theological enterprises, and they won few recruits to succeed them in their ministry.[22]

The New Divinity men were more successful. They acknowledged Jonathan Edwards as their hero, and they sought to establish their churches on strict principles of regenerate membership and on new, but sharply defined, standards of doctrinal orthodoxy. Almost all were graduates of Yale, and most of them were settled over churches in Connecticut and the Connecticut River Valley. Although they defended revivals and sought to fan the fires of religious fervour anew, their concern with doctrine and metaphysics tended to hinder those efforts. Their churches were often beset by declining membership, factional troubles or open schism. Moderates and liberals often dismissed them as a 'metaphysical school', yet they persisted, and, at the end of the century, though it was not directly of their doing, they were rewarded by a Second Great Awakening.[23]

The New Divinity men's contribution to American religious history was almost entirely in the realm of ideas. Building on the older Puritan divinity as it had been enlivened in the Awakening and set on a new course by Edwards, they maintained and extended the New England theology. As such, Sydney Ahlstrom has written, they 'contributed creatively to the single most brilliant and most continuous indigenous theological tradition that America has ever produced'. Among the leading contributors were Samuel Hopkins, Jonathan Edwards, Jr (Jonathan's son), and Nathanael Emmons. Joseph Bellamy provided the movement with its theological foundation.[24]

Bellamy, the first and most undeviating of Jonathan Edwards's disciples, trained for a time in Edwards's home. Not surprisingly, then, most of what Bellamy espoused was consistent with what Edwards had taught, but Bellamy did introduce some important shifts in emphasis. Among Bellamy's innovations was his concept of God as Moral Governor. As we have seen, this idea was already widespread in the early Republic, but in his hands it was prefatory to the most salient revisions of the Reformed tradition to be proposed by the New Divinity men. One of those revisions, and possibly the fundamental one, was the exoneration of God as the cause of sin through an emphasis on the divine permission of sin as the necessary means of achieving the greatest good in this best of all possible worlds. This was followed quite naturally by a muting of Edwards's argument for mankind's unity with Adam, which in turn opened the way for exorcising the idea of the imputation of Adam's sin. For Bellamy man was sinful because he sinned.[25]

A corollary was Bellamy's redefinition of reprobation, according to which God's punishment of sin was not seen as an expression of holy wrath, but rather as an essential means of maintaining the authority of God's Law. But perhaps best known of all was Bellamy's reinterpretation of the atonement, whereby God was no longer considered an offended party receiving Christ's death as satisfaction for man's infinitely evil ways and limited in its effect only to the elect. Bellamy took Christ's sacrifice as an outworking of God's love accomplished for the well-being of the universe.[26]

Historians have given the New Divinity movement mixed reviews. Herbert Schneider found it 'one of the most intricate and pathetic exhibitions of theological reasonings which the history of Western thought affords'. 'Modern Protestants', Schneider concluded, were 'so thankful to be rid of the Puritan incubus that they point to these post-Edwardseans as the death agony of a monstrous theology which should never have been born'. Joseph Haroutunian was just as harsh when he wrote: 'The profound tragedy of Edwards' theology was transformed into a farce by his would-be disciples, who used his language and ignored his piety.'[27]

Other scholars have given equal amounts of praise to the New Divinity movement. Frank Hugh Foster, for example, not only praised Edwards but also described the work of his successors as building on that tradition in meaningful ways and as existing at the summit of nineteenth-century theology. George Boardman regarded the New Divinity men as possessed of original power as thinkers and the power of the movement as 'really a matter of wonder'.[28] Sydney Ahlstrom, however, provided a more balanced assessment.

Ahlstrom offered praise but in the context of the time. The extenuating circumstance for the New Divinity men was that they existed during the Enlightenment, when the country was more concerned with political matters – government, law, trade, war and nation building – not theology. Nevertheless, he points out, 'they succeeded in doing what almost no one else in the Reformed tradition was then doing creatively. They maintained a dogmatic tradition and steadily developed it in the face of both revivalistic and rationalistic challenges to theological rigor':

> Never have theologians struggled against greater odds. Yet no one who reads their productions patiently can deny that they executed their task with brilliance. For the churches their works served as a highly effective sheet anchor during the period's political storms, enabling the New England tradition to move ahead again under the fair winds of the new century.[29]

The Second Great Awakening in New England

The years since the First Great Awakening were hard to understand for some. God seemed almost to have withdrawn his blessing from New England. There had been occasional local revivals, especially in the years 1763–4, but, until the end of the century, although the number of New Divinity men had grown from a small band to over 100, little followed. The first phase of the Second Great Awakening in New

England took place between 1797 and 1801, when many towns from Connecticut to New Hampshire felt 'refreshing showers'. 'I saw a continued succession of heavenly sprinklings . . .', wrote Edward Dorr Griffin, 'until, in 1799, I could stand at my door in New Hartford, Litchfield County, and number fifty or sixty contiguous congregations laid down in one field of divine wonders'. In 1801 the Awakening came to Yale, where one-third of the students were converted. And soon after, Bennet Tyler, one of the revival's leaders wrote:

> God, in a remarkable manner, was pouring out his Spirit on the churches of New England. Within the period of five or six years . . . not less than one hundred and fifty churches in New England were visited with times of refreshing from the presence of the Lord.[30]

Until it began to be influenced by the Great Awakening in the West, the New England Awakening was remarkably uniform in almost all of its appearances. Revivals came to the parishes of the New Divinity men with a consistency that they could interpret only as a sign of divine favour. In the words of the Edwardseans, it was the preaching of 'plain gospel truths, with which the people had long been acquainted, and had heard with indifference'. These 'plain gospel truths' were God's absolute sovereignty, man's total depravity and Christ's atoning love:

> It has been no uncommon thing for the subjects of the work, whose chief distress and anxiety antecedently arose from a sense of their being in the hands of God, unexpectedly to find themselves rejoicing in their very consideration . . . They have . . . apparently rejoiced in God's supremacy, and in being at this disposal, calmly leaving their case to his wise and holy decision.[31]

The revivals were without the hysteria and commotion that had brought the First Great Awakening into disrepute in many quarters, and that was arousing similar opposition in the West. That people were calm was something for which the New England ministers thanked God. They were not marked by 'outcries, distortions of the body, or any symptoms of intemperate zeal'. Indeed, they reported, 'you might often see a congregation sit with deep solemnity depicted in their countenances, without observing a tear or sob during the service'. Nevertheless, the fruits of conversion were incontestable, the New England ministers insisted. They could be seen in the renewed spiritual seriousness and reformation of morals among the converted.[32]

Whereas the First Great Awakening was heavily reliant on itinerants, the Second Great Awakening in New England was largely conducted by settled ministers within their own congregations. Prominent among the leaders of the Second Awakening were Timothy Dwight, Nathaniel William Taylor and Lyman Beecher. Dwight, grandson of Jonathan Edwards and President of Yale from 1795 to 1817, is often hailed as first among this select group of leaders. His primary crusade was against deism. Whether he was an Old Calvinist or a New Divinity man has been much debated, but to a large extent he was neither. As the founder of the New Haven Theology, as it came to be known, he started a new trend that was carried to completion by Nathaniel William Taylor.[33]

Taylor, arguably the best theologian of his time in New England, was both Dwight's most devoted student and the real architect of the New Haven Theology. Taylor ministered to the First Church of New Haven from 1811 to 1822, but his most important services were rendered as Professor of Theology at the Yale Divinity School. From that platform he became the Edwards of the Second Great Awakening, and his influence extended far beyond his own region and denomination.[34]

In spirit the New Haven Theology remained distinctly Reformed, for Taylor would never concede that he had departed from the Westminster Confession, Dwight, or Edwards. But he did gather together the innovations of the intervening New Divinity, based them firmly and knowledgeably on Scottish Philosophy, and propounded a plausibly rationalistic revival theology for mid-nineteenth-century America. Taylor condemned liberal Christianity for its overestimation of human reason, goodness and educability, but he also sought to modify orthodox Calvinism's doctrine of the total inability of man to effect his own salvation. He insisted that no man becomes depraved but by his own act, for the sinfulness of the human race does not pertain to human nature as such. 'Sin is in the sinning', and therefore 'original' only in the sense that it is universal. Though inevitable, it is not – as Edwards argued – causally necessary. Man always had, in Taylor's famous phrase, 'power to the contrary'.[35]

And finally there was Lyman Beecher, the self-asserting apostle of Taylorism. No other figure sums up better in his own life the many facets of the Second Great Awakening and its enormous consequences for American history. Beecher was the most methodical and pragmatic of the New England evangelicals, and his carefully organized techniques have been well documented. Within a movement that generally frowned upon itinerants, as they were employed in the First Great Awakening, Beecher enlisted regular clergy in parishes that had experienced revivals into pulpit exchanges with those who had not. He organized new converts into voluntary associations for organized missionary activities. When necessary, he emphasized or not principal points of Calvinism.

> I believe [he wrote] that both the doctrines of dependence and moral accountability must be admitted . . . [But] I also believe that greater or less prominence should be given to the one or the other of those doctrines according to the prevailing states of public opinion.[36]

While pursuing his career as a revivalist, Beecher brought to fullness the conception that most distinguishes the evangelistic resurgence of the next half-century: the intimate association of evangelism in its broadest sense with moral reform and social benevolence. As a reformer he was especially active in the temperance movement. When he was called in 1826 to Boston's Hanover Street Congregational Church, he brought the tactics of revivalism to the service of conservatism against liberals and Unitarians. In 1832 he moved west to become president of Lane Theological Seminary.[37]

A Concluding Note on the Second Great Awakening in New England

To conclude this section on the Second Great Awakening in New England, we should make two final points. Along with the redefinition of free moral agency, theologians of the Second Great Awakening in New England revised the concept of limited atonement. If, as they allowed, all men have free will, Christ could not have died for only a few predestined elect, but for whoever would accept God's offer of salvation. Further, they played down the idea that the atonement of Christ was a punishment he suffered for Adam's sin. Instead, they suggested that Christ came to earth to suffer as a man because he wished to sacrifice himself for the love of mankind.[38] It was a voluntary act of self-sacrifice that served both as a stimulus and as an example for believers, which relates to our second point.

The Second Awakening created a new kind of religious institution, the voluntary association of private individuals for missionary, reformatory or benevolent purposes. Usually these societies were chartered and governed independently, even when they had a nominal relation to some church body. Their membership grew wherever interest could be created, often on an interdenominational basis. Their activities were carried on without church or state controls, and in most cases they were focused fairly sharply on one specific purpose. This will be further explored in the Chapter 5.

The Great Awakening in the West

In 1814, on the occasion of the Yale commencement, Lyman Beecher addressed the leadership of New England's Second Great Awakening. Beecher informed his audience of the unprecedented number of new ministers required to serve the young nation, and he challenged them to provide financial assistance for worthy candidates. Declaring that the entire nation could boast only '3000 educated ministers of the Gospel', he called for 5000 new recruits, men who could train at a place such as Yale and thus rescue the people of America from another kind of religious leader who presumed to speak about divine matters:

> There may be, perhaps, 1500 besides who are nominally ministers of the Gospel. But they are generally illiterate men, often not possessed of a good English education, and in some instances unable to read or write. By them, as a body, learning is despised.[39]

Beecher went on to spell out the effects of people being 'exposed to the errors of enthusiastic and false teachers'. Illiterate teachers could not stand as pillars of civilization and moral influence, he explained, nor could they command the attention of 'that class of the community which is above their own', wielding 'that religious and moral literary influence which it belongs to the ministry to exert'. 'Illiterate men have never been the chosen instruments of God to build up his cause', Beecher continued, quickly explaining that the twelve disciples were instructed by Christ himself for three years 'to supply the deficiency of an education'.[40] Beecher, of course, was referring to those ministers who served as the vanguard of the Second Great Awakening in the West.

As is true of most other such events, it is difficult to date the beginning of the Second Great Awakening in the West. Most historians agree, however, that it began between the late 1780s and 1800. When the American Revolution ended, Americans moved west rapidly and in large numbers. They surged ahead of all trappings of civilization, including church and community. Bringing religion to them would require extraordinary measures, including the camp meeting. The camp meeting became the pre-eminent symbol of the Awakening in the West, which at least in its outward manifestation was quite different from the revivals in New England.[41]

The earliest major figure in the western Awakening was the Presbyterian minister James McGready, a bold and uncompromising Scotch-Irishman. McGready ministered in North Carolina until 1796, when he took charge of three parishes in south-western Kentucky. At the Gasper River Church in July 1800, he organized the first camp meeting.[42] Joining McGready was another Presbyterian, Barton W. Stone. Born in Maryland, Stone moved into western North Carolina, where he was converted under McGready. In 1800 he was serving the small Cane Ridge and Concord Churches in Bourbon, Kentucky. In August 1801 Stone organized a camp meeting at Cane Ridge that attracted a crowd of people estimated at from 10,000 to 25,000 – this at a time when nearby Lexington, the state's largest city, barely exceeded 2000.[43]

The Cane Ridge Revival lasted from six to seven days and would likely have lasted longer were it not for the failure of provisions for the unexpected crowd. When it was over, contemporaries referred to it as 'the greatest outpouring of the Spirit since Pentecost'. Historians labelled it a watershed in American religious history, but what happened nearly defies description. Barton Stone put it as simply as any:

> Many things transpired there, which were so much like miracles, that if they were not, they had the same effects as miracles on infidels and unbelievers; for many of them by these were convinced that Jesus was the Christ, and bowed in submission to him.[44]

Historian Sydney Ahlstrom has described the Cane Ridge crowd as including hardened, tobacco-chewing, tough-spoken and notoriously profane farmers, famous for their alcoholic thirst. They were joined by their 'scarcely demure wives and large broods of children' – all attracted in anticipation of participating in so large a social occasion in an otherwise lonely frontier farmer's life.[45]

William McLoughlin has argued that women in particular were drawn to camp meetings, because they bore the heaviest burdens of pain, sickness, sorrow, unremitting labour, and old age. 'For their labors there were few social rewards and no public victories.' They were excluded from most frontier pastimes, save joining religious institutions should they find their way into their communities. But, then, Christian fellowship was an important source of security for men and women: 'It gave regularity and order to life; it offered a source of strength beyond the self.'[46]

The most controversial element of the Cane Ridge Revival was the outward, physical manifestations of those overcome by religious emotions. Once again, we turn to Barton Stone's personal account:

> The bodily agitations or exercises, attending the excitement in the beginning of this century, were various and called by various names . . . The falling exercise was very common among all classes . . . The subject of this exercise would, generally, with a piercing scream, fall like a log on the floor, earth, or mud, and appear as dead . . .
>
> The jerks cannot be so easily described. Sometimes the subject of the jerks would be affected in some one member of the body, and sometimes the whole system. When the head alone was affected, it would be jerked backward and forward, or from side to side, so quickly that the features of the face could not be distinguished. When the whole system was affected, I have seen the person stand in one place, and jerk backward and forward in quick succession, their head nearly touching the floor behind and before . . .
>
> The dancing exercise . . . generally began with the jerks, and was peculiar to the professors of religion. The subject, after jerking awhile, began to dance, and then the jerks would cease. Such dancing was indeed heavenly to the spectators; there was nothing in it like levity, nor calculated to excite levity in the beholders . . . Thus they continued to move forward and backward in the same track or alley till nature seemed exhausted, and they would fall prostrate on the floor or earth . . .
>
> The barking exercise (as opposers contemptuously called it), was nothing but the jerks. A person affected with the jerks, especially in his head, would often make a grunt, or bark, if you please, from the suddenness of the jerk . . .
>
> The laughing exercise was frequent, confined solely with the religious. It was a loud, hearty laughter, but . . . it excited laughter in none else. The subject appeared rapturously solemn, and his laughter excited solemnity in saints and sinners . . .
>
> The running exercise was nothing more than . . . persons feeling something of these bodily agitations, through fear, attempt[ing] to run away, and thus escape from them; but it commonly happened that

they ran not far, before they fell, or became so greatly agitated that they could proceed no farther . . .

Stone concluded this chapter with a description of the singing exercise, wherein the subject in a very happy mind would 'sing most melodiously'. Such music, Stone concluded, 'silenced everything, and attracted the attention of all. It was most heavenly. How could you ever be tired of hearing it.' There were 'many eccentricities and much fanaticism in this excitement', he offered in closing, but 'the good effects were seen and acknowledged in every neighborhood'.[47]

Perhaps the most important figure to appear in the Second Great Awakening in the West was the Presbyterian revivalist Charles Grandison Finney. As the leading prophet of revivalism and perfectionism, he provides a transition to Chapter 5. Further, because Finney's work was largely in the Old Northwest, he, more than most frontier revivalists, came into contact with New Englanders of the Taylor/Beecher school. Indeed Taylor and Beecher and their disciples both feared and learned more from Finney than any other competitor. Under Finney the revivalism of the Old Northwest, now the Midwest, constituted the culmination of the northern phase of the Awakening. After 1830, however, Finney brought his revival methods back east to New England, New York City, Philadelphia and even the British Isles.[48]

Reports in New England portrayed Finney's revivals as fanatical affairs, and, fearing the ridicule they might bring on their own efforts, Taylor and Beecher arranged to meet Finney in New Lebanon, New York, in 1827. Taylor and Beecher hoped to persuade Finney to tone down his enthusiasm, but they failed. Finney simply countered that as he and his followers were winning so many converts it made no sense to change their ways. Finney agreed to discourage 'audible groaning', shouting, fainting and other convulsions, but little else. Indeed, he wrote:

> God has found it necessary to take advantage of the excitability there is in mankind to produce powerful excitements, among them before he can lead them to obey him. Men are so sluggish, there are so many things to lead their minds off from religion and to oppose the influence of the gospel, that it is necessary to raise an excitement among them till the tide rises so high as to sweep away the opposing obstacles.[49]

Finney largely repudiated Calvinism. He did not become a rationalist, but he did come to believe that 'reason was given us for the very

purpose of enabling us to justify the ways of God', and that 'the will is
free and . . . sin and holiness are voluntary acts of mind'. Conversion,
Finney declared 'is not a miracle or dependent on a miracle . . . It is
purely a philosophical result of the right use of constituted means.'
Therefore a revival is not a miracle; rather 'it consists entirely in the
right exercise of the powers of nature'. Drawing a parallel between
bringing about a revival and raising a crop of wheat, Finney insisted
that as the laws governing revivals were so clear and simple, anyone
following them could obtain the desired results.[50]

Finney developed a new concept of professional mass evangelism
and demonstrated that it could be used as effectively in the cities as in
rural camp meetings. He helped make revivalism a profession and
popularized the practice of protracted meetings – three or four day
revivalistic gatherings. Finney sometimes held these meetings in tents,
sometimes in large churches or auditoriums or even theatres, and, in
contrast to most other revivalists, his meetings were interdenominational, often sponsored by all the churches in a town. In that regard,
Finney and the professional revivalists that would follow in his foot-
steps served to supplement, rather than compete with, the regular
ministry, thereby becoming, as William McLoughlin put it, 'the most
powerful engine in the process of American church growth, frontier
acculturation, and benevolent reform'.[51]

Historians associate three major consequences with the Great Awakening in the West. First, because of that Awakening, revivalism became both symbol and impetus for the century-long process by which
the greater part of American evangelical Protestantism became revita-
lized. The organized revival became a major mode of church expansion.
Second, it in large part determined the country's denominational
expansion, most notably among Baptists and Methodists. And, third,
it helped advance the democratization of Christianity in America.[52]

The Democratization of Christianity in America

Between the American Revolution and 1845 the population of the
United States grew from 2.5 million to 20 million. This unprecedented
growth was due to a high birth rate and the availability of land, rather
than to heavy immigration; that would come later. Nevertheless, the
United States remained overwhelmingly rural, the ratio of people to
land barely doubling, while the number of Americans expanded tenfold.
Amidst this population boom, American Christianity became a mass

enterprise. The 1800 Christian ministers serving in 1775 swelled to nearly 40,000 by 1845. The number of preachers per capita more than tripled, and the colonial legacy of 1 minister per 1500 inhabitants became 1 per 500. This greater preaching density was remarkable given the spiralling population and the restless movement of peoples to occupy land beyond the reach of any church organization.[53]

The sheer number of new preachers in the Early Republic was not a predictable outgrowth of religious conditions in the British colonies. Rather, their sudden growth indicated a profound religious upsurge and resulted in a vastly altered religious landscape. Twice the number of denominations competed for adherents, and insurgent groups enjoyed the upper hand. One new denominational cluster, the Christians or the Disciples of Christ, for example, had an estimated 4000 preachers, equalling the number of clergy serving Presbyterian denominations. The Congregationalists, who had twice the clergy of any other American church in 1775, could not muster one-tenth the preaching force of the Methodists in 1845.[54]

We will look more carefully at the Christian movement, the Methodists, and the Baptists later in this section. For now, however, it should be noted that all three constituted mass movements, and were led by young men of relentless energy, who went about movement-building as self-conscious outsiders. They shared an ethic of unrelenting toil, a passion for expansion, a hostility to orthodox belief and style, a zeal for religious reconstruction, and a systematic plan to realize their goals. Further, however diverse their theologies and church organizations, they all offered common people compelling visions of individual self-respect and collective self-confidence.[55]

As common people became significant actors on the religious scene, there was increasing confusion and angry debate over the purpose and function of the church. A style of religious leadership that the public deemed 'untutored' and 'irregular' as late as the First Great Awakening became overwhelmingly successful, even normative, in the Second. Ministers from different classes vied with each other to serve as divine spokesmen, and democratic or populist leaders associated virtue with ordinary people and exalted the vernacular in word, print and song.[56]

Faced with problems beyond the ordinary experiences of easterners, westerners often rushed to biblical prophecy for help in understanding the troubled times that were upon them. Some demanded a return to revivals, the likes of those of the eighteenth century, while others felt free to experiment with new forms of organization and belief. By the end of the first decade of the nineteenth century, Nathan Hatch has argued, it became anachronistic to speak of dissent in America – as if there were still a commonly recognized centre against which new or emerging groups defined themselves. New groups were already vying to establish their identity as a counter-establishment.[57]

In at least three respects the popular religious movements of the Early Republic articulated a profoundly democratic spirit. First, they denied the age-old distinction that set the clergy apart as a separate order of men, and they refused to defer to learned theologians and traditional orthodoxies. Second, they associated virtue with ordinary people rather than with elites, and exalted the vernacular in word and song as the hallowed channel for communicating with and about God. And, third, they rejected the past as a repository of wisdom. In these ways, they reconstructed the foundations of religion in keeping with the values and priorities of ordinary people.[58]

These popular religious movements empowered ordinary people by taking their deepest spiritual impulses at face value rather than subjecting them to the scrutiny of orthodox doctrine and clergymen. Preachers from a wide range of new religious movements openly fanned the flames of religious ecstasy, and what had been defined as 'enthusiasm' was increasingly advocated from the pulpit as an essential part of Christianity. Such a shift in emphasis, accompanied by rousing gospel singing rather then formal church music, reflected the common people's success in defining the nature of faith for themselves.[59]

The Christian Movement

Characteristically, participants in the Christian Movement simply called themselves 'Christians'. They followed the lead of Elias Smith, a New England Jeffersonian, who sought a radical simplification of the gospel. Smith became a central figure in a loose network of religious radicals who between 1790 and 1815 chose the name 'Disciples of Christ'. They demanded, in the light of the American Revolution, a new dispensation free from the trammels of history, a new kind of church based on democratic principles, and a new form of biblical authority calling for common people to interpret the New Testament for themselves. Other major figures in the movement included James O'Kelly in Virginia, Barton Stone in Kentucky and Alexander Campbell in Pennsylvania. A Calvinist Baptist, a Methodist and two Presbyterians, all found traditional sources of authority anachronistic and moved toward similar definitions of egalitarian religion.[60]

From Portsmouth, New Hampshire, Smith, ordained a Baptist minister, launched the first religious newspaper in the Unites States, the *Herald of Gospel Liberty*, which he edited from 1808 to 1818. From that forum, and in scores of pamphlets and sermons, he and a band of fifty or so itinerants launched a blistering attack on Baptists, Congregationalists, Methodists and Federalists of any religious persuasion. By 1815 the newspaper had 1400 subscribers.[61]

In Virginia, James O'Kelly's Republican Methodists, founded in 1794, were taking the same route — undoing the 'ecclesiastical monarch' of the Methodist Church. An early leader among Virginia Methodists, O'Kelly could not abide the bishopric of Francis Asbury and withdrew with over thirty ministers to form a church that had as many as 20,000 members when it merged with Smith's Christians in 1809. 'As a son of America, and a Christian,' he declared to Asbury, 'I shall oppose your political measures and contend for the Savior's government. I contend for Biblical government, Christian equality, and the Christian name.'[62]

Barton Stone embarked upon the same pilgrimage in the wake of the Cane Ridge Revival in Kentucky in 1802, wherein he resolved that he could no longer live under Presbyterian doctrine or church organization. A year later he and five other ministers proclaimed that it was not just the Presbyterians who were wrong, but all churches. Signing a document entitled 'The Last Will and Testament of the Springfield Presbytery', they vowed to follow nothing but the Christian name and the New Testament. 'It was not without deep connotation', Nathan Hatch has pointed out, 'that Stone characterized his break with the Presbyterians as the "declaration of our independence".'[63]

Finally, there was Alexander Campbell, Scottish immigrant, the only college graduate of the four, and the only one not to participate in the American Revolution. Campbell found himself following the same trajectory of his fellow American Christians. Writing to his uncle in Scotland in 1815, he described his seven years in the United States:

During this period of years my mind and circumstances have undergone many revolutions. I have . . . renounced many of the traditions and errors of my early education. My mind was, for a time, set loose from all its former moorings. It was not a simple change, but a new commencement . . . The whole landscape of Christianity presented itself to my mind in a new attitude and position.[64]

By 1830 Alexander Campbell's quest for primitive Christianity led his movement, the Disciples of Christ, to unite with Stone's Christians. By 1860 their denomination claimed about 200,000 adherents, the fifth largest Protestant body in the United States. The Christians hammered relentlessly at the simple themes of sin, grace and conversion. They organized fellowships that resisted social distinctions and welcomed spontaneous experience, and they denounced any religion that seemed bookish, cold or formal. Further, the Christians espoused reform in three areas. First, they called for a revolution within the church to place laity and clergy on an equal footing and to exalt the conscience of the individual over the collective will of any congregation or church organization. Second, they rejected the traditions of learned theology altogether and called for a new view of history that welcomed inquiry and innovation. Finally, they advocated the inalienable right of every person to understand the New Testament for him- or herself.[65]

The Methodists

In 1806 Methodist Bishop Francis Asbury sent a report to his English colleague, Thomas Cooke, in which he expressed his growing confidence in the role of the Methodists in converting the New World. He spoke of the hundreds of gospel ministers under his charge, of the 8273 new members added during the last year, and of the pervasive sense that God's work was accelerating at an unprecedented rate. In particular, he delighted in the success of American camp meetings, describing the 'overwhelming power' of a four-day meeting twenty miles north-east of New York City, which, he estimated, 3000 lay people and 100 preachers had attended. Five years later he boasted that these occasions brought together as many as four million Americans annually – an estimated one-third of the total population.[66]

In the very years that Methodist leadership in Great Britain seemed willing to forego numerical growth as their primary goal, even accepting numerical losses in order to preserve discipline, American Methodists remained ruthlessly committed to arousing a following and creating new societies. Increasingly, Methodist leaders were sent out to call churches into existence, not to wait for churches to call them. Both roving evangelists and propagandists, they went from house to house looking for anyone who would listen, taking Francis Asbury's first 'discipline' seriously: 'You have nothing to do but to save souls. Therefore, spend and be spent in this work.'[67]

The Methodist Church was not the most democratic movement of the day, organizationally. Even under Francis Asbury's leadership, the Church refused to share ecclesiastical authority with the laity. Asbury was continually criticized for this by his more democratic competitors, but he never apologized for it or for its cadre of itinerant preachers being bound together by strict rules and discipline under one leader. Instead, he defended his own authority by linking it directly to the apostolic age, transcending the corruptions of the intervening centuries. More than any other church, Asbury insisted, the Methodists had restored the 'primitive order' of the New Testament, 'the same doctrine, the same spirituality, the same power in ordinances, in ordination, and in spirit'.[68]

While the structure of the Methodist Church may have seemed out of accord with the democratic stirrings of the times, the vital spring of Methodism under Asbury was to make Christianity profoundly a faith of the people. It was the Church's duty, he said, 'to condescend to men of low estate'. From Asbury and preachers like him, people received an invitation to join a movement promising them dignity of choice and beckoning them to involvement as a class leader, exhorter, local preacher and circuit rider. In these forms, lay preaching became the hallmark of American Methodism and served as a powerful symbol that the wall between a gentleman and commoner had been shattered.[69]

The Baptists

American Baptists have always viewed the General Missionary Convention in Philadelphia in 1814 as a watershed event in their history. The meeting was the first step in creating a national denomination out of hundreds of autonomous Baptist churches scattered along the Atlantic seaboard. For the thirty-two delegates at the organizing session of 'the Triennial Convention', this national undertaking was an important sign that the Baptist movement was coming of age. Baptist membership had grown tenfold since the Revolution, and its 2000 churches, 1600 ministers and 100 associations could no longer be overlooked. Already Baptists had begun to taste a measure of respectability and to look forward to a day when they would not have to bear the reproach of inferior social position.[70]

At least one prominent Baptist, however, took exception to this quest for respectability. John Leland was one of the most popular and controversial Baptists in America. He was most famous as an advocate of religious freedom in Virginia, but he was primarily a preacher and an itinerant evangelist. Leland was a persistent critic of clerical professionalism, which he believed was at the core of American Protestant denominations. He denounced the oppression of 'a hierarchical clergy – despotic judiciary – [and] an aristocratic host of lawyers', the mechanical operations of theological seminaries, the tyranny of formal structures and the burden of credalism – 'this Virgin Mary between the souls of men and the Scriptures'.[71]

Leland's opposition to creeds and confessions was a function of his firm identification with a popular audience, an instinct that even his radical predecessor Isaac Backus did not appreciate. Backus had defended his positions with learned tracts addressed to civil and religious elites. He opposed 'high and new things' in religion and was suspicious of rallying popular opinion. Leland relished a common audience, peppering his speeches and writings with blunt common sense and earthy humour. The greatest difference between Backus and Leland, however, was their contrasting view of the social order. While Backus never doubted the right of all to worship as they pleased, he was unconvinced that laymen could articulate their own theology. Leland rejected the idea of natural inequality in society, that some were set apart to lead and others to follow. He depicted the typical clergyman as venal and conniving, rather than capable of rising above self-interest. Like Jefferson, he perceived the organized church as corrupted by 'priestcraft', which he defined as the clerical quest for 'self-advantage'.[72]

Leland was a diligent publicist whose ideas had broad circulation, thereby assuring his legacy within the Baptist Church. That legacy consisted of a twofold persuasion that operated powerfully in the hinterland of Baptist church life: an aversion to central control and a quest for self-reliance. Whatever success Richard Furman and others had in building central institutions, their way was dogged at every step by serious defections to the antiformalist appeals of Leland and his successors. Thus, Baptists had the advantage not only of the peculiar rite of adult baptism but also of a democratic congregational polity, in which the members of each local church were subject to no higher ecclesiastical authority. Ordinary people gladly championed the promise of personal autonomy as a message they could understand and a cause to which they could subscribe, in God's name.[73]

Summary

American churches' profound commitment to their audience in the early decades of the nineteenth century shaped the way religious thinking was organized and carried out. When the commoner rose in power, people of ideas found their authority circumscribed. As a result, Nathan Hatch has argued, democratic America has never produced another theologian like Jonathan Edwards, just as it has never elected statesmen of the calibre of Johns Adams, Thomas Jefferson and James Madison. Insurgent religious leaders were not so much anti-intellectual as intent on destroying the monopoly of classically educated and university-trained clergymen. The insurgents considered people's common sense more reliable, even in theology, than the judgement of an educated few.[74]

This shift involved a new faith in public opinion as an arbiter of truth. Common folk were no longer thought to be irresponsible and wilful. Rather they were deemed ready to embrace truth, if only it was retrieved from academic speculation and the heavy hand of the past. These new ground rules flattened out uncomfortable complexity and often resolved issues by a simple choice of alternatives in the free market-place of ideas.

Notes

1. Nathan O. Hatch (1989), *The Democratization of American Christianity* (New Haven: Yale University Press), p. 3.
2. Roger Finke and Rodney Stark (1994), *The Churching of America, 1776–1990: Winners and Losers in our Religious Economy* (New Brunswick, NJ: Rutgers University Press), pp. 16, 55.
3. Arlin M. Adams and Charles J. Emmerich (1990), *A Nation Dedicated to Religious Liberty: The Constitutional Heritage of the Religion Clauses* (Philadelphia: University of Pennsylvania Press), pp. 10–11.
4. Adams and Emmerich, *Nation Dedicated to Religious Liberty*, p. 14.
5. Ibid., p. 15.
6. Leonard W. Levy (1985), *Emergence of a Free Press* (New York: Oxford University Press), pp. 220–236; Leonard W. Levy (1986), *The Establishment Clause: Religion and the First Amendment* (New York: Macmillan Publishing Company), pp. 65–6.
7. Thomas J. Curry (1986), *The First Freedoms: Church and State in America to the Passage of the First Amendment* (NY: Oxford University Press), p. 195.
8. Levy, *Establishment Clause*, p. 66; Curry, *First Freedoms*, p. 199.
9. Levy, *Establishment Clause*, pp. 75–7, 81.
10. Ibid., p. 82; Curry, *First Freedoms*, p. 207.
11. Curry, *First Freedoms*, p. 207. See also: Martin Marty (1997), *The One and the Many: America's Struggle for the Common Good* (Cambridge, MA: Harvard University Press).

12. Adams and Emmerich, *Nation Dedicated to Religious Liberty*, pp. 19–20; Curry, *First Freedoms*, pp. 199, 204–5.
13. Levy, *Establishment Clause*, pp. 32–33.
14. William G. McLoughlin (1971), *New England Dissent 1630–1833: The Baptists and the Separation of Church and State* 2 vols (Cambridge, MA: Harvard University Press), II: pp. 1088–106; Levy, *Establishment Clause*, pp. 32–3.
15. McLoughlin, *New England Dissent*, II: pp. 1160–85.
16. Levy, *Establishment Clause*, p. 35.
17. Ibid., p. 37.
18. Ibid., p. 38.
19. Adams and Emmerich, *Nation Dedicated to Religious Liberty*, p. 31.
20. Conrad Wright (1976), *Beginnings of Unitarianism in America* (Hamden, CT: Archon Books), pp. 59–186; Daniel W. Howe (1970), *The Unitarian Conscience* (Cambridge, MA: Harvard University Press); Charles H. Lippy(1981), *Seasonable Revolutionary: The Mind of Charles Chauncy* (Chicago: Nelson-Hall); David Robinson (1985), *The Unitarians and the Universalists* (Westport, CT: Greenwood Press), pp. 9–23.
21. Wright, *Beginnings of Unitarianism in America*, pp. 252–80; Conrad Wright (1989), 'Institutional reconstruction in the Unitarian Controversy', in Conrad Wright (ed.), *American Unitarianism, 1805–1865* (Boston: Massachusetts Historical Society and Northeastern University Press), pp. 3–29; Robinson, *Unitarians and the Universalists*, 30–8; Arthur W. Brown (1956), *Always Young for Liberty: A Biography of William Ellery Channing* (Syracuse, NY: Syracuse University Press).
22. William G. McLoughlin (1978), *Revivals, Awakenings, and Reform: An Essay on Religion and Social Change in America, 1607–1977* (Chicago: University of Chicago Press), pp. 98–101.
23. Sydney E. Ahlstrom (1972), *A Religious History of the American People* (New Haven: Yale University Press), pp. 404–5; McLoughlin, *Revivals, Awakenings, and Reform*, p. 101; Charles Roy Keller (1942), *The Second Great Awakening in Connecticut* (New Haven: Yale University Press,).
24. Ahlstrom, *Religious History of the American People*, pp. 405–7.
25. Ibid., p. 407.
26. Ibid., p. 407.
27. Herbert W. Schneider (1958), *The Puritan Mind* (Ann Arbor: University of Michigan Press), p. 208; Joseph Haroutunian (1932), *Piety versus Moralism: The Passing of the New England Theology* (New York: Henry Holt), pp. 71, 96, 127, 130, 176.
28. Frank H. Foster (1907), *A Genetic History of the New England Theology* (Chicago: University of Chicago Press); George N. Boardman(1899), *History of the New England Theology* (Chicago: University of Chicago Press), p. 14.
29. Ahlstrom, *Religious History of the American People*, p. 414.
30. Griffin is quoted in Keller, *Second Great Awakening in Connecticut*, pp. 37–8; Ahlstrom, *Religious History of the American People*, p. 416; Bennet Tyler (1846), *The New England Revivals . . . from Narratives First Published in the Connecticut Evangelical Magazine* (Boston: Massachusetts Sabbath Society), p. v.
31. Tyler, *New England Revivals*, p. 59.
32. Ahlstrom, *Religious History of the American People*, p. 417.
33. McLoughlin, *Revivals, Awakenings, and Reform*, pp. 109–10; Kenneth Silverman (1969), *Timothy Dwight* (NY: Twayne Publishers).

34. McLoughlin, *Revivals, Awakenings, and Reform*, pp. 111, 118.
35. Ahlstrom, *Religious History of the American People*, pp. 419–20; McLoughlin, *Revivals, Awakenings, and Reform*, pp. 114–15; Sidney E. Mead (1942), *Nathaniel W. Taylor* (Chicago: University of Chicago Press).
36. McLoughlin, *Revivals, Awakenings, and Reform*, pp. 111–14.
37. Ahlstrom, *Religious History of the American People*, p. 422; Lyman Beecher (1961), *Autobiography*, edited by Barbara Cross (Cambridge, MA: Harvard University Press).
38. McLoughlin, *Revivals, Awakenings, and Reform*, pp. 119–20.
39. Lyman Beecher (1814), *An Address to the Charitable Society for the Education of Indigent Pious Young Men for the Ministry of the Gospel* (New Haven, CT: no publisher), pp. 5–8.
40. Beecher, *Address to the Charitable Society*, pp. 5–8.
41. Catherine C. Cleveland (1916), *Great Revival in the West, 1797–1805* (Chicago: University of Chicago Press), p. 54; Charles A. Johnson (1955), *The Frontier Camp Meeting: Religion's Harvest Time* (Dallas, TX: Southern Methodist University Press), pp. 43–51; John Boles (1972), *The Great Revival, 1787–1805*: The Origins of the Southern Evangelical Mind (Lexington: University of Kentucky Press).
42. Ahlstrom, *Religious History of the American People*, p. 432; Johnson, *Frontier Camp Meeting*, p. 32; McLoughlin, *Revivals, Awakenings, and Reform*, p. 132.
43. Ahlstrom, *Religious History of the American People*, pp. 432–3.
44. Barton W. Stone (1954), 'A short history of the life of Barton W. Stone written by himself', in Rhodes Thompson (ed.), *Voices from Cane Ridge* (St. Louis, MO: Bethany Press), p. 68.
45. Ahlstrom, *Religious History of the American People*, p. 433.
46. McLoughlin, *Revivals, Awakenings, and Reform*, p. 133.
47. Stone, 'Short history of the life of Barton W. Stone', pp. 69–72; Johnson, *Frontier Camp Meeting*, pp. 55–62.
48. McLoughlin, *Revivals, Awakenings, and Reform*, pp. 122–3; Johnson, *Frontier Camp Meeting*, p. 172; Charles E. Hambrick-Stowe (1996), *Charles G. Finney and the Spirit of American Evangelicalism* (Grand Rapids, MI: W. B. Eerdmans), pp. 22–45; Whitney R. Cross (1950), *The Burned-Over District: The Social and Intellectual History of Enthusiastic Religion in Western New York, 1800–1850* (Ithaca, NY: Cornell University Press).
49. McLoughlin, *Revivals, Awakenings, and Reforms*, pp. 124–126; Hambrick-Stowe, *Charles G. Finney*, pp. 65–72.
50. Hambrick-Stowe, *Charles G. Finney*, p. 32; McLoughlin, *Revivals, Awakenings, and Reform*, p. 125.
51. McLoughlin, *Revivals, Awakenings, and Reform*, p. 127; Hambrick-Stowe, *Charles G. Finney*, pp. 228–6; William G. McLoughlin (1959), *Modern Revivalism: Charles Grandison Finney to Billy Graham* (New York: Ronald Press).
52. Ahlstrom, *Religious History of the American People*, pp. 435–6.
53. Hatch, *Democratization of American Christianity*, pp. 3–4.
54. Ibid., pp. 3–4.
55. Ibid., pp. 4–5.
56. Ibid., p. 5.
57. Hatch, *Democratization of American Christianity*, p. 7; Ruth H. Bloch (1985), *Visionary Republic: Millennial Themes in American Thought, 1756–1800* (New York:

Cambridge University Press); Donald G. Mathews (1969), 'The Second Great Awakening as an organizing process', *American Quarterly*, 21 (March): 23–43.

58. Joyce Appleby (1984), *Capitalism and a New Social Order: The Republican Vision of the 1790s* (New York: Oxford University Press), p. 79; Olivia Smith (1984), *The Politics of Language, 1791–1819* (New York: Oxford University Press).

59. George A. Rawlyk (1984), *Ravished by the Spirit: Religious Revivals, Baptists, and Henry Alline* (Kingston, Ontario: McGill-Queens University Press), p. 14; Richard L. Bushman (1984), *Joseph Smith and the Beginnings of Mormonism* (Urbana: University of Illinois Press), p. 59.

60. Hatch, *Democratization of American Christianity*, pp. 68–9.

61. McLoughlin, *New England Dissent*, II: pp. 745–9.

62. Charles Francis Kilgore (1963), *The James O'Kelly Schism in the Methodist Episcopal Church* (Mexico City: Casa Unida de Publicaciones); Edward J. Drinkhouse (1899), *A History of Methodist Reform*, 2 vols (Baltimore, MD: Board of Publication of the Methodist Protestant Church), especially volume one; Milo T. Morrill (1912), *A History of the Christian Denomination in America, 1794–1911* (Dayton, OH: Christian Publishing Association).

63. 'The last will and Testament of the Springfield Presbytery'(1847), in John Rogers (1972), *The Biography of Elder Barton Warren Stone* (Paris, KY: Cane Ridge Preservation Project), pp. 51–3; Robert Marshall and Barton W. Stone (1804), *An Apology for Renouncing the Jurisdiction of the Synod of Kentucky* (Lexington, KY: Joseph Charles); Hatch, *Democratization of American Christianity*, pp. 70–1.

64. Robert Richardson (1913), *Memories of Alexander Campbell* (Cincinnati, OH: Standard Publishing Company), I: pp. 465–6, 438.

65. Alexander Campbell (1863), 'An oration in honor of the Fourth of July, 1830,' in Alexander Campbell, *Popular Lectures and Addresses* (Philadelphia: J. Challen), pp. 374–5; Hatch, *Democratization of American Christianity*, pp. 71, 73.

66. Francis Asbury (1958), *The Journal and Letters of Francis Asbury*, edited by Elmer C. Clark, J. Manning Potts and Jacob S. Payton (Nashville, TN: Abindon Press), III: pp. 341–5, 453; Elizabeth Nottingham (1944), *Methodism and the Frontier Indiana Proving Ground* (New York: Columbia University Press).

67. David Hempton (1984), *Methodism and Politics in British Society 1750–1850* (Stanford, CA: Stanford University Press), p. 73; Mathews, 'The Second Great Awakening', p. 36.

68. Asbury, *Journal and Letters*, III: pp. 492, 475–8.

69. Hatch, *Democratization of American Christianity*, p. 85.

70. Ibid., pp. 93–5; James A. Rogers (1985), *Richard Furman: Life and Legacy* (Macon, GA: Mercer University Press), pp. 179, 293–5; Robert G. Torbet (1963), *History of the Baptists* (Chicago: Judson Press), p. 310.

71. McLoughlin, *New England Dissent*, II: pp. 915–38; Byron Cecil Lambert (1980), *The Rise of the Anti-Mission Baptists: Sources and Leaders, 1800–1840* (New York: Arno Press), pp. 116–52; John Leland (1802), *An Oration Delivered at Cheshire, Massachusetts, July 5, 1802, on the Celebration of Independence* (Hudson, NY: Charles Holt), p. 12.

72. Hatch, *Democratization of American Christianity*, p. 99.

73. Ibid., p. 101; see also Lambert, *Rise of the Anti-Mission Baptists*.

74. Hatch, *Democratization of American Christianity*, p. 162.

Recommended Readings

Adams, Arlin M., and Charles J. Emmerich (1990), *A Nation Dedicated to Religious Liberty: The Constitutional Heritage of the Religion Clauses*, Philadelphia: University of Pennsylvania Press.

Appleby, Joyce (1984), *Capitalism and a New Social Order: The Republican Vision of the 1790s*, New York: Oxford University Press.

Boardman, George N. (1899), *History of the New England Theology*, Chicago: University of Chicago Press.

Boles, John (1972), *The Great Revival, 1787–1805: The Origins of the Southern Evangelical Mind*, Lexington: University of Kentucky Press.

Brown, Arthur W. (1956), *Always Young for Liberty: A Biography of William Ellery Channing*, Syracuse, NY: Syracuse University Press.

Cleveland, Catherine C. (1916), *The Great Revival in the West, 1797–1805*, Chicago: University of Chicago Press.

Cross, Whitney R. (1950), *The Burned-Over District: The Social and Intellectual History of Enthusiastic Religion in Western New York, 1800–1850*, Ithaca, NY: Cornell University Press.

Curry, Thomas J. (1986), *The First Freedoms: Church and State in America to the Passage of the First Amendment*, New York: Oxford University Press.

Foster, Frank H. (1907), *A Genetic History of the New England Theology*, Chicago: University of Chicago Press.

Hambrick-Stowe, Charles E. (1996), *Charles G. Finney and the Spirit of American Evangelicalism*, Grand Rapids, MI: W. B. Eerdmans.

Haroutunian, Joseph (1932), *Piety versus Moralism: The Passing of the New England Theology*, New York: Henry Holt.

Hatch, Nathan O. (1989), *The Democratization of American Christianity*, New Haven: Yale University Press.

Howe, Daniel W. (1970), *The Unitarian Conscience*, Cambridge, MA: Harvard University Press.

Johnson, Charles A. (1955), *The Frontier Camp Meeting: Religion's Harvest Time*, Dallas, TX: Southern Methodist University Press.

Lambert, Byron Cecil (1980), *The Rise of the Anti-Mission Baptists: Sources and Leaders, 1800–1840*, New York: Arno Press.

Levy, Leonard W. (1986), *The Establishment Clause: Religion and the First Amendment*, New York: Macmillan Publishing Company.

McLoughlin, William G. (1959), *Modern Revivalism: Charles Grandison Finney to Billy Graham*, New York: Ronald Press.

McLoughlin, William G. (1971), *New England Dissent 1630–1833: The Baptists and the Separation of Church and State*, 2 vols, Cambridge, MA: Harvard University Press.

McLoughlin, William G. (1978), *Revivals, Awakenings, and Reform: An Essay on Religion and Social Change in America, 1607–1977*. Chicago: University of Chicago Press.

Marty, Martin (1997), *The One and the Many: America's Struggle for the Common Good*, Cambridge, MA: Harvard University Press.

Morrill, Milo T. (1912), *A History of the Christian Denomination in America, 1794–1911*, Dayton, OH: Christian Publishing Association.

Nottingham, Elizabeth (1944), *Methodism and the Frontier Indiana Proving Ground*, New York: Columbia University Press.

Robinson, David (1985), *The Unitarians and the Universalists*, Westport, CT: Greenwood Press.

Torbet, Robert G. (1963), *History of the Baptists*, Chicago: Judson Press.

Wigger, John H. (1998), *Taking Heaven by Storm: Methodism and the Rise of Popular Christianity in America*, New York: Oxford University Press.

Wright, Conrad (1976) *The Beginnings of Unitarianism in America*, Hamden, CT: Archon Books.

Wright, Conrad (ed.) (1989), *American Unitarianism, 1805–1865*, Boston: Massachusetts Historical Society and Northeastern University Press.

CHAPTER 5

Religion and the
Age of Reform

The first half of the nineteenth century witnessed the great age of American reform. Buoyed by the prospects of the prosperous new nation, middle-class Americans became inspired by a post-millennial perfectionism and set out to create the 'city on a hill' John Winthrop had promised two centuries earlier but never delivered. The earliest efforts at reform grew out of the missionary impulses of evangelical Protestant churches, but in time moved beyond the churches. Similarly women served as the rank and file of the reform movement, seeking to transform the nation but in the end being transformed themselves.

American Transcendentalism

American Transcendentalism was first and foremost a religious movement. Perry Miller warned that failure to recognize that point could lead to a misunderstanding of its direction, while Henry David Gray noted that religion was so important to American Transcendentalism 'that one is tempted to regard it not only as fundamental but all inclusive'. American Transcendentalism developed in the 1830s as a revolt against what Ralph Waldo Emerson called 'the corpse-cold Unitarianism of Harvard College and Brattle Street'. Seventeen of the Transcendental Club's twenty-six members were Unitarian ministers, and they hoped to use their belief in the intuitive perception of spiritual and moral truth to restore Unitarianism's idealism and pietism without losing its free-thinking and individualism and without resorting to the excesses of emotional revivalism.[1]

American Transcendentalism was but a distinctive phase of a far larger movement that existed in Western civilization. It was part of the Romantic Movement, which was itself a revolt against eighteenth-century rationalism. Thus American Transcendentalism's impulses came from abroad, especially in the works of English Romantics such as Scott, Wordsworth, Coleridge, and Carlyle, and in the English translations of

French and German writers like Cousin, Kant, Fichte and Schleiermacher. To a lesser extent ideas from the Orient were influential as well.[2]

Scholars often date the beginning of American Transcendentalism to 1836, the year the Transcendental Club met for the first time. It was also the year Emerson published his classic, *Nature*, wherein he presented the Transcendental prescription for losing one's egotistical self and becoming one with God. Through nature, Emerson argued, it becomes possible for man to enjoy firsthand contact with God. When contemplating nature, he wrote, 'I become a transparent eyeball; I am nothing; I see all; the currents of the Universal Being circulate through me; I am part or parcel of God'.[3]

Perhaps the principal event in the religious history of the American Transcendental Movement, however, was Ralph Waldo Emerson's 'Divinity School Address' delivered at Harvard on 15 July 1838. Asked by members of the graduating class to address them at their commencement, Emerson decided to take the opportunity to express opinions about religion which he had been turning over in his mind ever since leaving the ministry in 1832. As Donald Koster has put it, Emerson's address 'proved to be an intellectual grenade exploded in the very halls of authority'.[4] His address touched off an acrimonious controversy, but it also became one of the basic documents of the movement and a profound influence on American religion in the nineteenth century.

Emerson began his address by celebrating what he called 'moral sentiment', or intuitive insight into moral and spiritual laws which could never be received second hand. Everybody, he explained, possesses this sentiment. It represents the 'indwelling Supreme Spirit' in all men and women and it is 'the essence of all religion'. The Christian church, Emerson continued, had come to neglect the moral sentiment and in doing so had fallen into two serious errors: (1) It exaggerated the personal and miraculous authority of Jesus Christ; and (2) It looked upon revelation itself as past and dead and confined to biblical times. The 'assumption that the age of inspiration is past, that the Bible is closed', Emerson argued, and 'the fear of degrading the character of Jesus by representing him as a man, indicate with clearness the falsehood of our theology'.[5]

Erroneous views of miracles and of revelation, said Emerson, were responsible for a decaying church and waning belief. The only remedy for the erosion of faith was to recognize the reality of the moral sentiment and our ability, through it, to achieve 'eternal revelation in

the heart' today, as Jesus did centuries ago. Avoid secondary knowledge, Emerson advised the would-be ministers. Dare to love God
without mediator or veil, and in preaching try to acquaint people at first
hand with Deity. It was the office of a true teacher, he declared, to
'show us that God is, not was; that He speaketh, not spake'.[6]

Andrews Norton attacked Emerson's address in the Boston *Daily
Advertiser*. Norton was the leading Unitarian theologian of the time.
Recently retired as Professor of Sacred Literature in the Harvard
Divinity School, he had just published (in 1837) the first volume of
his three volume *Evidences of the Genuineness of the Gospels*. In that
volume Norton found the basic evidence for the Christian religion in
Jesus' miracles. When Emerson called them into question, Norton
charged him with weakening the very foundation of Christian theology
and with calling into question whether he believed in God at all.[7]

George Ripley attacked Norton for writing off as unbelievers all who
shared Emerson's views. To do this, he wrote, was to enforce the
exclusive principle that Calvinists had applied to Unitarians earlier in
the century, when the latter cast overboard the Trinity and other
orthodox Christian doctrines. Ripley recalled that Norton had once
been a champion of intellectual freedom and had formerly reprimanded
the orthodox for being so presumptuous as to define Christianity in
such a way as to exclude Unitarians.[8]

Theodore Parker, Unitarian minister in West Roxbury, followed the
controversy surrounding Emerson's 'Divinity School Address'. He
found the address to be 'the noblest and most inspiring strain I ever
listened to', but he was also amused by the commotion it had created. 'It
is thought that chaos is coming back', he told a friend, and that the
world was coming to an end. 'For my part', he added, 'I see that the sun
still shines, the rain rains, and the dogs bark, and I have great doubts
whether Emerson will overthrow Christianity at this time.'[9]

Parker's entry into the fray created a specially difficult situation for
Norton and his group, because, unlike Emerson and Ripley, Parker
remained in the church. In fact, the most controversial of his remarks on
Emerson's address came in an ordination sermon he delivered in South
Boston on 19 May 1841. He chose as his topic 'A Discourse on the
Transient and Permanent in Christianity', the title of which was drawn
from an essay by David Strauss, whose *Life of Jesus*, published in
Germany in 1835, was regarded as outlandish by liberal as well as
orthodox Christians.[10]

Parker argued that Christian forms, rites, creeds, doctrines, theology, and even the church itself, were transitory. Only the great truths intuited by Jesus had enduring value for the human race. In this regard, Parker quickly dismissed the infallible inspiration of both the Old and New Testaments, as well as the personal authority of Jesus. 'It is hard to see', he wrote, 'why the great truths of Christianity rest on the personal authority of Jesus, more than the axioms of geometry rest on the personal authority of Euclid or Archimedes.' Even if Jesus had never lived, said Parker, the truths he taught would stand firm, though, of course, the world would have lost the example of his beautiful character.[11]

The uproar over Parker's ordination sermon was even greater than that over Emerson's 'Divinity School Address'. He was ostracized publicly by most of his fellow-ministers, all but a handful refusing to allow him in their pulpits. 'As far as the ministers are concerned', lamented Parker, 'I am alone, ALL ALONE.' This was especially true after Parker delivered a series of lectures in Boston in 1841 and 1842, subsequently published as *A Discourse of Matters Pertaining to Religion* (1842), in which he announced: 'If Christianity be true at all, it would be just as true if Herod or Catiline had taught it.'[12]

The Boston Association of Unitarian ministers held a special meeting in January 1843, wherein they tried, unsuccessfully, to persuade Parker to resign. They could not muster the votes to expel him, but he remained a virtual pariah in the Unitarian community. In 1853 the executive committee of the American Unitarian Association, 'in a denominational capacity', separated itself from the errors of Transcendentalism and declared its faith in 'the Divine origin, the Divine authority, [and] the Divine sanctions of the religion of Jesus Christ'. Nevertheless, several of the younger ministers rallied to Parker's cause, and the breach was never sealed. Even when Parker lay near death in Italy in 1859, the Boston Association turned down a resolution to express sympathy for him in his suffering.[13]

Emerson's, Ripley's and Parker's critiques of miracles and Christ pulled the props out from under historical Christianity, but none of the three ever ceased to admire Jesus as a moral leader. Some Transcendentalists thought Emerson's view of religion was focused too much on the individual believer. Ripley, for example, believed that the purpose of Christianity was to redeem society as well as the individual from sin, and after resigning his pastorate he organized an experimental community at Brook Farm. William Henry Channing founded a church for workers in

New York City in 1836 and experimented with several independent churches dedicated to social reform in New York and Boston. And Orestes Brownson wrote *New Views of Christianity, Society, and the Church* (1836), in which he argued that a kind of transcendentalized Unitarianism, uniting spiritual Christianity with material social reform, could bring about the Kingdom of God on earth.[14]

Despite its roots in Europe, American Transcendentalism was nurtured in the soil of the New World. Some scholars point to its close times to the theology of Jonathan Edwards, especially where Edwards urged people to realize ideas with a sense of the heart as well as the head.[15] Others show how tenets that may have originated in Europe were adapted to the historical circumstances of the new republic, with its burgeoning democracy and its exaltation of the common man.[16] Catherine Albanese has argued that while evoking Western, even universal forms, American Transcendentalism was also new, and that newness bore the imprint of nineteenth-century America. 'The harmony with the cosmos which was the core of Transcendental religious experience', Albanese has written, 'turned also upon harmony with a world which included American historical manifestations', especially the age of Jackson – an era committed to a democratic, even romantic, view of the common and ordinary man.[17]

Religion and Reform

The first half of the nineteenth century bore witness to an unprecedented proliferation of reforms in which religion played a leading role. Once the War of 1812 ended, a combination of theological and economic developments led many men and women to assume that the world did not have to be the way it was, and that individual efforts mattered. These were the articles of faith for middle-class Americans, with their confidence in progress and human will. They were encouraged by the religious revivalism of the period, which taught that good deeds were the mark of godliness and that the millennium was near.[18]

Reform took place in a period that seemed much in need of reform. In the course of a half-century the nation had been transformed in ways unanticipated and not entirely welcome. Immigration, urbanization and industrialization had begun to change the social and cultural landscape. During the 1830s approximately 600,000 people came to the United States, a fourfold increase over the 1820s. In the next decade, the figure rose to 1,700,000 and then to 2,600,000 in the 1850s. At the same time, the proportion of Americans working in manufacturing and commerce and living in cities rose. New cities sprang up and old ones boomed. In 1810 there were 46 urban areas (defined as places with 2,500 or more population). In 1860 there were 393, including two cities – New York and Philadelphia – with over 500,000 residents.[19]

Cities were ripe for moral crusades. Reformers regarded them as dismal swamps of vice, disease and misery. But increasingly reformers turned their attention to slavery. Located almost entirely in the North, they came to see the South's peculiar institution as a relic of barbarism, and their own way of life as representing the course of civilization and progress. As Ronald Walters has pointed out, in this way economic differences strongly reinforced moral judgments.[20]

America's increased prosperity meant that there were more numerous middle-class men and women with education, income and leisure to devote to social causes. New technologies put powerful weapons in the hands of such people. The same transportation revolution that brought goods to distant markets also carried lectures to widely dispersed audiences reformers could not have reached a generation before. Innovations reduced the cost of printing to the point where reformers could produce newspapers, pamphlets and even books for a national readership.

Finally, the age of reform was marked by significant changes in the nature of politics. Not only had the Age of Jackson arrived, wherein the United States became more democratic and engaged in more democratic rhetoric, but a new style of politics emerged. With a rapidly increasing electorate and number of offices open to election, politicians began to court potential voters. Reformers reacted to this by complaining that a degraded and sinful majority was being manipulated by political machines, but many reformers nevertheless designed their crusades with politics in mind. If everything worked according to plan, for instance, temperance, Sunday schools and public education would produce a morally responsible electorate. Evangelical Protestants lobbied Congress in 1828 to stop postal employees from working on Sunday, and in the next decade abolitionists mounted a petition campaign urging Congress to take a stand against slavery. Ultimately, some reformers began to run their own candidates for political office.[21]

The Missionary Impulse

Antebellum reform was directly linked to the Second Great Awakening. Whether it came in camp meetings or from the pulpit of the local church, the evangelical message was proclaimed across the land and the public responded with explosions of spiritual zeal. Evangelicals both celebrated American freedom and economic prosperity and cautioned the American people against the potential such a new world presented for loss of commitment to God and community. Thus, at the same time that they shared in the nation's faith in progress, their sermons were filled with the rhetoric of sin, damnation, and salvation. Reformers shared this bifurcated world-view. Moreover, revivals provided reformers with techniques for organizing and propagandizing.[22]

Evangelical clergy and laymen engaged in moral crusades of their own and appeared in the lead of secular ones like temperance and antislavery. Such revivalistic institutions as Lane Seminary and Oberlin College were breeding grounds for reformers, many of whom had been inspired by Charles Grandison Finney and Lyman Beecher. In regions like the Western Reserve of Ohio and the 'burned-over district' of New York, reform movements followed close on the heels of revivals, while even reform political parties, like the abolitionist Liberty Party, did best in areas where religious enthusiasm had run high.[23]

The Second Great Awakening raised expectations for the Kingdom of God on earth. Pre-millennialists held that the return of Christ, the Day of Judgement and an end to history were imminent. Post-millennialists, however, were more numerous and of greater significance in antebellum reform. They may have disagreed over whether the reign of God was near or far, whether it would begin cataclysmically or quietly, but they agreed that it would be a real historical era occurring before the Final Judgement, and that it would consist of a thousand years of peace, prosperity, harmony and Christian morality. Their vision of the ideal society made the imperfections of their own day stark by comparison. Moreover, it assured them that a better world was possible, thereby spurring antebellum crusaders into action.[24]

Millennial optimism merged with a belief that the United States was chosen by God to fulfill a great mission, an old notion given new life in the antebellum period by territorial expansion and religious revivals (sure marks of divine favour). This idea of national destiny – manifest destiny – was a driving force in the conquest of a continent, but it was also employed by reformers. They claimed that America's special place in God's design not only justified their attempts to dominate lands and people in the West morally and physically but also meant that its sins were more heinous than those of other countries and that their reforms were urgently needed. The divine plan, indeed the millennium, depended on it.[25]

Millennialism's missionary impulse would not have been so strong if clergymen had not told mankind it could help God usher in his Kingdom. When nineteenth-century preachers made that claim, they were abandoning a line of theology stretching from John Calvin through early American Congregationalism and Presbyterianism. Calvinists maintained that human beings were innately sinful and could, of their own free will, do nothing pleasing to God. By the early years of the nineteenth century, clergy such as Charles Grandison Finney repudiated those propositions.[26]

Finney developed the concept of 'disinterested benevolence', which he saw as the sum of all holiness or virtue. The phrase itself had an honourable history in American Protestantism going back to Jonathan Edwards. Finney, however, took any trace of Calvinism out of it and turned it into an inspiration for reformers. Finney was certain that people could act virtuously if they wanted to, so he tried to persuade them of the 'utility of benevolence'. Using reasoning more reminiscent of Ben Franklin than John Calvin, Finney insisted that men and women not only could but also should, 'set out with a determination to aim at being useful in the highest degrees'. Of true Christians, Finney wrote: 'To the universal reformation of the world they stand committed.'[27]

Central to Finney's theology was a doctrine of perfectionism, the idea that individuals could become sanctified while on earth. He and the majority of evangelicals accepted a modern form of this doctrine, while staunchly rejecting a dangerous implication in it – the possibility that sanctified persons could do no wrong. Thus, perfectionism became an energizing principle, giving inspiration to people who wanted to impose absolute moral integrity upon their own lives and upon a changing world. Perfectionists believed that anything short of millennial standards should not be tolerated, and that belief was manifested in abolitionism, temperance and other reform movements, as well as in attempts to construct new social orders, or utopias.[28]

Reform Movements

Most of the early nineteenth-century Protestant voluntary organizations clustered in New England and the mid-Atlantic states. A few of them aimed at specific sins, but more were quite general in scope, like the

Connecticut Society for the Reformation of Morals, established in 1813. Such groups drew upon local clergy and pious laymen, who acted as a kind of moral police, pointing out immorality and lawbreaking that elected officials preferred to ignore.[29]

The largest Protestant voluntary associations, however, were dedicated to missionary activity rather than to harassing local wrongdoers. The first national association was the American Board of Commissioners for Foreign Missions, begun by Congregationalists in 1810, with Lyman Beecher among the founders. The American Bible Society came into existence in 1816, with the goal of putting the Scriptures into the hands of every family in the nation, while the American Sunday School Union (1824) established a similar goal for children. The most significant of all, however, was the American Tract Society, formed in 1825, and perhaps the first to use up-to-date presses issuing a never-ending stream of publications. By 1830 these voluntary associations covered the land with the printed word and had thousands of auxiliaries contributing to the cause. Firmly revivalistic, but also reformist, these groups preached against lack of faith as well as for moral causes.[30]

By 1830, Protestant voluntary associations constituted a loosely interconnected 'benevolent empire'. Although formally distinct from each other, these evangelical organizations propagated the same worldview, tapped the same financial resources, and had many of the same people on their boards of directors. They often held their conventions at the same times and in the same cities, thereby permitting a measure of coordinated action; in 1829, they mounted an especially energetic campaign in the West.[31]

The agencies of the benevolent empire had other things in common besides ideology, membership and sources of revenue. Many of them were significantly interdenominational. The managers of the Sunday School Union and the Bible Society, for example, included Presbyterians, Congregationalists, Methodists, Episcopalians, Baptists, Dutch Reformed and a few Moravians and Quakers. And the laity played a crucial role in such organizations. Clergy were never absent, but what is striking is the time, money and administrative skill contributed by laymen. People like Arthur and Lewis Tappan, wealthy New York merchants, were at the centre of nearly every one of the major religious and secular reforms of the day – antislavery, pacifism, temperance, health, education and women's rights, to name just a few.[32]

Religious Communitarianism

Since the War of 1812, John Humphrey Noyes wrote in 1870, 'the line of socialistic excitements lies parallel with the line of religious revivals'. Noyes had in mind the many experiments in living attempted by small groups of antebellum reformers. These were little utopias carved out of the American countryside, dedicated to one or another social or religious theory, and designed to serve as models for the rest of the world. Noyes pointed to the failings of revivalists and utopians: revivalists 'failed for want of regeneration of society' and utopians 'failed for want of regeneration of the heart'. The unwillingness of the two to unite 'their two great ideas' was all the more tragic, he continued, because they had so much in common. They shared a faith in the perfectible nature of mankind and a belief that the millennium was at hand. Both desired 'to bring heaven on earth'.[33]

Over 100 communitarian societies were built in the nineteenth century prior to the Civil War; the exact number is uncertain. The greatest wave of enthusiasm for utopian ventures came in the 1840s in the aftermath of the revivals of the 1820s and 1830s. Most communities lasted no more than a few years and involved only a small number of active members, but their importance as expressions of antebellum reform transcends such statistics. Communitarians aimed at creating a totally new order rather than improving the old one. As Noyes recognized, it was the ultimate expression of perfectionist and millennialist logic.[34]

It is difficult at first to see much coherence in anything so varied as antebellum communalism. The communities themselves ranged from highly structured to utterly unstructured, from theological to free-thinking, from celibate to 'free love'. To make sense out of the diversity, historians have developed different classifications. The simplest approach divides the communities between those that were primarily organized around religious doctrines and those that were primarily secular. We shall concentrate on the former.

Utopias of European Origin

Some of the largest and most stable utopian societies in antebellum America were neither antebellum nor American in origin. These ventures represent a particular kind of religious communalism, best labelled pietistic. The communities themselves were in the United

States but not especially of it. Several traced their ancestry to German sects, the rest to other seventeenth- or eighteenth-century European religious splinter groups. The most notable of the German-speaking communities – Ephrata, Harmony, Zoar and Amana – were especially adept at keeping their Old-World character in the midst of a rapidly changing new world. We shall consider only the first two and the Shakers.

1. Ephrata was not quite the first, nor was it the largest, utopian society in North America, but by the antebellum period it was the oldest. Ephrata's founder, Conrad Beissel, left the Palatinate in 1720 apparently with the idea of joining Woman in the Wilderness, a mystical community of German Pietists who gathered in the Pennsylvania forest to await the millennium. By the time Beissel arrived most members of the Woman in the Wilderness had scattered or died. Beissel remained, however, and spent much of the next twelve years in hermit-like spiritual contemplation. In 1724 he joined the Dunkers, a German sect, but in 1728 he published a work contradicting some of their doctrines. He attracted a few followers, and in 1732 he established Ephrata, near Lancaster, Pennsylvania, as a communitarian society or cloister.[35]

The days of those who lived at Ephrata were filled with work and worship. Their diet was sparse and vegetarian, and their dress was homespun. Men lived in one large building, women in another, and little in those dwellings distracted them from spiritual thoughts. The rooms were small and Spartan, and the residences were constructed and furnished without the use of metal, in imitation of Solomon's temple.[36]

For all its plainness and religiosity, Ephrata did not have absolutely rigid rules on two matters quite crucial to later communitarians – sexual relationships and private property. Beissel did not insist upon chastity, but he encouraged it and most of his followers were celibate in the mid-eighteenth century, when their numbers reached 300. The community punished 'the untimely intercourse of some of the brethren', but over the years there was a decline in celibacy as well as in membership. By 1800 most of the Ephratans were married. Beissel also did not demand that all property be held in common, although the community as a whole owned whatever was donated to Ephrata or produced by its residents. Those who valued worldly goods simply left the cloister, took housing nearby, and became 'outdoor' members, over whom Beissel and his successors exercised less rigorous discipline.[37]

By the early nineteenth century Ephrata was a relic. Beissel died in 1768. Peter Miller, his successor, survived him by twenty-eight years, leaving no one with his or Beissel's intellect and personal power to carry on. Ephrata inspired interest and at least one imitator in the nineteenth century, but by then it was not even the most vital of the German Pietistic communities, an honour that more properly belonged to George Rapp's Harmony Society.[38]

2. In 1791 Rapp, a thirty-three year old German farmer, told an official investigating his religious beliefs, 'I am a prophet and called to be one.' Rapp had been in conflict with the established Lutheran Church of Württemberg, and in 1803 that conflict caused him and several hundred disciples to leave for the United States. He purchased land in western Pennsylvania, and in February 1805 he incorporated the Harmony Society.[39]

Although living conditions were primitive at first, the Harmonists were steady and industrious. In a decade they cleared and cultivated over 2000 acres of land, and as early as 1807 they were selling goods to the outside world. In 1815, dissatisfied with the climate, the soil and the difficulty of getting their products to market, the Harmonists sold their Pennsylvania property and moved to Indiana, where they continued to grow and prosper, but, for reasons that are not clear, the society moved again in 1825. It sold everything to Robert Owen, the wealthy British social theorist, and returned to Pennsylvania to land north of Pittsburgh. This, the society's third home, was named Economy. At first the Harmonists did well, despite a slow drop in their population, but by 1874 they closed several factories for lack of a labour force. By 1900 the society had fewer than ten members.[40]

Harmony was a more worldly place than Ephrata, yet the two had some similar characteristics. Each was the creation of a vigorous and compelling founder. Rapp's control over his followers, although occasionally challenged, remained firm until his death in 1847, at ninety. Each community was millennialisitic. Rapp informed an inquirer in 1822 that Harmonists 'believe without doubt that the kingdom of Jesus Christ [is] approaching near'. If anything, Harmonists were more consistent in banning private ownership of property than Ephratans had been, but, like the Ephratans, Harmonists generally remained celibate. Rapp had advocated sexual abstinence as early as 1791, but he did not make it policy until 1807, and even then he made exceptions. Celibacy and unwillingness to proselytize non-Germans, however, had the same effect on the Harmony Society as on Ephrata. The membership grew old, died, and left none to keep the faith.[41]

3. The American career of the Shakers was rooted in the spiritual experiences of Ann Lee, the illiterate daughter of a Manchester blacksmith. Born in 1736, she took to factory and menial labour at an early age. While still a young woman she married Abraham Stanley, a blacksmith, like her father. It was an unhappy match. Ann Lee apparently felt repugnance at sexual intercourse and suffered through the birth and premature loss of four children. Before marrying Stanley, she had joined the Shakers, a small sect tracing its lineage to seventeenth-century France and so named for the convulsive dance that was part of their ritual. Fired with zeal, she preached, prayed and went into trances. She was also persecuted by mobs and by authorities, who occasionally threw Ann Lee and fellow-Shakers into prison. While in jail in 1770 she had a revelation and upon her release began to attract followers, who accepted her as 'Mother in Christ'. In 1774 another revelation directed her and eight followers to take passage to America. Her husband accompanied her, but abandoned her soon after they arrived in New York.[42]

Mother Ann and her tiny flock moved to Watervliet, New York, where they endured difficult times both because of the hardships of making a living and because of the hostility of neighbours, who suspected them of pro-British sympathies in the American Revolution. She died in 1784, three years before the sect formed its first true communal settlement in Mount Lebanon, New York.[43]

The Shakers began to grow after 1799, when a Baptist revival swept the country around Mount Lebanon. In what would prove to be a persistent pattern, they gathered in men and women who had been awakened by evangelical preaching but not satisfied by it. In 1805 the Shakers took advantage of revivals going on in the West by sending out preachers of their own. The result was another rich harvest of converts and formation of half a dozen new communities. At their height in the 1830s the Shakers numbered around 6000.[44]

Although Mother Ann was central to their theology, the Shakers owed their organizational success to her successors. In 1787 Joseph

Meacham and Lucy Wright became the first American-born leaders. In 1836 Frederick W. Evans became an elder, a position he held for fifty-seven years. All three proved to be effective administrators and propagandists for the Shakers. For all their ability, however, much of the Shakers' strength was in their distinctive and compelling way of life.[45]

Mother Ann Lee had taught that God was both male and female in nature, with Jesus representing the masculine side. Since Mother Ann represented the feminine side, her coming marked completion of God's revelation and the beginning of the Kingdom of Heaven on earth. This was a variety of millennialism and an assertion of the spiritual equality of men and women. Both sexes shared authority throughout the sect's hierarchy, from its 'Head of Influence' at Mount Lebanon to the 'families' (or smaller groups of men and women) that were the basic unit within each community. There were few places in American society where females were so emancipated from their usual roles as wives and mothers and granted so much genuine influence. Thus it is not surprising that by the middle of the nineteenth century most Shakers were women.[46]

Shaker men and women lived in chastity as well as relative equality. Mother Ann made 'Virgin Purity' a pillar of her faith and insisted that her followers be celibate. Shakers believed that sexuality was an animal passion belonging to a lower, less spiritual order of existence. Even though many non-Shakers shared that belief, few antebellum Americans went to the extreme of trying to ban sexual intercourse altogether, and Shakerism struck many observers as being cold and contrary to human nature.[47]

Yet one of the secrets of Shakerism's appeal was the way it alternated self-denial with emotional release. Much of a Shaker's day was spent in silence, hard work, and emotional restraint. Various rituals, however, provided moments of sheer ecstasy. The most curious of these, and the best known, was the dance that was part of Shaker services. The dance and its accompanying music changed over time, but it always was a performance in which both sexes participated, parading in what visitors described as odd, regimented movements, sometimes dignified, sometimes spasmodic. The Shakers also went through periods of special enthusiasm, as in the late 1830s and early 1840s, when each of their communities was swept by spiritualism, mystical experiences and speaking in tongues. The

Shakers gave regular expression to evangelical emotionality, and made it all the more intense by mixing it with asceticism.[48]

Finally, on the matter of private property the Shakers were among the most radical of utopians. They did away with distinctions in 'temporal blessings' about as completely as any American commune ever has. But theirs was 'Christian Communism', to use Ronald Walters's phrase, not the modern, secular variety. 'They shared their possessions because they did not did not value them much; their eyes were on heaven.'[49]

American Communitarian

Although pietistic societies were beginning to fade as early as the 1820s, they had lessons to teach later communitarians. The pietistic communities had begun the process of breaking away from conventional notions of family relationships and private property. Their pacifism, millennialism and ability to survive provided a model and inspiration. American communitarians after 1825 generally operated within the Christian tradition, just as eighteenth-century Pietists did; but each took different components from it, which in turn led to different modes of behaviour. The Pietists drew upon the communalism, monasticism and mysticism of the primitive church. Later utopians lived out a social gospel, bringing Protestant principles to bear upon the wider world around them, as well as within the community. Brook Farm and Oneida provide two instructive examples of the later group.

1. Brook Farm, located in West Roxbury, Massachusetts, was a product of New England culture. Compared to communities like Hopedale, Brook Farm was not as infused with reform zeal; if anything, it was more individualistic. But it was also religious in inspiration. Elizabeth Peabody spoke of an early plan for it as 'Christ's Idea of Society', and it originated in conversations between two Unitarian ministers, William Ellery Channing and George Ripley. In 1841 Ripley and some colleagues purchased land and began the community.[50]

    Brook Farm is sometimes characterized as a 'Transcendentalist Utopia', but what it owed to Transcendentalism is not completely clear. Transcendentalism itself was not a coherent set of doctrines. It was more a sensibility and a set of attitudes about mankind and nature. Ripley may have found in Transcendentalism a belief in the limitless potential of human beings, but, as Ronald Walters has pointed out, other communitarians got the same belief from evangelical Protestantism, through its perfectionist strain. Moreover, reform was at the heart of American Transcendentalism, but there was no hope of social betterment, from the Transcendentalist point of view, unless people took their cues from the 'great inward Commander'. Thus Ralph Waldo Emerson, for one, agonized over whether to join Brook Farm and finally convinced himself that he was more valuable preserving his autonomy and remaining unaffiliated.[51]

Brook Farm encouraged serious self-development. George Ripley had hoped 'to insure a more natural union between intellectual and manual labor than now exists'. The community, accordingly, was organized so that all members not only worked with their hands but also had the means 'for intellectual improvement and for social intercourse, calculated to refine and expand'. Some, like Nathaniel Hawthorne, were not enchanted by having to do farm chores, but others were enthusiastic about the other arts. 'The weeds', George William Curtis recalled fondly, 'were scratched out of the ground to the music of Tennyson and Browning.' And whatever the effect upon weeds, Brook Farm's cultural ferment was unparallelled among American utopian societies. In 1845 Brook Farm took over publication of the *Phalanx*, a New York Fourierist periodical, renamed it the *Harbinger*, and made it into an important weekly journal. Brook Farm's schools were well staffed and remarkably flexible for the times. They had a broad liberal arts curriculum, broke with the practice of rote memorization, and attempted to combine learning with doing.[52]

From its beginnings, Brook Farm was economically marginal. It was organized as a dividend paying joint-stock venture, but it was too Transcendental to be profit-making. The founders hoped to make 'the acquisition of individual property subservient to upright and disinterested uses'. They nonetheless sought to 'reserve sufficient private property, or means of obtaining it, for all purposes of independence'. The result was a muddle of community and private interests, which would have been troublesome if Brook Farm had been prosperous. As it was, the real problem was making ends meet. In 1846, after a brief period or reorganization as a Fourieristic Phalanx, a disastrous fire swept the expensive and uninsured new main building. The community closed and the remaining property was sold in 1849.[53]

2. Where Brook Farm was shaped by Ripley's Unitarianism and Transcendentalism, Oneida was a product of evangelical Protestantism. Its

founder was John Humphrey Noyes, a Vermonter by birth, a Dartmouth, Andover Theological Seminary and Yale man, by education, and a lawyer and clergyman by training. He had what was probably the most original mind of any American communitarian.[54]

While at Yale Divinity School Noyes came to believe that once a person was saved, he or she became perfect, that is, incapable of sinning. He believed he had reached that state on 20 February 1834. In 1837 Noyes first voiced his unorthodox sexual ideas. Abigail Merwin, an early convert whom Noyes loved, spurned both him and his doctrines, and married another man. Much grieved, Noyes wrote to a follower that 'when the will of God is done on earth as it is in heaven there will be no marriage'. Among those who become perfect, all will belong to each other; there will be no exclusive attachments. Thus, Merwin would be his bride in spirit, even if she was another man's under human law.[55]

In June 1838 Noyes wed Harriet Holton and the couple settled in Putney, Vermont, where Noyes's tiny congregation of disciples printed his works and developed his doctrines and practices. In 1841 the group began to organize and to pool its resources, and three years later Noyes, his brother George and two of his brothers-in-law created a financial partnership, which they soon opened to anyone who cared to invest in it. By 1846 the Putney perfectionists were evolving the legal and economic structure of a communal society, but they also were beginning the marital experiments that would cause them to be driven from Vermont. That spring, John and Harriet Noyes and George and Mary Cragin began a system of 'complex marriage', maintaining that it was not a sin for any sanctified man and woman to have intercourse. Noyes's two sisters and their husbands joined the complex marriage, and by the end of 1846 the central members of the Putney group declared themselves a community of persons as well as of property. By the fall of 1847 Noyes fled to New York City to avoid prosecution on charges of adultery, and, shortly after, he and some of the Putney group joined a communal settlement begun by fellow-perfectionists in Madison County, New York. Together they formed the Oneida Association.[56]

In addition to complex marriages, Noyes's program at Oneida involved birth control and planned reproduction. Of the few methods available in the early 1840s, Noyes chose male continence, or intercourse without ejaculation. He promoted male continence for various reasons, including health: it freed women from pregnancy and spared men the expenditure of seminal fluid, which Noyes, like many nineteenth-century Americans, believed to be debilitating. He also added theological arguments. Male continence, he maintained, was part of God's design. It would 'give speed to the advance of civilization and refinement'. With fear of pregnancy banished, sexual intercourse would become 'a joyful act of fellowship' or even a religious ritual.[57]

Sexual encounters at Oneida were subject to a variety of rules and regulations. By the 1860s all requests for intercourse had to be made through a third party and were duly recorded in a ledger. In 1869 the community began to experiment with planned reproduction, or 'stir-piculture'. A committee approved, even suggested, 'scientific combinations' of community members to become parents. Since Noyes believed moral characteristics were passed on to children, the men and women selected were supposed to be the most spiritually advanced in the community, but some attention was given to physical conditions as well. During the next decade fifty-eight children were born at Oneida, thirteen conceived accidentally and forty-five as stirpiculture babies. Nine of the children were fathered by Noyes, the most spiritually advanced member of all.[58]

Oneida flourished in spite of the hostility its sexual practices aroused. Noyes attributed the community's endurance to what he saw as two of the essential features of stable utopian societies: community ownership of property and an emphasis on manufacturing and commerce rather than agriculture. By the 1870s, however, younger members absorbed new ideas from their college education on the outside. The result was an undercurrent of questioning of the old ways and a decline in religious fervour. Noyes's failing leadership was an even greater problem. Although he clearly was the driving force of Oneida, he was too often absent. In 1875 he tried to impose his son Theodore, a Yale-trained physician, as head of the community. The community balked, however, and Noyes faced open rebellion.[59]

In 1879 a quarrel erupted over the question of which male ought to act as 'first husband' to virgin females in the community, a duty Noyes had taken upon himself. Noyes feared being charged with statutory rape and fled to Canada. Like many other communal ventures, Oneida depended on the personal power of its central figure. With him gone, with the leadership divided, and with a group of local clergymen attacking the community, Oneida's governing council reluctantly decided that the system of complex marriage had to be abandoned. On 1 January 1881, Oneida ceased to be a community and became a joint-stock company.[60]

Women, Reform, and Religion

Until 1800, in the colonies and new nation, there existed a traditional sexual division of labour. Each member of the household contributed to the well-being of all, in a manner consistent with a world of farms, small shops and cottage industries, where young and old, male and female, each had a role. Economic development after 1800 changed that by widening the range of careers available and by altering the chances for individuals to rise or sink on the social scale. The best of the new opportunities were reserved for males and required spending long hours away from the rest of the family. The home increasingly became a female domain, cut off from business and public affairs. If she were middle class, a woman no longer worked in ways society recognized as work.[61]

Antebellum images of masculinity and femininity both reflected those social changes and helped shape them. Men, according to most writers, were naturally strong in body and mind, aggressive and sexual. Women were innately weak, passive, emotional, religious and chaste. These were complimentary virtues and vices – men supported women, and women provided the sensitivity men lacked. Such stereotypes, Ronald Walters has pointed out, reassured each sex that it belonged where it was: 'Woman was too fair a flower to survive in business or politics, where man's cunning and intellect were prime virtues; in the home she was protected, her goodness blossomed, and she refined man's coarseness.'[62]

Linda Kerber has argued that a level of ambivalence resulted from those gender roles. On the one hand, by way of example, republican ideology called for a sufficiently educated female citizenry to educate future generations of sensible republicans; on the other hand, domestic tradition viewed highly educated women as unnatural and 'perverse threats to family stability'. Further, at least from a twentieth-century perspective, such notions implied female inferiority. Nevertheless, many antebellum commentators suggested that females had a great social role to play, if not in politics and the professions, then through their influence over men and children in the home. Although a woman 'may never herself step beyond the threshold', one clergyman gushed, 'she may yet send forth from her humble dwelling, a power that will be felt round the globe'.[63]

That sort of rhetoric – recently labelled the 'cult of domesticity' – may have described only some lives. To poor women, who often worked outside the home, it represented, at best, a standard to which they might aspire; at worse, it was a measure of their failure. Some females, however, discovered that the common assumptions about them could justify activities other than being a housewife. Reform was one of these. If woman's influence was so beneficial, why should it be kept at home? Why not bring to the outside world all those feminine virtues necessary to counteract masculine vices? The first step involved wo-men, a majority in many church congregations, participating actively in early-nineteenth-century religious and charitable enterprises. By the 1830s they moved into more secular causes: health reform, temperance, antislavery and campaigns to redeem prostitutes and curb licentious-ness. Many joined the nation's first women's rights movement, while a few became interested in communitarian ventures and talked about rearranging relations between the sexes.[64]

Few of the first generation of female reformers posed any direct challenge to the *status quo*. By mid-century, however, that was no longer the case, and resistance to their efforts grew proportionately. By the 1850s most reformers, including women, began to realize that moral suasion, which had been at the heart of their involvement in the public sphere, had failed to transform American society. Increasingly, reformers turned to electoral means, which had largely excluded women. As Lori Ginzburg has put it: 'Voteless, women discovered that benevolent work's growing dependence on electoral means had by the 1850s rendered "female" means for change less effective and thus less popular.' Until the Civil War ended it all, women continued to be involved in the American Reform Movement, but with less attachment to their religious origins.[65]

As early as 1840 there was talk of creating a formal institutional structure to advance the cause of women. In that year Elizabeth Cady Stanton was in London with her abolitionist husband, a delegate to a World's Antislavery Convention. After an acrimonious debate, female representatives were excluded from the Convention, and Stanton's indignation at the insult coincided with her discovery of those whom she later called 'the first women I had ever met who believed in the equality of the sexes'. Among them was an American Quaker and abolitionist, Lucretia Mott. The two became close friends and resolved to hold a convention as soon as they returned home. That convention was held in Seneca Falls, New York, in July 1848.[66]

For the opening of the Seneca Falls Convention, Stanton, Mott and others prepared a Declaration of Sentiments modelled on the Declaration of Independence. Reminding Americans of the natural rights ideology of the American Revolution, their Declaration began with the premise that 'all men and women are created equal' and substituted 'man' for King George as the tyrant. They submitted 'to a candid world' a bill of indictment against male domination, just as their forefathers had done against the British seventy-two years earlier.[67]

Stanton and her collaborators accused man of endeavouring, 'in every way that he could, to destroy her [woman's] confidence in her own powers, to lessen her self-respect, and to make her willing to lead a dependent and abject life'. They specifically objected to the lack of the vote and educational and professional opportunities for women, as well as to laws depriving wives of control over property and awarding children to fathers in cases of divorce. They included eleven resolutions asserting sexual equality, advocating a single moral standard for males and females, and urging women not simply to stay at home but to 'move in the enlarged sphere which her great Creator has assigned her'. They added a resolution calling for 'the overthrow of the monopoly of the pulpit, and for the securing to woman an equal participation with men in the various trades, professions, and commerce'.[68]

The importance of the women's rights movement that produced the Seneca Falls Convention should not be underestimated. Its immediate accomplishments may have been few, but, as Robert Abzug has argued, any understanding of the drive toward sexual equality in America must begin with recognition of what happened in the debate over women in the antebellum period, in which reformers articulated the most dynamic vision of womanhood in American history. The women's rights movement began when they served reform in other areas of American society. By the 1840s, realizing inequities within their own lives, they sought to improve their own lot as well. They began by exercising their newly gained power in the family and in the church, and then entered the world beyond.[69]

The Feminization of American Religion

Women played a major role in the Reform Movement in antebellum America. Indeed, the abolitionist, temperance and peace societies depended on women for their existence, and, in terms of their place in American society, women, especially middle-class women, benefitted from their participation. Women increased their influence on American religion – American Protestantism, in particular – thereby altering the course of American religious history so significantly as to have historians point to their efforts as causing 'the feminization of American religion'.[70]

In the period following the American Revolution, the previously mentioned political and economic activities were deemed critically important to the nation, and therefore more masculine, more competitive, more aggressive and more responsive to shows of force and strength. Religion and the family – America's official and conventional cultural life itself, Ann Douglas has argued – was not as important, and so became the property of the ladies. Religion entered a process whereby it became more domesticated, more emotional, softer and more accommodating – more feminine.[71]

Although it would not last, at the height of the evangelical democratization of the Second Great Awakening, many women became preachers, especially among Methodists, Baptists and Christians. Thereafter, women and ministers became allies in opposition to that from which they had been excluded. The hierarchy of ministers, limited to males, remained unchanged, but those same male ministers, operating in a world where persuasion had replaced coercion, found themselves answerable to a larger degree to the women who filled their pews than the men, who remained members in name only. Cut off from their masculine heritage, they feminized their teachings, de-emphasizing harsher Calvinist doctrines such as those related to original sin and emphasizing family morals and the concept of superior female morality.[72]

Observers of the American scene frequently made note of this development. Frances Trollope referred to the women-filled pews and remarked that

> it is only from the clergy that the women of America receive that sort of attention which is so dearly valued by every female heart throughout the world. I never saw, or read, of any country where religion had so strong a hold upon the women, or a slighter hold upon the men.

When Orestes Brownson complained about a 'female religion', he was referring to the prominent role women were playing in the congregations and revivals. He caricatured ministers as domesticated pets of those women, fit only 'to balance teacups and mouth platitudes'.

Brownson's solution was to join the Catholic Church, as yet a holdout against such changes.[73]

The 'male principle', as it has been called, came under attack in antebellum American Protestant churches. It continued to be the case that God was referred to as male, but there was an increasing tendency to elevate the importance of femaleness, which is to say the idea of a Father–Mother God, and even the concept of a male–female Saviour. In contrast to his Calvinist counterpart, the new Christ – the feminized Christ – was the exemplar of meekness and humility, the sacrificial victim. If Christ assumed the role of a human dominated by love, sacrificing himself for others, asking nothing but giving everything and forgiving his enemies into the bargain, he was playing the same role as the true woman.[74]

Summary

In nineteenth-century America, religion was given over to women, in its content and in its membership. In the process, religion became the repository for those female values that were seen having no place outside the home and church in the business of building a nation. Women and virtue became almost synonymous. In order to do this, it was necessary first to assign certain virtues to women and then to institutionalize those virtues. The family, popular culture and religion were the vehicles by which feminine virtues were institutionalized. Barbara Welter may have summarized all of this best, when she wrote that

> religion in its emphasis on the brotherhood of man developed in women a conscious sense of sisterhood, a quality absolutely essential for any kind of meaningful women's movement. The equality of man before God, expressed so effectively in the Declaration of Independence, had little impact on women's lives. However, the equality of religious experience was something they could personally experience, and no man could deny it to them.[75]

Notes

1. Perry Miller (ed.) (1960), *The Transcendentalists: An Anthology* (Cambridge, MA: Harvard University Press), pp. ix, 8; Henry David Gray (1917; 1958), *Emerson: A Statement of New England Transcendentalism as Expressed in the Philosophy of Its Chief Exponent* (New York: Frederick Ungar Publishing Co.), p. 7; Walter G. Muelder, Laurence Sears and Anne V. Schlabach (eds) (1960), *The Development of American Philosophy: A Book of Readings* (Boston: Houghton Mifflin Company), p. 109; Paul

Boller, Jr (1974), *American Transcendentalism, 1830–1860: An Intellectual Inquiry* (New York: G. p. Putnam's Sons), p. xix; Octavius Brooke Frothingham (1876; 1965), *Transcendentalism in New England, A History* (Gloucester, MA: Peter Smith), p. 114; William G. McLoughlin (1978), *Revivals, Awakenings, and Reform: An Essay on Religion and Social Change in America, 1607–1977* (Chicago: University of Chicago Press), p. 102.

2. Merle Curti (1951), *The Growth of American Thought* (New York: Harper Donald N. Koster (1975), *Transcendentalism in America* (Boston: Twayne Publishers), pp. 13–14; Arthur E. Christy (1932), *The Orient in American Transcendentalism: A Study of Emerson, Thoreau, and Alcott* (New York: Columbia University Press).

3. Ralph Waldo Emerson (1950), *Nature in Emerson: The Selected Writings of Ralph Waldo Emerson*, ed. Brooke Atkinson (New York: The Modern Library), p. 6.

4. Koster, *Transcendentalism in America*, p. 36.

5. Ralph Waldo Emerson (1967), 'The Divinity School Address', in Sydney E. Ahlstrom (ed.), *Theology in America: The Major Protestant Voices from Puritanism to Neo-Orthodoxy* (Indianapolis, IN: The Bobbs-Merrill Company), pp. 298, 311.

6. Emerson, 'Divinity School Address', pp. 311–16.

7. Boller, *American Transcendentalism*, pp. 8–9.

8. Ibid., pp. 12–13.

9. Ibid., pp. 15–16.

10. Ibid., pp. 17–18; Miller, *Transcendentalists*, p. 106.

11. Theodore Parker (1960), 'A discourse on the transient and permanent in Christianity', in Muelder, Sears and Schlabach, *Development of American Philosophy*, pp. 112–13.

12. Boller, *American Transcendentalism*, p. 19.

13. Sydney E. Ahlstrom (1972), *A Religious History of the American People* (New Haven: Yale University Press), p. 607; Boller, *American Transcendentalism*, pp. 20–1.

14. Boller, *American Transcendentalism*, pp. 27–9.

15. Koster, *Transcendentalism in America*, p. 32; Sherman Paul (1952), *Emerson's Angle of Vision* (Cambridge, MA: Harvard University Press), p. 13; Stephen E. Whicher (1953), *Freedom and Fate: An Inner Life of Ralph Waldo Emerson* (Philadelphia: University of Pennsylvania Press), pp. 40–3.

16. Alice Felt Tyler (1962), *Freedom's Ferment: Phases of American Social History from the Colonial Period to the Outbreak of the Civil War* (New York: Harper Torchbooks); John S. Harrison (1910), *The Teachers of Emerson* (New York: Sturgis Keith J. Hardman (1987), *Charles Grandison Finney, 1792–1875: Revivalist and Reformer* (Syracuse, NY: Syracuse University Press).

17. Catherine L. Albanese (1977), *Corresponding Motion: Transcendental Religion and the New America* (Philadelphia, PA: Temple University Press), pp. xiii-xiv, 129.

18. C. S. Griffin (1967), *The Ferment of Reform, 1830–1860* (Arlington Heights, IL: Harlan Davidson), pp. 1–8; Robert H. Abzug (1994), *Cosmos Crumbling: American Reform and the Religious Imagination* (New York: Oxford University Press), pp. 3–8.

19. Ronald G. Walters (1978), *American Reformers, 1815–1860* (New York: Hill and Wang), p. 5.

20. Walters, *American Reformers*, p. 6; Timothy L. Smith (1957), *Revivalism and Social Reform: American Protestantism on the Eve of the Civil War* (Nashville, TN: Abington Press), pp. 34–44, 148–62; Griffin, *Ferment of Reform*, pp. 21–7. See also: Avery O. Craven (1967), 'The Northern attack on slavery', in David Brion

Davis (ed.), *Antebellum Reform* (New York: Harper and Row), pp. 19–37; Clifford S. Thistlewaite (1967), 'The Anglo-American world of humanitarian endeavor', in Davis, *Antebellum Reform*, pp. 81–96; Charles C. Cole (1954), *The Social Ideals of the Northern Evangelists* (New York: Columbia University Press).

21. Walters, *American Reformers*, pp. 7–8; Tyler, *Freedom's Ferment*, pp. 21–2; Richard Carwardine (1978), *Transatlantic Revivalism: Popular Evangelism in Britain and America, 1790–1865* (Westport, CT: Greenwood Press), pp. 1–132. See also: Daniel Walker Howe (1991), 'The evangelical movement and political culture in the North during the Second Party System', *The Journal of American History*, 77 (March): 1216–39.

22. Catherine A. Brekus (1998), *Strangers and Pilgrims: Female Preaching in America, 1740–1845* (Chapel Hill: University of North Carolina Press), pp. 12–15; Donald G. Mathews (1969), 'The Second Great Awakening as an organizing process, 1780–1830', *American Quarterly*, 21 (March): 23–43.

23. Walters, *American Reformers*, p. 23; Smith, *Revivalism and Social Reform*, pp. 45–62, 103–13. See also: John R. Bodo (1954), *The Protestant Clergy and Public Issues, 1812–1848* (Princeton: Princeton University Press); Whitney R. Cross (1950), *The Burned-Over District: The Social and Intellectual History of Enthusiastic Religion in Western New York, 1800–1850* (Ithaca, NY: Cornell University Press).

24. Smith, *Revivalism and Social Reform*, pp. 225–37; Tyler, *Freedom's Ferment*, pp. 23–45. See also: James H. Moorhead (1984), 'Between progress and the Apocalypse: A reassessment of millennialism in American religious thought, 1800–1880', *The Journal of American History*, 71 (December): 524–42.

25. Walters, *American Reformers*, p. 26. See also: William R. Hutchison (1987), *Errand to the World: American Protestant Thought and Foreign Missions* (Chicago: University of Chicago Press).

26. Walters, *American Reformers*, pp. 26–7; Smith, *Revivalism and Social Reform*, pp. 148–62; Abzug, *Cosmos Crumbling*, pp. 30–76.

27. Walters, *American Reformers*, p. 27; Charles E. Hambrick-Stowe (1996), *Charles G. Finney and the Spirit of American Evangelicalism* (Grand Rapids, MI: W. B. Eerdmans), pp. 183–6.

28. Walters, *American Reformers*, p. 28; Hambrick-Stowe, *Charles G. Finney*, pp. 183–6. See also: Hardman, *Charles Grandison Finney*, and William G. McLoughlin (1959), *Modern Revivalism: Charles Grandison Finney to Billy Graham* (New York: Ronald Press).

29. Walters, *American Reformers*, pp. 30–1; Smith, *Revivalism and Social Reform*, pp. 80–94.

30. Walters, *American Reformers*, pp. 31–2; Tyler, *Freedom's Ferment*, pp. 31–5.

31. Walters, *American Reformers*, p. 33.

32. Walters, *American Reformers*, p. 33. See also: Bertram Wyatt-Brown (1969), *Lewis Tappan and the Evangelical War against Slavery* (Cleveland, OH: Case-Western Reserve University Press).

33. Walters, *American Reformers*, p. 39; John Humphrey Noyes (1870; 1966), *Strange Cults and Utopias of Nineteenth Century America* (formerly titled: *History of American Socialisms*) (New York: Dover Publications), pp. 25–9.

34. Walters, *American Reformers*, p. 40; Noyes, *Strange Cults and Utopias of Nineteenth Century America*, pp. 10–20.

35. Walters, *American Reformers*, p. 41; Tyler, *Freedom's Ferment*, p. 111.

36. Tyler, *Freedom's Ferment*, p. 114; Mark Holloway (1966), *Heavens on Earth: Utopian Communities in America* (New York: Dover Books), pp. 45–6.
37. Noyes, *Strange Cults and Utopias of Nineteenth Century America*, pp. 133–4; Holloway, *Heavens on Earth*, pp. 47–8.
38. Tyler, *Freedom's Ferment*, pp. 114–15.
39. Walters, *American Reformers*, pp. 42–3; Tyler, *Freedom's Ferment*, p. 121; Holloway, *Heavens on Earth*, p. 89.
40. Tyler, *Freedom's Ferment*, pp. 121–5; Holloway, *Heavens on Earth*, pp. 90–2.
41. Walters, *American Reformers*, pp. 43–4; Tyler, *Freedom's Ferment*, pp. 121–5; Noyes, *Strange Cults and Utopias of Nineteenth Century America*, p. 135. See also: Karl J. R. Arndt (1965), *George Rapp's Harmony Society, 1785–1847* (Philadelphia: University of Pennsylvania Press).
42. Marguerite Fellows Melcher (1941; 1960), *The Shaker Adventure* (Cleveland, OH: The Press of Western Reserve University), pp. 3–16; Holloway, *Heavens on Earth*, pp. 55–9.
43. Melcher, *Shaker Adventure*, pp. 16–40.
44. Walters, *American Reformers*, pp. 40–5; Melcher, *Shaker Adventure*, pp. 57–83.
45. Melcher, *Shaker Adventure*, pp. 52–3, 56, 79–80, 179, 255, 276.
46. Walters, *American Reformers*, p. 46; Tyler, *Freedom's Ferment*, pp. 148–9.
47. Melcher, *Shaker Adventure*, pp. 9–10; Holloway, *Heavens on Earth*, pp. 65–7.
48. Tyler, *Freedom's Ferment*, pp. 155–60; Holloway, *Heavens on Earth*, pp. 75–7.
49. Walters, *American Reformers*, p. 47.
50. Noyes, *Strange Cults and Utopias of Nineteenth Century America*, pp. 104–6; Koster, *Transcendentalism in America*, p. 17.
51. Walters, *American Reformers*, p. 51; Koster, *Transcendentalism in America*, pp. 101–7; Abzug, *Cosmos Crumbling*, pp. 18–20. See William R. Hutchison (1959), *The Transcendentalist Ministers: Church Reform in the New England Renaissance* (New Haven: Yale University Press).
52. Walters, *American Reformers*, p. 52; Tyler, *Freedom's Ferment*, pp. 177–82; Noyes, *Strange Cults and Utopias of Nineteenth Century America*, pp. 109–13.
53. Walters, *American Reformers*, pp. 52–3; Tyler, *Freedom's Ferment*, pp. 183–4; Koster, *Transcendentalism in America*, pp. 21–2.
54. Noyes, *Strange Cults and Utopias of Nineteenth Century America*, pp. 614–15; Robert David Thomas (1977), *The Man Who Would Be Perfect: John Humphrey Noyes and the Utopian Impulse* (Philadelphia: University of Pennsylvania Press), pp. 1–41.
55. Thomas, *Man Who Would Be Perfect*, pp. 20–41, 86–90, 92–3.
56. Tyler, *Freedom's Ferment*, pp. 187–9; Noyes, *Strange Cults and Utopias of Nineteenth Century America*, pp. 624–33, 638–40; Thomas, *Man Who Would Be Perfect*, pp. 105–11, 143–5.
57. Walters, *American Reformers*, p. 57; Thomas, *Man Who Would Be Perfect*, pp. 101–5.
58. Walters, *American Reformers*, pp. 57–8; Thomas, *Man Who Would Be Perfect*, pp. 173–5.
59. Tyler, *Freedom's Ferment*, pp. 190–1; Noyes, *Strange Cults and Utopias of Nineteenth Century America*, pp. 641–5; Thomas, *Man Who Would Be Perfect*, pp. 167–76.
60. Holloway, *Heavens on Earth*, pp. 194–6; Thomas, *Man Who Would Be Perfect*, p. 176. See also: Maren Lockwood Carden (1969), *Oneida: Utopian Community to Modern Corporation* (Baltimore, MD: Johns Hopkins University Press).

61. Linda K. Kerber (1980), *Women of the Republic: Intellect and Ideology in Revolutionary America* (Chapel Hill: University of North Carolina Press), p. 7.
62. Walters, *American Reformers*, pp. 102–3; Barbara Welter (1966), 'The cult of true womanhood: 1820–1860', *American Quarterly*, 18 (Summer): 151–74.
63. Kerber, *Women of the Republic*, p. 10; Abzug, *Cosmos Crumbling*, pp. 183–203; Walters, *American Reformers*, p. 103.
64. Kerber, *Women of the Republic*, p. 111; Glenda Riley (1987), *Inventing the American Woman: A Perspective on Women's History* (Arlington Heights, IL: Harlan Davidson), pp. 75–6, 96–8.
65. Lori D. Ginzberg (1986), '"Moral Suasion is Moral Balderdash": Women, politics, and social activism in the 1850s', *The Journal of American History*, 73 (December): 601–22.
66. Walters, *American Reformers*, pp. 106–7.
67. Ibid., p. 107.
68. Ibid., pp. 107–8.
69. Abzug, *Cosmos Crumbling*, pp. 184–5.
70. Barbara Welter (1976), *Dimity Convictions: The American Woman in the Nineteenth Century* (Athens: Ohio University Press), p. 83.
71. Welter, *Dimity Convictions*, p. 84; Ann Douglas (1988), *The Feminization of American Culture* (New York: Anchor Press), pp. 17–19; Riley, *Inventing the American Woman*, pp. 26–7, 51–2, 75–6.
72. Riley, *Inventing the American Woman*, p. 76; Douglas, *Feminization of American Culture*, pp. 7–9, 42–3; Brekus, *Strangers and Pilgrims*, chaps 3–6.
73. Frances Trollope (1832; 1949), *Domestic Manners of the Americans* (New York: Random House), p. 75; Welter, *Dimity Convictions*, pp. 86, 221 FN9.
74. Welter, *Dimity Convictions*, pp. 87–8. See also: Eliza W. Farnham (1964), *Woman and Her Era* (New York: A. J. Davis).
75. Welter, *Dimity Convictions*, p. 102.

Recommended Readings

Abzug, Robert H. (1994), *Cosmos Crumbling: American Reform and the Religious Imagination*, New York: Oxford University Press.
Albanese, Catherine L. (1977), *Corresponding Motion: Transcendental Religion and the New America*, Philadelphia, PA: Temple University Press.
Boller, Paul, Jr. (1974), *American Transcendentalism, 1830–1860: An Intellectual Inquiry*, New York: G. p. Putnam's Sons.
Brekus, Catherine A. (1998), *Strangers and Pilgrims: Female Preaching in America, 1740–1845*, Chapel Hill: University of North Carolina Press.
Carwardine, Richard (1978), *Transatlantic Revivalism: Popular Evangelism in Britain and America, 1790–1865*, Westport, CT: Greenwood Press.
Cole, Charles C. Jr (1954), *The Social Ideals of the Northern Evangelists 1826–1860*, New York: Columbia University Press.
Cross, Whitney R. (1950), *The Burned-Over District: The Social and Intellectual History of Enthusiastic Religion in Western New York, 1800–1850*, Ithaca, NY: Cornell University Press.
Davis, David Brion (ed.) (1967), *Antebellum Reform*, New York: Harper and Row.
Douglas, Ann (1988), *The Feminization of American Culture*, New York: Anchor Press.

Francis, Richard (1997), *Transcendental Utopias: Individual and Community at Brook Farm, Fruitlands, and Walden*, Ithaca, NY: Cornell University Press.

Gray, Henry David (1917), *Emerson: A Statement of New England Transcendentalism as Expressed in the Philosophy of Its Chief Exponent*, rpt 1958 New York: Frederick Ungar Publishing Co.

Hambrick-Stowe, Charles E. (1996), *Charles G. Finney and the Spirit of American Evangelicalism*, Grand Rapids, MI: W. B. Eerdmans.

Hardman, Keith J. (1987), *Charles Grandison Finney, 1792–1875: Revivalist and Reformer*, Syracuse, NY: Syracuse University Press.

Holloway, Mark (1966), *Heavens on Earth: Utopian Communities in America*, New York: Dover Books.

Hutchinson, William R. (1959), *The Transcendentalist Ministers: Church Reform in the New England Renaissance*, New Haven: Yale University Press.

Kerber, Linda K. (1980), *Women of the Republic: Intellect and Ideology in Revolutionary America*, Chapel Hill: University of North Carolina Press.

Koster, Donald N. (1975), *Transcendentalism in America*, Boston: Twayne Publishers.

McLoughlin, William G. (1959), *Modern Revivalism: Charles Grandison Finney to Billy Graham*, New York: Ronald Press.

McLoughlin, William G. (1978), *Revivals, Awakenings, and Reform: An Essay on Religion and Social Change in America, 1607–1977*, Chicago: University of Chicago Press.

Melcher, Marguerite Fellows (1941; 1960), *The Shaker Adventure*, Cleveland, OH: The Press of Western Reserve University.

Miller, Perry (ed.) (1960), *The Transcendentalists: An Anthology*, Cambridge, MA: Harvard University Press.

Noyes, John Humphrey (1870), *Strange Cults and Utopias of Nineteenth Century America* (formerly titled: *History of American Socialisms*), rpt.1966, New York: Dover Publications.

Smith, Timothy L. (1957), *Revivalism and Social Reform: American Protestantism on the Eve of the Civil War*, rpt 1965, New York: Harper and Row.

Stein, Stephen J. (1992), *The Shaker Experience in America: A History of the United Society of Believers*, New Haven: Yale University Press.

Thomas, Robert David (1977), *The Man Who Would Be Perfect: John Humphrey Noyes and the Utopian Impulse*, Philadelphia: University of Pennsylvania Press.

Tyler, Alice Felt (1962), *Freedom's Ferment: Phases of American Social History from the Colonial Period to the Outbreak of the Civil War*, New York: Harper Torchbooks.

Walters, Ronald G. (1978), *American Reformers, 1815–1860*, New York: Hill and Wang.

Welter, Barbara (1976), *Dimity Convictions: The American Woman in the Nineteenth Century*, Athens: Ohio University Press.

CHAPTER 6

A People Apart

Although a constant part of the history of religion in America, the first half of the nineteenth century witnessed the appearance of an unusually large number of religious groups that lay outside America's religious mainstream. A few, like Jews, had been present in small numbers during the Colonial Period, but were granted religious freedom and social toleration only grudgingly; Roman Catholics, whose numbers exploded in the first half of the nineteenth century, faced considerable resistance. African-Americans were forced to make the Christianity imposed on them their own. As slaves they worshipped under their masters' supervision and secretly with their own exhorters; as free men they formed their own related, yet separately constituted Christian denominations. Still others, like the Mormons, Seventh-Day Adventists, and Disciples of Christ – inspired by perfectionism, holiness, adventism, universalism and spiritualism – broke away from already established denominations to form their own sects, thereby further cultivating the soil of a nation that more than any other has become a virtual breeding ground for new religions.

Perry Miller ascribed this proliferation of new religions in the nineteenth century to the centripetal power of the Second Great Awakening.[1] While the rhetoric of unity was omnipresent in American churches, centrifugal forces were never more acute. The chief culprit, Nathan Hatch has argued, was the democratic dissent born of American independence. Between 1800 and 1860 a wildly diverse religious culture made both denominational identity and authority fragile creations. The result was a period of religious ferment, chaos and originality unmatched in American history.[2]

In this chapter we shall discuss only three of the hundreds of such religious outsiders – three of the most prominent examples of the nineteenth century: African-Americans, Roman Catholics, and Mormons. All three succeeded in achieving a position of acceptance, if not fully equal status, among the nation's array of religious denominations. In some cases they were forced to make significant changes in their own beliefs or rituals to become accepted; in all cases, by their struggle, they fuelled the ongoing process in America of defining and redefining what is acceptable and, ultimately, what is American.

R. Laurence Moore and Catherine Albanese have pointed to the importance of these new or marginalized religious groups. Moore has argued that they played a vital role in American religious history by posing innovative ideas that in time were adopted, in some form, and that forced the Protestant American mainstream to continually revise, and make more inclusive, what was deemed acceptable. Albanese has argued that they 'pursued a more totalizing vision' than the mainstream churches. Departing from the normative Protestantism of the era, the everyday became the centre of their religious reality, bringing together what had previously been seen as ordinary with the extraordinary.[3]

African-American Religion

American slaves came mainly from West Africa, and their traditional West African religion provided an integrated world view. As G. J. A. Ojo has written: 'African life in general is thoroughly permeated by religion. It is no overstatement to say that religion is not just one complex of African culture but the catalyst of the other complexes.' For American slaves religion was the vital way by which the entire human body collectively expressed its essence.[4] Historians continue to debate, however, the extent to which the character and development of the cultural life of African-Americans retained ties to, or elements of, their African past.

In 1969 E. Franklin Frazier wrote that 'because of the manner in which the Negroes were captured in Africa and enslaved, they were practically stripped of their social heritage'. Forty-five years earlier, however, Melville J. Herskovits argued that elements of African culture could be found in all phases of African-American life, including religion. C. Eric Lincoln and Lawrence Mamiya have combined both perspectives, explaining that 'the black sacred cosmos or the religious worldview of African Americans is related both to their African heritage, which envisaged the whole universe as sacred, and to their conversion to Christianity'. Blacks 'created their own unique and distinctive forms of culture and worldviews as parallels rather than replications of the culture in which they were involuntary guests'.[5]

In parts of Latin America and on the larger plantations of the Southern states, slaves were able to retain a considerable measure of their African heritage. This was less clear where they existed in smaller numbers, which was most often the case in the United States. Where they lived alone, or in the company of only a few, slaves were inducted into the white world in such a manner as to loosen all social bonds among them and to destroy the traditional basis of social cohesion. This process was made even more effective by the dominance of young men among slaves until 1840 and the precarious nature of the slave family, both of which have long been seen as factors detrimental to traditional religious forms among whites and blacks.[6]

Regardless of the degree to which most historians believe African religion survived among slaves, most agree that Christianity became the dominant element in African-American religion. Slaves reshaped the Christianity they embraced, however, leading many to conclude that: 'They conquered the religion of those who had conquered them.' In its new formulation African-American Christianity lacked both the sense of guilt and mission central to Western Christendom, but gained a 'humanism that affirmed joy in life in the face of every -trial'.[7]

If there was any initial opposition to their christening, that soon disappeared as new laws made clear that slaves would not become free through their acceptance of Christianity. Thus by the close of the seventeenth century and early decades of the eighteenth century, some slaves were baptized either soon after their arrival or as they became the first generation born into slavery. At first the Anglican Church took the lead, but in the wake of the First Great Awakening the most significant missionary efforts toward African Americans came at the hands of Methodists and Baptists. Even after Methodist opposition to slavery vanished, large numbers of slaves and free Blacks continued to be attracted to the type of religious worship Methodists and Baptists provided, especially in the revivals of the Second Great Awakening.[8]

Baptist and Methodist preachers, who generally lacked the formal education of Anglican ministers, were more effective in appealing to the poor, ignorant and outcast. Similarly, slaves found in their fiery message of salvation hope for, and even the prospect of, escape from their earthly woes. The emphasis which the preachers placed on feeling as a sign of conversion found a ready response in slaves who were repressed in so many ways, as did the opportunity for the social solidarity camp meetings and other revivals offered.[9]

Some owners feared teaching slaves the Bible, much as they did reading and writing, for what use they might make of such knowledge. Slaves might well find in the Bible implications of human equality which would incite them to take steps to free themselves. Others saw religion as a means of control and even exhibited genuine concern for the spiritual welfare of their slaves.[10]

The Bible nonetheless provided the means by which slaves acquired a new theology. From the Bible slaves learned that God, ultimately revealed in Jesus, was the ruler of the universe and superior to all other gods, and that God punished and rewarded men, black and white, for their deeds. Whites might stress those passages that encouraged slaves to accept their lot in this world, and, if they were obedient, honest and truthful, to believe that they would be rewarded in the next. Slaves adapted this and other messages and passages from the Bible, however, to their own psychological and social needs. The Old Testament notion of God as avenger, conqueror and liberator became an important part of their faith, as did the image of Moses as the deliverer of his people. From the New Testament the reality of Jesus as the Son of God made flesh found a deep response among blacks. The experience of oppression found immediate resonance with the incarnational view of the suffering, humiliation, death and eventual triumph of Jesus in the resurrection. In sum, the Bible presented a pervasive theme of deliverance.[11]

One of the best examples of how slaves adapted Christianity to their peculiar needs is the sacred folk music known as the 'negro spiritual'. Although adopted from whites, African-Americans invested spirituals with elements of their African and American experiences and made them their own. There has been considerable effort on the part of scholars to invest black spirituals with a revolutionary meaning, or to claim that they represented disguised plans for escape from slavery. Clearly such messages were incorporated. Slave spirituals, however, were also religious in sentiment and otherworldly in outlook. They expressed the awe and wonder of the slave in regard to life and death, his emotional reactions to the complexity of his existence, and his desire to escape from the uncertainties and frustrations of this world. Simply put, slaves did not have to choose between the two; their spirituals could be worldly, spiritual, or both.[12]

Slaves had too strong a grip on reality to identify the frequent references in their spirituals to deliverance solely with any promise of the Kingdom of God on Earth. Deliverance had a more limited and immediate meaning. Though militant and even revolutionary on occasion, American slaves never mounted a sustained militant millennialism. Theirs was a quietest version of millennialism. Neither was the slaves' religion messianic in the political sense. The deliverer of the people was to be God, and He – in the image of Moses–Jesus – was to be called forth by faith.[13]

The single most persistent image of the slave spirituals was that of the chosen people. The force of this image cannot be diminished by the observation that similar images were present in the religious singing of white evangelical churches during the first half of the nineteenth century. White Americans could be expected to sing of triumph and salvation, given their long-standing heritage of the idea of a chosen people, but for this message to be expressed by slaves who were told endlessly that they were members of the lowliest of races is significant. As Lawrence Levine put it: 'It offers an insight into the kinds of barriers the slaves had available to them against the internalization of the stereotyped images their masters held and attempted consciously and unconsciously to foist upon them.'[14]

Many slave holders tried to control African-American religion by employing white preachers, upon whose biblical interpretations and spiritual messages they could rely. A few of those preachers appear to have earned the slaves' respect, both by their preaching and their concern for the slaves' welfare. Most were greeted with indifference and a few with hostility, forcing an increasingly large number of slaves to worship in private. It was the invisible institution of the African-American church that took root among slaves, more than the visible.[15]

Since all forms of organized social effort were forbidden among the slaves, in the absence of an established priesthood, the black preacher played an important role in the invisible church. The black preacher was 'called' to his office and through his personal qualities achieved a position of dominance. The call was supposed to have come through some religious experience which indicated that God had chosen him as a spiritual leader, and, as a result, he became a leader among slaves. Quite often, however, black preachers were forced to hide their calling from their masters.

The African-American preacher had to combine his knowledge of the sacred Scriptures with an ability to speak and communicate his special knowledge to the slaves. As W. E. DuBois found, black slave religion depended on three particular characteristics: 'the preacher, the music, and the frenzy'. If you had the first two, the third followed. The preacher was an orator who could deliver a plain message that could reach the heart. Slaves looked to him because he could understand and address them, their hopes and their misery. But he also had to be able to sing. Employing both, he could move his congregation toward an ecstatic form of worship intended to provide a purifying emotional catharsis and a moment of spiritual ecstasy by which, at least for the moment, they could escape the harshness of their reality.[16]

Where he was unknown to his master, the black preacher was free to exercise his gifts and to direct his followers as he saw fit. Where he was known, he was always subject to at least some supervision, and that supervision grew more intense over time. Each insurrection scare – Gabriel Prosser's (1800), Denmark Vesey's (1822) and Nat Turner's (1831), each connected in some way to black preaching – provoked further repression. Nat Turner was not a preacher in the formal sense of the word, but he was an exhorter, and he convinced his fellow slaves in Southampton County, Virginia, by the power of his message, that he was the anointed one of God for their deliverance. They killed fifty-seven white men, women and children. The governor of Virginia blamed the revolt on the evil doings of black preachers, and state legislatures throughout the South passed laws forbidding free blacks to preach to slaves, to register and control black preachers, and to require whites to be present when they preached.[17]

At the same time, many historians have argued that the period after 1831 constituted a very fruitful period for the spread of Christianity among the slaves. After 1831, their evidence suggests, Southern planters, motivated both by fear of insurrection and desire for social control, as well as a sincere concern for the salvation of slaves, heavily promoted Christianity in a spiritually starved slave community. The result was a dramatic increase in the number of conversions. As Albert Raboteau found: slaves 'remained only minimally touched by Christianity by the second decade of the 19th century', but, as a result of this considerable effort by planters and the receptivity of the slaves, 'widespread conversion of slaves to Christianity [occurred] by the time of the Civil War'.[18]

The first black church in America is generally acknowledged to have been the African Baptist, or Bluestone, Church established on the William Byrd plantation in Mecklenberg, Virginia, in 1758. The Silver Bluff Baptist Church, located in South Carolina not far from Augusta, Georgia, was founded between 1773 and 1775 by George Liele. Liele was converted and baptized by local Baptists, and, because of his 'unusual ministerial gifts', his master permitted him to preach on neighbouring plantations, including the Galphin plantation where the Silver Bluff Baptist Church was erected. His master was killed in the Revolutionary War, and, when heirs raised some question about his status, Liele fled behind British lines in Savannah and later followed the British when they evacuated the city. Before he left Savannah, however, Liele baptized Andrew Bryan and some other blacks who founded the First African (Baptist) Church in Savannah around 1788. When Bryan died in 1812, he was the acknowledged leader of African-American religious life in Georgia.[19]

The pioneering work of black Baptist preachers was most successful in those areas of the South where the interests of the ruling whites were not so deeply rooted in the plantation system – in the cities of Virginia, for example. A few even preached to whites, but there was always some question concerning the propriety of blacks preaching to whites or even their worshipping together. Where large numbers of black communicants existed, they worshipped in separate wings of congregations and under different preachers. Presbyterians, Episcopalians, Baptists and Methodists built separate churches for their black members, and in those churches blacks tended to conduct their services according to their own mode of religious expression.[20]

In the North, as in the South, a number of black preachers acquired some distinction and preached to mixed congregations, but similar problems arose. Among the most famous of early African-American preachers in the North was Richard Allen, both because of his preaching and because of the role he played in organizing an independent black church. Allen was born a slave in Philadelphia but was sold to a planter who took him to Delaware, where he came under the influence of Methodist preachers and converted. He was allowed to conduct prayers and preach in the house of his master, and he and his brother were permitted to purchase their freedom from their master, when he became convinced that slavery was wrong.[21]

In 1780 Allen became a preacher, and Methodist Bishop Asbury gave him assignments whereby he was allowed to travel with white Methodist ministers. Six years later he was invited to preach in the St George Methodist Episcopal Church in Philadelphia, where he observed the need of blacks for religious leadership and a benevolent voluntary association. Allen and others organized the Free African Society. He also proposed that a separate church be established for blacks, but his proposal was opposed by both whites and blacks until blacks attending St George Church were removed from the seats around the wall and ordered to sit in the gallery. Mistaking the section of the gallery which they were to occupy, Allen and Absalom Jones were almost dragged from their knees as they prayed.[22]

After Allen and Jones left St George Church, they differed as to whether blacks should model their church organization after the Methodist or the Episcopal Church. Jones organized the St Thomas African Protestant Episcopal Church and became the first black Protestant Episcopal priest, but the majority of seceding blacks followed Allen, who organized the Bethel Church, for which a building was purchased and dedicated in 1794. Bishop Asbury ordained Allen a deacon. Later he became an elder and the movement spread to other cities, largely in the North. The representatives of those churches met in Philadelphia in 1816 and established the African Methodist Episcopal Church. Allen was elected bishop and a book of discipline was adopted which embodied the same articles of religion and rules as the Wesleyans.[23]

The secession of blacks from the white Methodist church in Philadelphia was followed by secessions in New York City. Peter Williams, a sexton for a number of years in the John Street Methodist Church, was distinguished for his piety and faithfulness among white communicants. However, being influenced by the general movement among African-Americans to establish their own churches, he joined with other blacks in organizing the Zion Church out of which, in 1801, developed the African Methodist Episcopal Zion Church. The African Methodist Episcopal Zion Churches did not completely separate from the Methodist Church until after the Methodists' 1824 General Conference, the Zion Churches' First General Conference being held in 1828.[24]

African-Americans also sought asylum from 'the spirit of slavery and the spirit of caste' in independent Baptists churches, which were being established by blacks in the southern states like Maryland, Virginia, Georgia and Kentucky, and in the Northern cities of Boston, New York City and Philadelphia. By 1850 the number of black Baptists reached 150,000 and by 1870, 500,000, but it was only later that the black Baptist churches were brought together in a national convention.[25]

The Civil War and emancipation destroyed whatever stability and order that had developed among African-Americans under the slave regime. Nevertheless, the strength of the slaves' religion became clear.

The religious intensity of the ex-slave Union troops, the freed men's translation of their political position into religious terms and the extraordinary mushrooming of black churches told their story. Emancipation provided the opportunity for the fusion of the invisible institution of the African-American church, which had taken root among the slaves, and the visible institutional church that had grown up among free blacks before the Civil War. The result was rapid growth in the size of the black church. But there was a more important result of this merger, namely the structuring or organizing of African-American life to an extent that had not previously existed. Religious life became the chief means by which this organization came about.[26]

Roman Catholicism

Historian Arthur M. Schlesinger, Sr, once described anti-Catholicism as 'the deepest bias in the history of the American people'. Schlesinger did not mean to suggest that it was the most violent of American prejudices, though violent it was at times, but that it struck, and continues to strike, a chord in the depth of the American consciousness. As Michael Schwartz has put it:

> It is woven into the fabric of our culture. For the most part unconsciously and unintentionally, as a sort of tacit assumption, this prejudice has helped to shape our national character, mold our institutions, and influence the course of our history.[27]

Although by the end of the nineteenth century it would become the largest denomination in the United States, for the first two centuries of the nation's history Roman Catholicism had to do battle for freedom and dignity in a Protestant empire. As noted in the opening chapter of this book, the oldest colonial power in what is now the United States was Catholic Spain; the first permanent Spanish continental settlement was established at St Augustine, Florida, in 1565. Catholic France also planted settlements in Maine as early as 1604, eventually spreading along the St Lawrence River Valley into the Ohio River Valley and south along the Mississippi. As a result of the treaty process, westward expansion, purchases and war, Spanish and French Catholic lands, and the people therein, became part of the United States by the Civil War.[28]

As discussed in Chapter 2 the British settlements of North America – the civilization and culture that laid the foundation of the United States

— was overwhelmingly Protestant and hostile to Roman Catholics. As the result of the cruelties of the English Reformation, alleged subversive activities such as the Gunpowder Plot, and continued international quarrels with Catholic France and Spain, opposition to Roman Catholicism was widespread and deeply imbedded throughout the colonies. The intellectual centre of English America developed in Puritan Massachusetts, and the Puritans not only representing the dissenting wing of England's Reformation but also the most ardent opposition to Roman Catholicism. For Puritans, Catholicism was a corruption of the Christian message, Rome was Babylon, and the Pope was the anti-Christ — images that would not be lost in the United States throughout the period covered in these pages.[29]

The threat of Catholicism concerned more than religion. The freedom of humanity was at stake in the battle between Catholicism and Protestantism, as well. New Englanders believed that Catholics were part of a vast international conspiracy to seek world domination. They believed that Catholics owed their loyalty first and foremost to that conspiracy and its leader, the Pope. They held that the Pope used his religious influence to maintain his tyrannical grip, and, because they owed their allegiance to the Pope, Catholics could not be trusted with any civil power in Protestant countries.[30]

A Massachusetts statute of 1647 identified any Catholic priest discovered on its territory as 'an incendiary and disturber of the public peace and safety, and an enemy to the true Christian religion' and, if apprehended, subject to 'perpetual imprisonment' or, for second offenders, possible death. Similar laws could be found in most colonies, making it at least theoretically the case that Catholics could enjoy full civil and religious rights only in Rhode Island. But in fact, in the colonial period, prosecutions of Catholics were rare, largely because there were so few Catholics in the colonies.[31]

Roman Catholics did find their way to English America, especially to Maryland and Pennsylvania. The most substantial Catholic settlement was in Maryland, a proprietary colony founded by the Lords Baltimore and dedicated to religious toleration for Catholics. Toleration was provided for by law beginning in 1639, but made more specific in the 1649 Act Concerning Religion, and for a time Roman Catholics enjoyed most of the civil rights guaranteed Protestants under English law. But, as they soon became a distinct minority among Protestants, acts concerning Catholic toleration were repeatedly rescinded until England's

Glorious Revolution of 1688, whereupon toleration was lost for the duration of the colonial period.[32]

Significant numbers of Roman Catholics migrated to William Penn's Holy Experiment, as well. Although not as obviously a Catholic haven as Maryland, Pennsylvania offered Catholics religious toleration. And Catholics were treated comparatively well, even if the colony did require oaths of allegiance and supremacy and a test act that denied them membership in the assembly and other public offices.[33]

By 1763 there were about 20,000 to 25,000 Roman Catholics in the thirteen colonies, or about 1 per cent of the population. But as the colonies slipped toward war with England, anti-Catholic sentiment among Protestants continued – even among rebel leaders. Sam Adams, for example, insisted that there was 'much more to be dreaded from the growth of Popery in America than from the Stamp Act', while even Harvard College had its Dudlein Lectures, the fourth in each annual series devoted to 'detecting, convicting and exposing the idolatry, errors and superstitions of the Romish church'. At least in New England, the belief that it was becoming 'popish' contributed to the growing antipathy of Whigs toward Britain.[34]

The Quebec Act, which British colonists assumed was promulgated in response to the Boston Tea Party, and further evidence of the influence of Catholicism on the British throne, was 'intolerable'. It inflamed prejudice by establishing the Roman Catholic religion in Canada – where most residents were, in fact, Catholic – but, when the first shots of the Revolutionary War were fired, attempts to establish friendly relations with Catholic Canada, France and Spain required efforts on the part of revolutionary leaders to suppress at least outward expressions of hostility toward that faith. Canadians were never persuaded to join the colonial effort for independence, and some American Roman Catholics joined the Tory side, but most Roman Catholics in the thirteen colonies did rally to the independence movement.[35]

Maryland's Charles Carroll was among the most eloquent spokesmen for independence. Employing the pseudonym 'First Citizen', Carroll challenged Tory Daniel Dulany in public debate over colonial grievances, only to be criticized by Dulany for even calling himself a citizen, having been disqualified by law from any legal participation in colonial government simply because he was not a Protestant. Citizen or not, Carroll served on Maryland's Committee of Correspondence, in its state Senate, as representative to the Continental Congresses, and as

signer of the Declaration of Independence. 'When I signed the Declaration of Independence', he later wrote, 'I had a view not only of our
independence from England but the toleration of all sects, professing
the Christian religion, and communicating to them all great rights.'
Carroll and his cousin John Carroll, a former Jesuit priest, joined the
nation's first, if failed, diplomatic mission to Canada in 1776.[36]

With independence and the creation of new state constitutions,
several states continued established Protestant churches, while most
continued restrictions of one sort or another on Roman Catholics.
Typically, state law required office-holders not to 'deny the being of
God or the truth of the Protestant religion'. Nevertheless, conditions
were more favourable for Catholics and step by step, state by state, by
1868 such restrictions fell and religious freedom was extended to them –
but not without a period of heightened hostility toward Catholics.[37]

Following the signing of the peace treaty with Great Britain, steps
had to be taken to organize the Roman Catholic Church in the United
States. That, of course, would be a delicate matter, given Protestant
Americans' antipathy both to Catholics and bishops, the latter issue
dating to opposition to the establishment of an Anglican bishop in the
colonies. Beginning in 1782 John Carroll began the process of organizing America's Catholics by working out a 'Constitution of the Clergy',
which detailed financial arrangements and rules of behaviour, as well as
a panel for arbitration and conciliation. But a replacement had to be
found for the English vicar apostolic of the London district who had
previously exercised church authority over American Catholics. Until
such time, two sacraments – holy orders and confirmation – could not
be conferred. In 1784 Rome named Carroll Superior of the Mission in
the United States; in 1789 it made Carroll the nation's first bishop.[38]

It fell to Carroll and his successors to deal not only with increasing
anti-Catholic sentiment in the face of Catholic immigration, but also the
problem of reconciling a native Catholic tradition, that had grown up in
a Protestant environment and adopted some Protestants ways, and the
ethnic divisions that developed within American Catholicism. Given
the Protestant tradition of congregational autonomy, which American
Catholics had come to appreciate, the establishment of a traditional
Roman Catholic hierarchy – and even its trusteeship over church
property – was problematic.

Given the peculiar American situation in which he was raised,
Carroll had a strong sense of the need for a national church that

would largely shape its own destiny, including a comparatively autonomous body of clergy, that might choose its own bishops and be
presided over by the bishop of its own choosing. He envisioned a
local church in communion with the see of Rome, but internally
autonomous, self-perpetuating and free of any taint of foreign jurisdiction. Carroll's plan would not be realized, as the Roman Church's
magisterium – traumatized by actions taken against the Church during
the French Revolution – took steps toward greater centralization
throughout the Catholic world. His failure to achieve such ends not
only caused dissent among American Catholics but also added fuel to
the fire of Protestants who saw opposition from Rome to such republican ideas indicative of the retrogressive and harmful authority with
which it had to deal.[39]

Nevertheless, the American Roman Catholic Church flourished in
the nineteenth century, largely because of unprecedented immigration –
about 250,000 in the 1830s, 700,000 in the next decade, and a million in
the ten years before the Civil War. By 1860 there were nearly 2.5 million
American Catholics, making them second in number only to American
Methodists. By 1890 they topped 7.3 million and all other American
denominations. As James Hennesey put it, in reference to this great
migration: 'Many shed their ancestral religion along with allegiance to
European princes, but most retained it. Those who remained Catholic,
and their descendants, became American Catholicism.' Nativism, however, had not completely disappeared during the era of toleration, and,
with the dramatic growth of Roman Catholicism in the early nineteenth
century, it reappeared with unprecedented hostility.[40]

Early nineteenth century Catholic immigrants, largely Irish and
German, found themselves tied to the industrialization and urbanization
that swept the nation beginning in this period and posed a direct threat
to what was seen as the traditional Protestant way of life. Indeed, Irish
Catholics became indelibly linked with that threat. Their growing
involvement in urban Democratic politics and insistence on their own
schools only added to feelings of hostility. As even the father of
American theological liberalism, the Reverend Horace Bushnell of
Hartford, Connecticut put it in 1847: 'Our first danger is barbarism,
Romanism next.'[41]

A spate of anti-Catholic literature followed. Samuel F. B. Morse, the
inventor, wrote *Foreign Conspiracy against the Liberties of the United
States* (1834), in which he charged various European missionary support

organizations, such as the Leopoldine Foundation, with papal support, and with using poor ignorant immigrants as its shock troops to bring about a monarchist-papist putsch in the United States. Lurid tales of convent horrors appeared, such as Rebecca Reed's *Six Months in a Convent* (1835) and Maria Monk's Awful *Disclosures of the Hotel Dieu Nunnery in Montreal* (1836). The first told of atrocities committed among the Ursuline sisters, often running to the pornographic, with tales of priest–nun rendezvous and murdered infants (the product of those rendezvous). Reed and Monk became regulars on the lecture circuit, and a storm of violence brewed.[42]

The first violence occurred in Charlestown, near Boston, at a convent school run by sisters of the Ursuline community. Enjoying the heavy patronage of more liberal Protestants for the education of their children, the area's more conservative Protestants – especially Congregationalists (also engaged in a struggle with those same liberal Protestants, mostly Unitarians) – increased their anti-Catholic rhetoric, which literally burst into flames in 1834. Rebecca Reed came to town for a public lecture. One of the Ursulines, Elizabeth Harrison, later determined to be suffering from mental depression, briefly fled the community, creating a public stir. And Lyman Beecher of Cincinnati's Lane Theological Seminary delivered sermons intended to raise money for the seminary, but focused on the need to do so in order to deter papal plans to take over the Mississippi River Valley. Charlestown selectmen inspected the Ursuline convent and reported that nothing was amiss, but a mob gathered, and, when they could not be persuaded that they had nothing to fear, they ransacked and burned the convent to the ground. Only one rioter was ever convicted, and he was pardoned.[43]

Philadelphia burst into flames in the spring and summer of 1844 over complaints of the city's Catholics against the reading of the King James Version of the Bible in the public schools. When, on 3 May, the nativist American Republican Party held a meeting in the Irish district of Kensington, thirty homes and an Irish volunteer fire department went up in flames. In July rumours spread of the stock-piling of arms in one of the city's Catholic churches. When muskets were actually found in the church – having been supplied by the state arsenal for self-defence – a mob marched on the church, only to be met by a heavily armed group of Irish Catholic defenders. Before it was over, fourteen lay dead or dying. Another fifty were wounded.[44]

Bishop Kendrick of Philadelphia was criticized for his passive role in the Philadelphia riots; not so Bishop Hughes of New York. When nativist disturbances threatened his city, he demanded a meeting with Mayor Robert Morris and his successor James Harper, where he demanded protection and, failing that, issued a thinly veiled threat by allusion to the fires that welcomed Napoleon to Moscow in 1812. A nativist rally was subsequently cancelled and the city, though tense for some time, did not burn.[45]

The nativist movement spilled over into national politics with the formation of the American Republic Party in 1843. It reorganized into the Native American Party and was soon joined by the Order of the Star Spangled Banner, devoted to excluding Roman Catholics from public office, and even from the country. It spawned the Know Nothing Movement, which took political shape as the American Party. Governors, senators, congressmen, and a host of state and local officials owed their election to Know Nothing support, especially in the northeastern, border and southern states.[46]

In 1853 papal diplomat Archbishop Gaetano Bedini visited the United States. His arrival went peacefully enough; he even met with President Franklin Pierce. But he was soon attacked by the nativist press and when he travelled to the Midwest trouble started. A former priest turned anti-Catholic spokesman, Alessandro Gavazzi, charged Bedini, when Papal Governor of Bologna, with being responsible for executions carried out there by Austrian military authorities. Mobs promptly labelled him the 'Butcher of Bologna' and hounded his every step until he was spirited out of the country.[47]

When the Know Nothing phase of nativism died in the 1850s, it did so not because of any lessening of antipathy toward Catholics, but rather because American concern with Catholics was overcome by concern with slavery. Hostility toward Catholics would rise again, at the end of the nineteenth century.

The Mormons

In some respects, the Church of Jesus Christ of Latter-day Saints was distinctly American. It was born of the evangelically sowed seeds in the soil of the American frontier, reflecting elements of both evangelicalism and the frontier in its character. Its founder, Joseph Smith, Jr, was born in 1805 into a struggling farm family in Vermont. In 1816 the family moved to Palmyra, in the 'burned-over district' of western New York, so known because of the frequency of religious revivals in the area in the first half of the nineteenth century. The Great Revival of 1816–17 was in progress when the Smiths arrived in Palmyra, and it was in the immediate wake of that revival that the twelve-year-old Joseph first became concerned about religion. 'My mind became seriously impressed with regard to the all important concerns for the welfare of my immortal soul', he later reported, 'which led me to searching the scriptures.' Two years later the Methodists organized a camp meeting nearby and he was tempted, but for the moment resisted, making any formal commitment to them. Soon he had little good to say about it or any other denomination.[48]

Financially, the Smiths were no more successful in their new home than in their old, and in time Joseph took up treasure hunting and money digging. At one point he was arrested and found guilty of being 'a disorderly person and an impostor', the specific evidence used against him being that he employed a 'seer stone'. In 1827, however, his luck began to change, if in ways he did not anticipate. He became the author of a new bible and the founder of a new religion, that would outdistance every other sect brought into being in America. As Smith's biographer Fawn Brodie wrote: 'Joseph's was no mere dissenting sect. It was a real religious creation, one intended to be to Christianity what Christianity was to Judaism: that is, a reform and a consummation.'[49]

Smith reported that his first vision came to him in 1820, but that he did not fully understand it. By the time he reported it in 1832, Smith knew that the vision was one of the steps in 'the rise of the church of Christ in the eve of time' and the restoration of the Aaronic Priesthood. 'The Lord opened the heavens upon me and I saw the Lord and he spoke unto me saying Joseph my son thy sins are forgiven thee, go thy way, walk in my statutes, and keep my commandments.' Like countless other revival subjects who had come under conviction, Joseph Smith received assurance of forgiveness from the Lord. His 'soul was filled with love' and for many days he could 'rejoice with great joy'; the Lord was with him.[50]

Smith's conversion was different from nearly all others brought about by the revivals of the period. Smith claimed that the angel Moroni appeared to him in a vision and led him to a cache of gold plates inscribed in 'reformed Egyptian' hieroglyphics, as well as to a set of seer stones (Urim and Thummim) with which he was able to read the plates. Although Martin Harris and Oliver Cowdery claimed to have received visions attesting the existence and authenticity of them, no one else ever actually saw the plates. Smith translated them   he on one side of a curtain, his wife, Cowdery and two other copyists on the other. The task was completed in 1829 and in March 1830 the *Book of Mormon* was offered for sale.[51]

Although interspersed with exhortations on topics of doctrinal and social consequence, the *Book of Mormon* is primarily historical in form. It is a 500-page account of the wanderings and experiences of America's pre-Columbian inhabitants: first, the Jaredites, who left the Tower of Babel and crossed the Atlantic to America, only to extinguish their numbers through continuous internecine wars; second, the evil sons of Laman (the Lamanites), who were the American Indians; and third, the good sons of Nephi, who after many battles were all but extinguished by the Lamanites. Only Mormon and his son Moroni were left, and they buried their chronicles in 384 CE so that whenever God chose they could be revealed again to their spiritual descendants, who would establish the Nephite stake in Zion before the Last Day.[52]

Controversy surrounded the *Book of Mormon* from its first appearance. Actual authorship of the *Book of Mormon* has been contested, as has the very existence of the golden plates, but most scholars agree that the book and its subsequent use at the hands of its author captured both the spirit and needs of those in the region. Joseph Smith may, or may not, have had a decisive religious crisis in which his agony over the multiplicity of sects led to the vision that made him a seer and prophet, but he clearly had experienced revival preaching, and he was familiar with the large number of doctrinal issues it raised. His father had been influenced by Universalism, Methodism and even scepticism; his mother was a seeker after cultic certainties; and in 1824 Joseph himself had heard a local preacher consign his dead brother to hell. He was also well versed in the King James Version of the Bible, a point made clear by his having appropriated from it about 27,000 words for the *Book of Mormon*, as well as its English style and heterogeneous structure.[53]

As Sydney Ahlstrom has written, the *Book of Mormon*

brought a satisfying answer to many needs: it undercut sectarian pluralism and emotionalism with objectivity, moral legalism, a liberal answer to many old issues, a positive this-worldliness, and even a kind of rationalism that had grown out of Joseph's own disdain for frontier sermonizing.

Smith himself made his opposition to sectarian pluralism clear, when he wrote that 'if God had a church, it would not be split into factions'. Such factions, he insisted, were 'devoted to destruction'. The book, however, did not make Mormonism. Joseph Smith, and, after Smith's death, Brigham Young did that.[54]

Soon after publication of the *Book of Mormon* in 1830, Smith baptized six of his followers and formed a church. Within a month forty people acknowledged Smith a seer, translator, prophet and apostle of Jesus Christ. Church doctrine, rules of ritual and direction as to the myriad of other organizational concerns with which churches are normally concerned were minimal at first. Joseph Smith, however, spoke for the Lord, and his revelations were non-stop. A steady flow of revelations began to define the shape and goals of Mormonism. Infant baptism was ruled out in favour of limiting receipt into the church to those old enough to be accountable for their sins before God and to repent. The Calvinist principle of irresistible grace was struck down in favour of the idea that 'there is a possibility that man may fall from grace and depart from the living God'. But at least for the first few years there was little to distinguish Mormon belief from that of other Protest denominations. Richard Bushman has suggested that the articles promulgated in the first years of the church's history made no effort to distinguish the new church from other denominations. Instead, the purpose was to identify the new organization as a respectable Christian church, holding to the established principles of the gospel. 'Joseph's visions were not flaunted before the world. They were simply acknowledged as part of the church's history.'[55]

Smith's well-staged and publicized healings drew converts, as did his warnings about the imminent Second Coming, but they also drew an increasing number of critics. Hecklers and then mobs began to frequent Mormon gatherings, threatening bodily harm as well as creating a situation where Smith was subjected to arrest warrants for disturbing the peace. Smith began advocating a move west and, five months after the church's founding, Smith announced that the New Jerusalem would be found 'on the borders by the Lamanites'. Mormonism's first westward trek began.[56]

In Kirtland, Ohio, the 'United Order of Enoch' took form from Smith's continued revelations. A theocratic government was established, and the notion that the Latter-day Saints were soon to rule on the earth became widely accepted among them. As in New York, however, hostility arose among the group's neighbours in part fuelled by fear of the potential political power of the large group of new settlers, but also by concern for reports of Smith's anti-republican civil and unorthodox spiritual ways. Converts continued to pour in and a temple was built and dedicated with festivities pervaded by pentecostal fervour. What amounted to a bank, though called the Kirtland Safety Society Anti-Banking Company, was organized, notes issued, and a large debt accumulated until the panic of 1837 burst the bubble and brought creditors to its gates. Schism, rioting and fires followed. Smith fled to Missouri, but his woes did not end.[57]

The Mormons were chased out of Jackson County, Missouri, by an angry mob that resented their presence and feared they would incite an Indian uprising against them. Rumours abounded that the Mormons were taking their faith to the Indians and slaves – a situation made worse by Smith's promise on 4 July 1838 that he would wreak vengeance on his oppressors, and that he would be a 'second Mohammed'. Violence escalated. Missouri Governor Lilburn Boggs called out the militia, vowing to run Smith out of the state. Smith was arrested, and his followers left Missouri for Illinois, where they founded the town of Nauvoo.[58]

It was election time 1840, and with Whigs and Democrats vying for support in the newly settled territory both parties sought the 15,000 Mormon votes. Nauvoo was promptly given a charter that made it almost an autonomous theocratic political unit, and Nauvoo became the fastest growing city in Illinois. By 1842 it boasted a population of about 10,000 people. Evangelistic efforts were extended even to the poor of England, who began emigrating by the thousands, and Smith organized a military force known as the Nauvoo Legion. Smith was declared King of the Kingdom of God, and he gathered to him ever increasing civil and spiritual powers. He continued to receive revelations, including, between 1841 and 1843, the concept of plural marriage.[59]

In 1844 Joseph Smith announced his candidacy for the presidency of the United States. Some argue that his decision to run for office was motivated by his desire to publicize his grievances against the federal government after he had tried unsuccessfully to enlist the aid of federal officials to secure compensation for losses suffered during the Mormon expulsion from Missouri. Others insist that he was encouraged by a strong sense of millennialism – by his belief that the US government was on the verge of collapse to be replaced by the just rule of the King of Kings. A few have concluded that Smith believed that his election would dissolve all distinctions between sacred and secular and make them one.[60]

Regardless of his motives, Smith's candidacy provoked dissidence, apostasy, fear and violence. Non-Mormons accused him of conspiring to establish a theocratic empire. Ex-Mormons like John C. Bennett published lurid tales of polygamy, corruption and lawlessness, and dissidents set up a rival newspaper called the *Nauvoo Expositor*. Smith responded with crushing authority, and the Illinois militia threatened to intervene. Joseph and Hyram Smith surrendered to authorities, whereupon they were moved to a Carthage, Illinois, jail. While awaiting trial, a mob broke into the jail and lynched both of them.[61]

Although challenged in his bid for leadership of the church by Sidney Rigdon and Joseph's younger brother William Smith, and faced with a separationist movement led by James Strang, Brigham Young was recognized as Smith's successor. Young, born to a devout Vermont Methodist family, moved to western New York as a young man. Like Smith, he was influenced by the religious enthusiasm of the burned-over district, but he became a Methodist exhorter. In 1830 Young came into contact with Mormonism when Samuel Smith, one of Joseph's younger brothers, arrived in the town where Young was living to preach Mormonism and to sell copies of the *Book of Mormon*. It took two years, but in 1832 Young cast his lot with the new church. He travelled to Kirtland, Ohio, where he met Joseph Smith, and in 1835 Smith appointed Young to the newly created Council of Twelve.[62]

In the midst of the controversy surrounding Joseph Smith, the Illinois state legislature revoked the Nauvoo charter. Upon his assuming power over the church, a warrant was issued for Young's arrest, and although Young was able to persuade those who came to arrest him to at least temporarily allow him his freedom he had little choice but to leave. On 15 February 1846, Young departed Nauvoo, beginning the harrowing Mormon trek across America to the Great Salt Lake basin. They arrived in July 1847. A constitutional convention was held in 1849, and the autonomous state of Deseret took shape. Within a decade ninety communities were formed and the future of Mormonism seemed assured, at least for the moment.[63]

In 1850 Utah became a United States territory. Young tried to have Utah admitted to the union as a state, bypassing territorial status and thereby strengthening control by the Mormon majority. He was made territorial governor, but old quarrels were renewed, including word, once again, of the continued practice of plural marriage among the Mormons. Rather than avoid the issue, Young and other leaders of the church sought to defend plural marriage. First, they defended it on hereditary grounds, as an essential practice for procreation. Polygamy would facilitate the peopling of this world by producing numerous posterity through a righteous chosen (Mormon) lineage. Second, they pointed to the Old Testament precedents of Abraham, Isaac and Jacob. And third, they argued that it was consistent with man's nature, meaning that his basic sexual drive was polygamous and should be allowed legitimate outlet. Women, by nature, were monogamous.[64]

Mormon attempts to defend polygamy did not persuade many to their cause, and the conflict between the Mormons and federal troops in the region escalated. When the Mormons were blamed for the Indian killings of eight members of a US Army Topographical Survey team, known as the Gunnison Massacre, federal troops were assigned to the area against Young's wishes. In 1857, when President James Buchanan replaced Young with a non-Mormon as territorial governor, Young decided that the Mormons must stand their ground and what became known as the Utah, or Mormon, War began.[65]

Although the war was officially declared ended in 1858, a cold war of sorts continued between the Mormons and the US government for the rest of the century. Though it lies beyond the limits of this study, it should be noted that in 1879 the US Supreme Court ruled against polygamy, by upholding the constitutionality of an 1862 Act of Congress against bigamy, noting that religious freedom did not involve the right to subvert an institution upon which 'society may be said to be built'. The Edmunds Act of 1882 brought stringent political pressures to bear on the Mormons, to which was added a federal act of 1884 applying economic penalties. Finally, in 1890, the church revised its teaching on polygamy, thus bringing peace to the area and opening the way to statehood, which was granted in 1896. Over the course of the next century, the Church of Jesus Christ of Latter-day Saints gained not only acceptance but also numbers sufficient to make it one of the largest religious bodies in the United States, with adherents worldwide.[66]

Summary

Jon Butler has described antebellum America as a 'spiritual hothouse', both for the expansion of already established denominations and for the creation of new ones. Sydney Ahlstrom called it a 'sectarian heyday' and Nathan Hatch 'a sea of sectarian rivalries'. As Christianity – Protestant Christianity, to be more specific – advanced, however, so too did new and sometimes ugly demands for government guarantees of

Christian hegemony. In the case of African-Americans, control was intended to preserve the slave economy and racial social hierarchy. In the case of Roman Catholics and Mormons, nativists responded to what they saw as a threat to their divinely ordained Protestant empire. Resistance emerged from strong, unresolved tensions accompanying America's advancing religious complexity, Protestant institutional prowess and persistent desires for simplification and individual freedom. The players would change, but the nation's even greater future religious complexity would continue.[67]

Notes

1. Perry Miller (1961), 'From convenant to the revival', in James Ward Smith and A. Leland Jamison (eds), *The Shaping of American Religion* (Princeton: Princeton University Press), p. 354.
2. Nathan O. Hatch (1989), *The Democratization of American Christianity* (New Haven: Yale University Press); Roger Finke and Rodney Stark (1994), *The Churching of America, 1776–1990: Winners and Losers in Our Religious Economy* (New Brunswick, NJ: Rutgers University Press).
3. R. Laurence Moore (1986), *Religious Outsiders and the Making of Americans* (New York: Oxford University Press), p. 19; Catherine Albanese (1992), *America: Religions and Religion* (Belmont, CA: Wadsworth Publishing), p. 223.
4. G. J. A. Ojo (1984), *Yoruba Culture: A Geographical Analysis* (London: University of London Press), p. 158; Eugene D. Genovese (1976), *Roll, Jordan, Roll: The World the Slaves Made* (New York: Vintage Books), p. 210.
5. E. Franklin Frazier (1969), *The Negro Church in America* (New York: Schocken Books), p. 1; Melville J. Herskovits (1924; 1990), *The Myth of the Negro Past* (Boston: Beacon Press); C. Eric Lincoln and Lawrence H. Mamiya (1990), *The Black Church in the African American Experience* (Durham, NC: Duke University Press), p. 2. See also: Genovese, *Roll, Jordan Roll*, p. 162; Sidney W. Mintz and Richard Price (1997), 'The birth of African-American culture', in Timothy E. Fulop and Albert J. Raboteau (eds), *African-American Religion: Interpretive Essays in History and Culture* (New York: Routledge), pp. 37–53.
6. Frazier, *Negro Church in America*, p. 1; E. Franklin Frazier (1969), *The Negro Family in the United States* (Chicago: University of Chicago Press), Part 1; Genovese, *Roll, Jordan, Roll*, p. 184.
7. Genovese, *Roll, Jordan, Roll*, pp. 211–12; Albert J. Raboteau (1997), 'The Black experience in American evangelicalism: The meaning of slavery', in Fulop and Raboteau, *African-American Religion*, pp. 89–106.
8. Genovese, *Roll, Jordan, Roll*, pp. 183, 185; Frazier, *Negro Church in America*, pp. 6–7; Donald G. Mathews (1965), *Slavery and Methodism* (Princeton: Princeton University Press), pp. 293–9; Raboteau, 'Black experience in American evangelicalism', pp. 92–3.
9. Frazier, *Negro Church in America*, p. 9. See also: Catherine C. Cleveland (1916), *The Great Revival in the West, 1797–1805* (Chicago: University of Chicago Press); Elizabeth K. Nottingham (1941), *Methodism and the Frontier Indiana Proving Ground* (New York: Columbia University Press).

10. Susan M. Fickling (1924), *Slave Conversion in South Carolina: 1830–1860* (Columbia: University of South Carolina), p. 18.; Genovese, *Roll, Jordan, Roll*, p. 189; William Sumner Jenkins (1935; 1960), *Pro-Slavery Thought in the Old South* (Gloucester, MA: Peter Smith), pp. 13, 17; Clement Eaton (1961), *Growth of Southern Civilization, 1790–1860* (New York: Harper and Row), p. 87.
11. Lincoln and Mamiya, *Black Church in the African American Experience*, pp. 3–4; Genovese, *Roll, Jordan, Roll*, pp. 252–3.
12. Lawrence W. Levine (1997), 'Slave songs and slave sonsciousness: An exploration in neglected sources', in Fulop and Raboteau, *African-American Religion*, pp. 60–2; Miles M. Fisher (1953), *Negro Slave Songs in the United States* (Ithaca, NY: Cornell University Press); Frazier, *Negro Church in America*, pp. 12–13; Howard Thurman (1947; 1975), *The Negro Spiritual Speaks of Life and Death* (Richmond, IN: Friends United), pp. 17, 27–8, 38, 51; Lawrence Levine (1971), 'Slave songs and slave consciousness', in Tamara K. Hareven (ed.), *Anonymous Americans* (Englewood Cliffs, NJ: Prentice Hall), p. 114; Vincent Harding (1997), 'Religion and resistance among antebellum slaves', in Fulop and Raboteau, *African-American Religion*, pp. 109–11.
13. Genovese, *Roll, Jordan, Roll*, p. 272.
14. Levine (1953), 'Slave songs and slave consciousness', p. 69.
15. Genovese, *Roll, Jordan, Roll*, pp. 202–9; Lincoln and Mamiya, *Black Church in the African American Experience*, p. 24.
16. Genovese, *Roll, Jordan, Roll*, p. 258; Frazier, *Negro Church in America*, p. 18; Lincoln and Mamiya, *Black Church in the African American Experience*, pp. 5–6.
17. Genovese, *Roll, Jordan, Roll*, pp. 257, 259; Harding, 'Religion and resistance among antebellum slaves', pp. 117–18; Herbert Aptheker (1966), *Nat Turner's Slave Rebellion* (New York: Humanities Press).
18. Albert Raboteau (1978), *Slave Religion: The 'Invisible Institution' in the Antebellum South* (New York: Oxford University Press), pp. 155–62; Genovese, *Roll, Jordan, Roll*, pp. 187–88.
19. Frazier, *Negro Church in America*, pp. 23–4; Lincoln and Mamiya, *Black Church in the African American Experience*, pp. 23–4.
20. Leroy Fitts (1985), *A History of Black Baptists* (Nashville, TN: Broadman); Frazier, *Negro Church in America*, pp. 25–6; Genovese, *Roll, Jordan, Roll*, pp. 235, 240.
21. Will B. Gravely (1997), 'The rise of African churches in America (1786–1822): Reexamining the contexts', in Fulop and Raboteau, *African-American Religion*, pp. 136–7; Richard Allen (1960), *The Life, Experience and Gospel Labors of Rt. Rev. Richard Allen*, ed. George A. Singleton (New York: Abingdon Press), p. 12; Charles H. Wesley (1935), *Richard Allen, Apostle of Freedom* (Washington, DC: Associated Publishers), pp. 15–17.
22. Wesley, *Richard Allen*, pp. 52–3; Lincoln and Mamiya, *Black Church in the African American Experiences*, pp. 50–1.
23. Carter G. Woodson (1972), *The History of the Negro Church* (Washington, DC: Associated Publishers), pp. 75–7; Lincoln and Mamiya, *Black Church in the African American Experience*, pp. 51–2; Daniel A. Payne (1891; 1969), *History of the African Methodist Episcopal Church* (New York: Arno Press).
24. Lincoln and Mamiya, *Black Church in the African American Experience*, pp. 56–7; Frazier, *Negro Church in America*, p. 28. See also: William J. Walls (1974), *The African Methodist Episcopal Zion Church: Reality of the Black Church* (Charlotte,

NC: AME Zion Publishing House); Howard D. Gregg (1980), *History of the African Methodist Episcopal Church* (Nashville, TN: AMEC Publishing House).

25. Lincoln and Mamiya, *Black Church in the African American Experience*, p. 25; Frazier, *Negro Church in America*, p. 28.

26. Frazier, *Negro Church in America*, pp. 29–30; Lincoln and Mamiya, *Black Church in the African American Experience*, p. 7; Raboteau, *Slave Religion*.

27. Michael Schwartz (1984), *The Persistent Prejudice: Anti-Catholicism in America* (Huntington, IN: Our Sunday Visitor), pp. 13–14.

28. James Hennesey (1981), *American Catholics: A History of the Roman Catholic Community in the United States* (New York: Oxford University Press), chaps 1–3.

29. Hennesey, *American Catholics*, pp. 36–7; Ray Allen Billington (1938), *The Protestant Crusade, 1800–1860* (New York: Macmillan Company), pp. 1–4.

30. Francis D. Cogliano (1995), *No King, No Popery: Anti-Catholicism in Revolutionary New England* (Westport, CT: Greenwood Press), p. 14.

31. Hennesey, *American Catholics*, p. 37; Billington, *Protestant Crusade*, pp. 7–9.

32. Hennesey, *American Catholics*, pp. 37–42; Billington, *Protestant Crusade*, pp. 5–7.

33. Hennesey, *American Catholics*, p. 49.

34. Hennesey, *American Catholics*, pp. 55–6; Charles H. Metzger (1962), *Catholics and the American Revolution: A Study in Religious Climate* (Chicago: Loyola University Press), p. 14; Cogliano, *No King, No Popery*, pp. 8–9, 35.

35. Cogliano, *No King, No Popery*, p. 51; James H. Hutson (ed.) (1975), *A Decent Respect for the Opinions of Mankind, Congressional State Papers 1774–1776* (Washington, DC: Library of Congress), p. 29; Hennesey, *American Catholics*, p. 59.

36. Daniel Dulany (1974), *Maryland and the Empire, 1773: The Antilon-First Citizen Letters*, ed. Peter S. Onuf (Baltimore, MD: Johns Hopkins University Press), pp. 121–2; Edmund C. Burnett (ed.) (1921–31), *Letters of Members of the Continental Congress*, 8 vols (Washington, DC: Carnegie Institution), I: p. 354; Martin I. J. Griffin (1907–11), *Catholics and the American Revolution*, 2 vols (Ridley Park, PA: Published by the Author), I: p. 352; Hennesey, *American Catholics*, pp. 64–5.

37. John E. Semonche (1985), *Religion and Constitutional Government in the United States* (Carrboro, NC: Signal Books), pp. 22–3.

38. Hennesey, *American Catholics*, pp. 69–70.

39. Ibid., pp. 85, 89.

40. Hennesey, *American Catholics*, p. 102. For a discussion of the controversy surrounding the counting of American Catholics, see Finke and Stark, *Churching of America*, pp. 110–15.

41. Hennesey, *American Catholics*, pp. 118–19.

42. Billington, *Protestant Crusade*, pp. 90–2, 99–108, 122–5.

43. Ibid., pp. 68–76; Hennesey, *American Catholics*, p. 122.

44. Billington, *Protestant Crusade*, pp. 220–34; Michael Feldberg (1975), *The Philadelphia Riots of 1844: A Study of Ethnic Conflict* (Westport, CT: Greenwood Press).

45. Richard Shaw (1977), *Dagger John: The Unquiet Life and Times of Archbishop John Hughes of New York* (New York: Paulist Press), p. 197.

46. Billington, *Protestant Crusade*, pp. 200–11.

47. James F. Connelly (1960), *The Visit of Archbishop Gaetano Bedini to the United States, June 1853–February 1854* (Rome: Universita Gregoriana).

48. Richard L. Bushman (1984), *Joseph Smith and the Beginnings of Mormonism*

(Urbana: University of Illinois Press), pp. 52–3; Marvin S. Hill (1989), *Quest for Refuge: The Mormon Flight from American Pluralism* (Salt Lake City, UT: Signature Books), pp. 9, 12, 28.

49. Sydney E. Ahlstrom(1972), *A Religious History of the American People* (New Haven: Yale University Press), p. 502; Fawn M. Brodie (1979), *No Man Knows My History: The Life of Joseph Smith* (New York: Alfred A. Knopf), p. viii.

50. Bushman, *Joseph Smith*, pp. 56–7.

51. Ibid., pp. 61–4, 87–102; Ahlstrom, *Religious History of the American People*, p. 502.

52. Bushman, *Joseph Smith*, pp. 115–19; Ahlstrom, *Religious History of the American People,* pp. 502–3.

53. Bushman, *Joseph Smith*, pp. 115–140; Ahlstrom, *Religious History of the American People*, pp. 503–4.

54. Ahlstrom, *Religious History of the American People*, p. 504; Hill, *Quest for Refuge*, pp. xi, xiv.

55. Bushman, *Joseph Smith*, p. 157.

56. Bushman, *Joseph Smith*, pp. 149–68; Ahlstrom, *Religious History of the American People*, pp. 503–5.

57. Hill, *Quest for Refuge*, pp. xix, 55–98; Kenneth H. Winn (1989), *Exiles in a Land of Liberty: Mormons in America, 1830–1846* (Chapel Hill: University of North Carolina Press), pp. 63–84; Newell G. Bringhurst (1986), *Brigham Young and the Expanding American Frontier* (Boston: Little, Brown and Company), pp. 32–5.

58. Bringhurst, *Brigham Young*, pp. 36–41; Winn, *Exiles in a Land of Liberty*, pp. 85–105.

59. Bringhurst, *Brigham Young*, pp. 44–9, 51–4; Leonard J. Arrington (1985), *Brigham Young: American Moses* (New York: Alfred A. Knopf), pp. 79–97; Ahlstrom, *Religious History of the American People*, p. 506.

60. Bringhurst, *Brigham Young*, p. 60; Hill, *Quest for Refuge*, p. 138.

61. Winn, *Exiles in a Land of Liberty*, pp. 182, 212–14; Arrington, *Brigham Young*, p. 103; Bringhurst, *Brigham Young*, p. 62; Ahlstrom, *Religious History of the American People*, p. 506.

62. Bringhurst, *Brigham Young*, pp. 1–29, 64–8; Arrington, *Brigham Young*, pp. 19–49.

63. Arrington, *Brigham Young*, pp. 128–9; Bringhurst, *Brigham Young*, pp. 82–3; Ahlstrom, *Religious History of the American People*, p. 507.

64. Bringhurst, *Brigham Young*, p. 111.

65. Arrington, *Brigham Young*, pp. 250–68; Bringhurst, *Brigham Young*, pp. 112–18, 136–9.

66. Ahlstrom, *Religious History of the American People*, p. 507.

67. Jon Butler (1990), *Awash in a Sea of Faith: Christianizing the American People* (Cambridge, MA: Harvard University Press), pp. 225, 284; Ahlstrom, *Religious History of the American People*, p. 472; Hatch, *Democratization of American Christianity*, p. 62.

Recommended Readings

Aptheker, Herbert (1966), *Nat Turner's Slave Rebellion*, New York: Humanities Press.

Arrington, Leonard J. (1985), *Brigham Young: American Moses*, New York: Alfred A. Knopf.

Billington, Ray Allen. (1938), *The Protestant Crusade, 1800–1860*, New York: Macmillan Publishing Company.

Bringhurst, Newell G. (1986), *Brigham Young and the Expanding American Frontier*, Boston: Little, Brown and Company.

Brodie, Fawn M. (1979), *No Man Knows My History: The Life of Joseph Smith*, New York: Alfred A. Knopf.

Bushman, Richard L. (1984), *Joseph Smith and the Beginnings of Mormonism*, Urbana: University of Illinois Press.

Cogliano, Francis D. (1995), *No King, No Popery: Anti-Catholicism in Revolutionary New England*, Westport, CT: Greenwood Press.

Eaton, Clement (1961), *Growth of Southern Civilization, 1790–1860*, New York: Harper and Row.

Feldberg, Michael (1975), *The Philadelphia Riots of 1844: A Study of Ethnic Conflict*, Westport, CT: Greenwood Press.

Frazier, E. Franklin (1969), *The Negro Church in America*, New York: Schocken Books.

Fulop, Timothy E. and Albert J. Raboteau (eds) (1997), *African-American Religion: Interpretive Essays in History and Culture*, New York: Routledge.

Genovese, Eugene D. (1976), *Roll, Jordan, Roll: The World the Slaves Made*, New York: Vintage Books.

Herskovits, Melville J. (1924), *The Myth of the Negro Past*, rpt 1990, Boston: Beacon Press.

Hill, Marvin S. (1989), *Quest for Refuge: The Mormon Flight from American Pluralism*, Salt Lake City, UT: Signature Books.

Jenkins, William Sumner (1935), *Proslavery Thought in the Old South*, rpt 1960 Gloucester, MA: Peter Smith.

Lincoln, C. Eric and Lawrence H. Mamiya. (1990), *The Black Church in the African American Experience*, Durham, NC: Duke University Press.

Mathews, Donald G. (1965), *Slavery and Methodism: A Chapter in American Morality, 1780–1845*, Princeton: Princeton University Press.

Metzger, Charles H. (1962), *Catholics and the American Revolution: A Study in Religious Climate*, Chicago: Loyola University Press.

Moore, R. Laurence (1986), *Religious Outsiders and the Making of Americans*, New York: Oxford University Press.

Raboteau, Albert (1978), *Slave Religion: The 'Invisible Institution' in the Antebellum South*, New York: Oxford University Press.

Schwartz, Michael (1984), *The Persistent Prejudice: Anti-Catholicism in America*, Huntington, IN: Our Sunday Visitor.

Sernet, Milton C. (1975), *Black Religion and American Evangelism: White Protestants, Plantation Missions, and the Flowering of Negro Christianity, 1787–1865*, Metuchen, NJ: Scarecrow Press.

Thurman, Howard (1947), *The Negro Spiritual Speaks of Life and Death*, rpt 1975 Richmond, IN: Friends United.

Walls, William J. (1974), *The African Methodist Episcopal Zion Church: Reality of the Black Church*, Charlotte, NC: AME Zion Publishing House.

Wesley, Charles H. (1935), *Richard Allen, Apostle of Freedom*, Washington, DC: Associated Publishers.

Winn, Kenneth H. (1989), *Exiles in a Land of Liberty: Mormons in America, 1830–1846*, Chapel Hill: University of North Carolina Press.

Woodson, Carter G. (1972), *The History of the Negro Church*, Washington, DC: Associated Publishers.

CHAPTER 7

Civil War and the Churches

The American Civil War was a moral war, not because one side was good, the other evil, nor because purity of motive was more pronounced on one side than on the other. Rather, as Sydney Ahlstrom has argued, it was a moral war because it sprang from a moral impasse on issues which Americans in the mid-nineteenth century could no longer avoid or escape. 'Had there been no slavery, there would have been no war. Had there been no moral condemnation of slavery, there would have been no war.'[1]

The Civil War was shaped by politicians seeking secular and material gain, but both the North and South invoked the name of God in their struggle. At the root of the conflict were fundamental disagreements over the morality of slavery and the churches' responsibilities toward the institution. American evangelical churches promoted a theology that had considerable implications for public discourse. They spawned an ecclesiastical sectionalism, and in the process were themselves torn asunder. In 1860 Henry Clay reflected on the importance of those divisions: 'If the churches divide on the subject of slavery, there will be nothing left to bind our people together but trade and commerce.' Let their passions be aroused and they will fight 'even if you show them that ruin to themselves and families will be the probable result'. Divided, and aroused they became, and, much as Clay predicted, fighting and ruin resulted.[2]

Origins of the Antislavery Movement

By the end of the seventeenth century African slavery became an accepted way of life throughout the South, and almost simultaneously the first protests against the South's peculiar institution were heard. The earliest known petition against slavery was published in Pennsylvania in 1688 by Francis Daniel Pastorius. In 1700 Judge Samuel Sewall of Boston published his *Selling of Joseph*, and soon after the Quakers began adding their condemning testimony, most notably in John Woolman's *Considerations on the Keeping of Negroes* (1754).[3]

In the aftermath of the American Revolution, the acceptance of Enlightenment concepts regarding natural rights and human liberty led some denominations to incorporate condemnations of slaveholding in their disciplines. In 1775 the Quakers organized the country's first antislavery society, and in 1776 Anthony Benezet led the Society of Friends in expelling its slaveholding members. John Wesley persuaded the Christmas Conference of 1784, from which American Methodism dates its formal origins, to institute measures that would exclude slave-owners or dealers from membership. This early burst of antislavery vigour did not last, however. As slavery continued to grow and become the source of more heated debate, the Methodist proscription was relaxed, as it was among the other leading denominations. In 1816 some church leaders helped organize the American Colonization Society, whose mission was to encourage manumission by sending former slaves out of the country, especially to its African outpost, Liberia.[4]

If accommodation was the rule for over two centuries, the 1830s would prove to be a turning point. The story of William Lloyd Garrison, the principal leader of the Abolitionist Movement, is representative. In 1829, while running a small Baptist temperance journal, Garrison was converted to the antislavery cause by Benjamin Lundy, a New Jersey Quaker.[5] Garrison helped Lundy publish his *Genius of Universal Emancipation* but was jailed for libel. When he was released, he went to Boston to found *The Public Liberator and Journal of the Times*, in the inaugural issue of which appeared the following pledge:

> I will be harsh as truth, and as uncompromising as justice. On this subject [of slavery] I do not wish to think, or speak, or write with moderation . . . I am in earnest – I will not equivocate – I will not excuse – I will not retreat a single inch – AND I WILL BE HEARD.[6]

No longer a gradualist – urging emancipation sometime 'between now and never' – Garrison, like an increasing number of abolitionists, demanded abolition immediately. 'Immediate emancipation' became the new battle cry, but even Garrison did not insist that slavery cease right away. Rather, he demanded that people decide immediately to renounce slavery, thereby setting the process of emancipation in motion.[7] In 1846 abolitionist Presbyterian minister Albert Barnes spelled out what such a commitment on the part of the nation's churches would mean:

> Let the time come when, in all the mighty denominations of Christians, it can be announced that the evil [slavery] is ceased with them forever; and let the voice of each denomination be lifted up in kind, but firm and solemn testimony against the system . . . and the work is done. There is no public sentiment in this land . . . that would resist the power of such testimony.[8]

As Lyman Beecher said of Garrison, his zeal was commendable but misguided. His absolutism, his lack of charity, his incapacity – or unwillingness – to understand the hesitancy of others, and his branding of the US Constitution a diabolical compact alienated many initially sympathetic Northerners. It provoked heightened Southern opposition to emancipation as well. States in the upper South, including Virginia, debated emancipation until 1830, but the Nat Turner Revolt of 1831 and the growing din of Northern abolitionism of the early 1830s ended that. In 1832 Garrison organized the New England Antislavery Society on a platform of immediatism. In 1833, with the help of the wealthy merchant Arthur Tappan, he established the American Antislavery Society (AAS), and by 1838 the AAS claimed a membership of 250,000.[9]

Adding fervour to the abolitionist movement were the idealism generated by, and expressed publicly by, clerical and lay leaders of the American Revolution and the religious heat of the Second Great Awakening. The Declaration of Independence served as a symbolic bench mark dividing the ages of monarchic despotism from a new era of political liberty and self-determination, and American reformers pictured their own moral revolutions as the fulfilment of their destiny as God's chosen people. Suggestive of this, David Walker, the militant free black abolitionist, concluded his manifesto, *Appeal to the Colored Citizens of the World*, by quoting the Declaration of Independence and exclaiming: 'See your Declaration, Americans!!!'[10]

That same spirit of reform was advanced by the Second Great Awakening, and, in particular, the revival activity of Charles Finney in the Old Northwest. In contrast to the First Great Awakening, the participants of which generally remained silent on more worldly matters, conversion and Christian commitment to a social relevant cause, like antislavery, was an earmark of the Second Awakening. The revivalists believed in a new, more immediate relation between man and God and man and his fellow-creatures – one that emphasized perfectibility rather than inability, activity rather than passivity, benevolence rather than piety.[11]

The Second Great Awakening encouraged abolitionists and most antebellum crusaders to see reform as something akin to an act of repentance. Evangelists instilled in their audiences a sense of personal responsibility for slavery and an obligation to act against it, as sin. In their bleak images of the slaveholder, the slaver and the South, evangelical abolitionists constructed a model of what happened when any people did not conquer their worst cravings. They characterized slaveholders as lazy, irreligious and disrespectful of family, and the slaveholding South as a place where tyranny and disorder prevailed. Moral dissolution turned the South into a cursed land. Such condemnation slighted social, political and economic factors, and it could be narrow and self-righteous, but it had a passion and moral firmness badly needed when men and women agitated unpopular issues in a society where the instinct to compromise was second nature. Immediate emancipation jolted people out of their complacency and infused antislavery with a fervour it did not have before 1830.[12]

In 1834 Theodore Dwight Weld, one of Finney's converts and for a time one of Finney's 'holy band' of assistant revivalists, was also converted to abolitionism, and he brought the antislavery gospel to Lane Theological Seminary in Cincinnati. The seminary students' nearly unanimous indictment of gradualism in the debates that resulted not only produced a number of leading abolitionists, but also provoked administrators to adopt disciplinary measures, which in turn led one vocal group of dissidents to migrate to Oberlin. Oberlin, under the leadership of Asa Mahon and Charles Finney, and with the financial assistance of Arthur and Lewis Tappan of New York – both of whom had also felt Finney's influence – became a centre of both abolitionism and revivalism.[13]

Other influential figures joined forces with the new movement. In 1835 James G Birney, a former slaveholder, then colonizationist, was converted to abolitionism by Theodore Dwight Weld. Birney began his work in Kentucky, but when threatened by mob action he moved to Cincinnati, Ohio, where he began publishing a crusading journal. The murder of Elijah Lovejoy in Alton, Illinois, in 1837 while defending his printing press electrified the North and led even more to conclude that slavery and freedom were incompatible. Among those brought into the movement at that point was Edward Beecher, President of Illinois

College. Beecher not only condemned the Alton riots, but also issued a series of articles on 'organic sin', which gave evangelical abolitionism some of its major ethical and theological insights.[14]

The antislavery axis of Tappan, Garrison, Weld, Lovejoy and Birney was forged, transforming what had been a minor, ineffective protest movement into a nationally organized crusade. The American Anti-Slavery Society printed and distributed thousands of pieces of abolitionist literature, even in the South, and in 1837 it began to encourage and coordinate the circulation of antislavery petitions directed at Congress. In 1840 the American Antislavery Society broke in two over Garrison's insistence on involving women leaders and on nonpolitical moral suasion, but any negative impact on the movement as a whole was brief. Antislavery was soon thoroughly politicized, leading to the creation of the Liberty and Free Soil Parties. As long as antislavery remained a third party issue, it could not carry the day. But as Ronald Walters has concluded: 'In a highly political nation, electioneering and losing can serve as a valuable form of propaganda.' With the rise of the Republican Party in the 1850s, they would lose no more.[15]

As noted earlier, rallying in support of slavery in the South was due to the Nat Turner revolt of 1831 and the inflammatory, vituperative language of the Abolitionist Movement. The South, which had not until that point spoken with one voice on its peculiar institution, rapidly closed ranks. Abolitionist hopes for an awakening of Southern slaveholders' consciences were dashed, and an elaborate scriptural argument that soothed Christian consciences on slavery was fused with a new Southern nationalism. By the 1850s treatises by Thomas Dew, John C. Calhoun, Edmund Ruffin, Henry Hughes, William Grayson, George Fitzhugh and others provided elaborate sociological defences of African slavery, often by comparing it to the 'wage slavery' of the North. Southern clergy added appeals to slaveholders to live up to the ideals expounded in those treatises and to treat their slaves humanely.[16]

Proslavery literature involved an effort to construct a coherent Southern social philosophy. In defending what they referred to as the cornerstone of their social order, Southerners presented a world-view that included social legitimization and their self-conscious definition of themselves. Non-evangelical Southerners responded to antislavery polemics with anger and indignation. Southern evangelicals responded differently. They found it necessary to challenge the abolitionist's premise that slavery was a sin before God.[17]

Southern evangelicals argued that scripture sanctioned slavery in passages like Genesis 14: 14, Leviticus 25: 44–55 and I Corinthians 7: 21–4. They pointed to the Old Testament story of Ham. In summary form, they explained that Noah had three sons, Ham, Shem and Japeth, from whom the earth was populated. One day when Noah lay in a drunken stupour, Ham, the father of Canaan, saw his nakedness. He told Shem and Japeth, who covered their father without looking at him. Upon waking, Noah realized what had happened and cursed Ham. 'Cursed be Canaan; a servant of servants shall he be unto his brethren.' Noah blessed Shem, adding that Canaan would be his servant, and prophesied that God would 'enlarge Japeth', who would dwell in the tents of Shem and be served by Canaan as well (Genesis 9: 20–9). Southerners understood Ham to be black, Japeth white, and Shem Indian – all prototypes of the races of America, thus offering one resolution to a tension in white Southern Christian thought: how blacks could be fellow-human beings and yet deserve to be slaves.[18]

Turning to the New Testament, Southern evangelicals pointed out that Christ and his apostles, though living where it existed and was recognized by Roman law, did not denounce slavery. Indeed they received into the church slaves and slaveholders alike and called upon slaves to be obedient to their masters, and masters to act with humanity toward their slaves. Why should things be any different in the Christian South? As Mark Noll has pointed out, the South was largely successful in its exegetical defence of slavery through direct appeal to Scripture, forcing Northern clergy to find other grounds for their claim of slavery's sinfulness. Their appeal to a Higher Law to condemn slavery constituted not an appeal to the Bible but to an individual conscience that stood above not only the Constitution but also the revealed Word of God.[19]

Southern Christian missions to the slaves burgeoned during the 1840s and 1850s. Such missions, Southern evangelicals insisted, provided 'a most merciful deliverance' from the 'savage idolatry' of unredeemed Africa to a Christian land where they became 'the most contented and happy people on earth'. In sum, as Carwardine has concluded, Southerner evangelicals 'accepted slavery not because it was a positive good, but because it was consistent with Scripture and involved fewer evils than would result from emancipation'.[20]

It should be noted that although quite effective, the enormous pressures for conformity were never entirely successful in eliminating Southern opposition to slavery. There were clergy who dissented from the Southern proslavery position, and they paid a dear price for that dissent. Given their low profile, their exact numbers cannot be determined, but they were a distinct minority. Most were located in the upper South, as was true of dissent in the general population. Even there, however, making their sentiments known, or having them discovered, often led to severe punishment (frequently at the hands of mobs), imprisonment and even death.[21]

Antislavery and the Churches

Church history was intrinsic to both Northern and Southern anti- and proslavery developments. The many voluntary associations for evangelism and moral reform became inseparable from the humanitarian crusades that marked the firsthalf of the nineteenth century, including the antislavery movement. The churches were slow in joining the antislavery cause, but as the movement gained momentum the countless auxiliary organizations of mainstream Protestantism became radiating centres of concern and agitation. The national antislavery societies, now moribund and faction-ridden, were superseded by ecclesiastical organizations in which an antislavery social gospel was forging ahead, winning new leaders, trampling on compromisers and bringing schism or conflict when the occasion demanded.[22]

Black involvement in the antislavery movement is best known for the efforts of prominent figures such as Frederick Douglass, Sojourner Truth and Harriet Tubman. Less well known and underestimated are the efforts of black ministers. Similarly, clerical efforts to undermine slavery were not limited to a few notables; they can be seen among black ministers in small parishes and on the itinerant circuit, who 'despite their less favorable circumstances, were able to stoke the fires of antislavery sentiment by suggesting new options to the black folks who heard them from day to day'. Like white abolitionist, black ministers were also most active after 1830, in their case because their churches had weathered the storms of organization, legitimacy and autonomy by then and could act with greater confidence and experience.[23]

Participation in antislavery activities did create a black clerical elite. They tended to belong to traditionally white churches. They interacted with white abolitionists and were generally freer and better situated to be visibly active. Among their ranks were Congregationalists Amos Beman and Charles Ray, Episcopalians Alexander Crummell and Peter Williams, Presbyterians Samuel Cornish and Theodore Wright, and others. A much larger group of ministers served in middle-class or historically black churches (for example the African Methodist Episcopal [AME] Church), while most worked in small congregations and on itinerant circuits. We know very little about the second two groups. Their actions were less public and their sermons seldom found their way into print.[24]

Most black ministers opposed slavery through the counselling of their church members in self-respect and a 'higher manhood' and by providing aid to fugitives, often at stations on the underground railroad. Some offered ideological support and even antislavery activism, but most offered constant support for moral reform. Their theology, like that of most of their white abolitionist ministerial colleagues, was nineteenth-century evangelical Protestant, but it was more heavily weighted in the direction of a human god and liberating Christology. Carol George has written:

> They took special pains to balance the claims of the sacred and the secular, a reflection, in part, of the duality of Protestantism itself. More than that, it was the result of seeing God acting in history on behalf of oppressed people.

Nevertheless, as the Civil War approached, black ministers lived in an increasingly dangerous world. As one AME minister put it: 'Every colored man is an abolitionist, and slaveholders know it.'[25]

The South witnessed the anomaly of its equally fervent religiosity and equally strident moralism marked by a diametrically opposed view of slavery, that can be accounted for only with reference to their different cultural conditions and ethics. As Sydney Ahlstrom put it: 'The South channeled the social impact of evangelicalism and its perfectionist demands against the weaker provinces of Satan's kingdom.' In other words, it was used to keep the work of the evangelical united front aimed at the tasks it had pursued before 1830.[26]

Slavery was not entirely ignored. Richard Furman's biblical argument was adopted by the South Carolina Baptist Association in 1822, and by 1841, when John England, the Roman Catholic bishop of Charleston, published his defence of slavery, this line of thought had sunk deep into the Southern consciousness. Theologians and laity alike learned to recite the standard biblical texts on African inferiority, patriarchal and Mosaic acceptance of servitude and Saint Paul's counsels of obedience to masters. Evangelization of the slaves was pursued with increased vigour, at the same time that the emotionalism of revivalism contributed to extremist views on slavery in the South, as it had in the North. As the nation reached mid-century, evangelicals both in the North and South became increasingly more polarized and less willing to compromise.[27]

Churches Rent Assunder

William Lloyd Garrison never anticipated that abolitionism would cause any conflict within American churches. He and others in the antislavery movement were church leaders 'tenacious of their theological views, [and] full of veneration for the organized church and ministry', confident that both would rally to their cause. They never dreamed that their opposition to the nation's 'distinctive, all-conquering sin' would breed such opposition and divide American denominations so badly. Those clergy who had not yet spoken out on slavery were simply preoccupied with subjects nearer home or ignorant of the true nature of the institution.[28]

Even the ranks of the Quakers, who were the first to oppose slavery in large numbers, were divided – not on the issue of slavery, of which they were rid, but on abolition. Benjamin Lundy, James and Lucretia Mott and others actively engaged in abolition, but theirs were individual efforts, and many of their co-religionists refused to join them. Moreover, antislavery was a factor in the struggle between 1827 and 1829 that led to separations within Quaker meetings. Elias Hicks, whose principles precipitated those separations, authored the antislavery pamphlet *Observations on the Slavery of the Africans and Their Descendents* (1810), in which he urged Friends to boycott rice, cotton, and sugar, as long as they were products of slave labour. Hicks primary concerns were doctrinal, however, and the Hicksites were not necessarily antislavery.[29]

Similarly, the Presbyterian church did not explicitly divide on the issue of slavery until after secession. The Old School–New School division of 1837 can be regarded as the first great ecclesiastical North–South separation. Old School men had grown suspicious of the new kind of revivalism that swept the nation after 1800. Many were suspicious of its growing emphasis on conversion and religious experience, and disturbed by the apparent corresponding laxity with regard to doctrine and the sacraments. They were also sceptical of the results of an alliance New England Presbyterians had entered into with Congregationalists – the Plan of Union – whereby the two worked toward interdenominational harmony and the championing of evangelical Christianity on the region's sparsely settled frontier. By the 1830s, however, Old School Southern Presbyterians began to sense a growing antislavery spirit in the New School. That spirit, though not explicitly articulated, underscored the accusations of heresy and complicity exchanged at the Presbyterian Assembly of 1837, and that led to the two groups' separation. Antislavery memorials presented to the General Assembly of 1837 were tabled without discussion, and four synods representing the 'New School' were expelled, even though they were supported by some 60,000 Presbyterians, all in the North.[30]

In 1818 the General Assembly of the undivided Presbyterian church unanimously adopted a manifesto that declared the institution of slavery 'utterly inconsistent with the law of God'. It also voted, however, that 'hasty emancipation' was an even 'greater curse'. This compromise continued to mark the official position of both the New and Old Schools after 1837. Both continued to have minorities that represented anti- and proslavery positions, and leaders of both factions feared further divisions.[31]

Within the New School more and more members made their antislavery sentiments known. The Reverend Albert Barnes of New Jersey published the influential *Inquiry into the Scriptural View of Slavery* (1846). In 1846 and 1849 a few churches even left the New School to form an antislavery union, but it was shortlived. Finally, in 1850 the New School General Assembly repudiated the view that slavery was a divinely sanctioned institution. In 1853 it took steps to implement that position and tension increased until, in 1857, the small number of remaining proslavery presbyteries withdrew to form their own assembly. After the war it merged with the Old School Church, South. The Old School Church was more successful in suppressing any official discussion of the slavery issue until 1861, when the newly constituted Presbyterian Church of the Confederate States of America declared: 'We have no right, as a church, to enjoin [slavery] as a duty, or to condemn it as a sin.'[32]

The Methodist Church was just as poorly equipped to deal with the slavery controversy. It was organized in a strict and inflexible way, so that disagreements over matters of consequence had to be formally resolved at a national level. Thus, when it sought to extend its membership into the South, Methodists were forced to modify John Wesley's original regulations on slavery. By 1843 there were 1200 Methodist ministers and preachers owning about 1500 slaves, and 25,000 members with about 208,000 slaves. If the church was going to maintain its unity, it would have to maintain a strict neutrality and silence on the slavery question. By 1836 neither was any longer possible.[33]

At first the Methodists followed the Presbyterians' example. At their General Conference of 1836 Methodists formally conceded the evils of slavery, but they condemned as well, in very forceful terms, 'modern abolitionism'. This measure managed to get the church through its annual meeting in one piece, but it only incited the increasing number of Methodist abolitionists, led by the Vermont circuit preacher Orange Scott. Scott, influenced by William Lloyd Garrison and the *Liberator*, turned the Methodist organ, *Zion's Herald*, to antislavery, while his 'Appeal to the Methodist Episcopal Church', printed in 1838 in the *Wesleyan Anti-Slavery Review*, made the struggle within the church for a change in its stern anti-abolitionist policy inevitable.[34]

By the General Conference of 1844 a sizable number of Methodists was prepared to call for separation. The debate was precipitated by an outcry over the slaveholding of Bishop James Andrew of Georgia. When a motion to force Andrew to 'desist from the exercise of his functions' as long as he owned slaves passed – voted along sectional lines – all was lost. Neither side was willing to compromise and the two sides agreed to 'an amicable plan of separation', in which the two groups pledged to remain in fellowship with each other.[35]

On 1 May 1845, the Methodist Episcopal Church, South, was born at a convention in Louisville, Kentucky. Since the South had been able to stave off any attempt to condemn slavery in the undivided church, no changes in the new church's constitution were necessary. In the North, however, the process of reorganization did not go as smoothly. Northern Methodists condemned the Compromise of 1850, but they did not formally commit themselves to the Abolitionist Movement. Instead, foreshadowing the response of Lincoln and Unionists to Southern secession, when word of the separation of Southern Methodist congregations reached the membership in the North, several leaders, including abolitionists, issued charges of unconstitutionality. At the 1848 General Conference, the South's delegate was rebuffed and the Plan of Separation declared null and void. The Northern Methodist Church did not redress its actions of 1848 by sending a delegate southward until 1872; by then the issue of slavery had been settled, but not separation. Northern and Southern Methodists had gone their own way.[36]

Finally, there were the Baptists. In theory, the Baptists were better prepared for the challenge of slavery than either the Presbyterians or Methodists, in that their polity was primarily congregational; Baptist national organization was no more than a cooperative agency of the churches, a 'General Convention . . . for Foreign Missions'. Founded in 1814 to support missionaries to foreign countries, the Convention met triennially, after 1832 in conjunction with the new Home Missionary Society. During the volatile 1830s, the Convention managed to avoid the issue of slavery. In 1840 antislavery Baptists organized the National Baptist Anti-Slavery Convention and tried to force the issue among their brethren. In the same year, however, the Foreign Missions Board formally declared its neutrality, and in 1843 it was supported in this by the General Convention.[37]

The Anti-Slavery Convention continued to meet and to agitate, and by 1844 abolitionism gained in both numbers and stridency among Baptists in the North. Antislavery talk began to be heard in state conventions, and soon both mission boards were faced with decisions deliberately thrust upon them by the South in an attempt to head off any actions by the North. In October 1844 the Home Board declined to appoint as a missionary the nominee of the General Baptist Convention, James Reeves, because he was a slaveholder. It insisted, however, that it would continue to embrace slaveholding members and contributions.[38]

Two months later the Foreign Board took a similar position when petitioned to state its policy by the Alabama Baptist Convention. The Southern response was predictable. They called for a meeting of their similarly aggrieved brethren to take a united stand against what they saw at the aggression of their Northern brethren. Delegates from nine states met on 8 May 1845 in Augusta, Georgia, and gave birth to the Southern Baptist Convention. Its first regular triennial session was held in 1846. The Southern Baptist Convention issued no formal statement on slavery. Northern Baptists avoided further division by retaining their congregational format, but their American Baptist Missionary Union excluded proslavery members from its ranks.[39]

Churches that Escaped Schism

None of the several American churches of the antebellum period could escape the impact of the slavery debate. Some, however, were able to escape the full brunt of its divisiveness. Some of those churches were able to survive schism because they did not have significant membership in both regions, North and South. Congregationalists and Unitarians, for example, not only made their antislavery position public but also made major contributions to the antislavery movement. Their members, however, were almost entirely from the North and increasingly anti-slavery.[40]

Other churches – the Lutheran, Episcopal and Roman Catholic churches, for example – remained undivided until secession. Despite their having comparatively large constituencies in the North and South and contributing vigorous polemicists to both sides of the controversy, they were able to avoid any showdown on the matter. Lutheran synods and Episcopal and Roman Catholic dioceses tended to be organized on a territorial basis, thereby limiting the meeting of controversial issues at the national level. The Lutheran General Synod, for example, which did take a strong antislavery stand, had little more than advisory or coordinating functions, thereby leaving each territorial synod to deal with the issue much as it chose.[41]

The general conventions of the Episcopal Church did provide the opportunity for controversy, but the church was able to avoid schism by remaining extraordinarily passive. Historians remain divided in explaining this, but they agree that Episcopalians were generally conservative and satisfied with the *status quo*. In the end, separate dioceses could and did adapt themselves to local conditions with no interference from above.[42]

The Roman Catholic Church was unique among all the previously mentioned American denominations in that it was international, and the official position of the church in the antebellum period – issued from the Vatican – was that slavery as a principle of social organization was not in itself sinful. In 1838 Pope Gregory XVI did reiterate the church's condemnation of the slave trade, but not slavery itself. As Archbishop of Baltimore, thereby occupying the most influential post in the American hierarchy, Bishop Francis Kenrick continually sought to interpret the church's teachings on slavery. He regretted that there were so many slaves whose liberty and education were so restricted, but he otherwise equivocated, thereby placing himself much in the same company with episcopal leaders who favoured the *status quo*.[43]

Much the same can be said of the pastoral letters of the assembled American Catholic bishops, which studiously avoided any reference to the national dilemma. The single exception was a letter of 1840 in which the bishops made an ambiguous, indirect allusion to the nation's political parties having avoided the issue of slavery. Historians have interpreted that letter as an admission that the hierarchy was divided, and divided it remained. Even when the war came and churches existed in the Union and Confederacy, the church at large maintained its position on slavery, while bishops North and South continued to keep in contact with each other 'so far as circumstances would allow'.[44]

One last interesting example of compromise comes from none other than the African Methodist Episcopal Church. When a majority report on slavery, denying membership to those who held slaves, was presented to the 1856 AME general convention, it was labelled radical and hotly debated. Obviously, there were few slaveholders, if any, in their ranks, but they feared that adoption of the proposed measure would result in closings of its Southern congregations and encourage the intimidation of its itinerants in border states. The convention passed a milder compromise report.[45]

Historian William Warren Sweet has argued that 'there are good reasons to support the claim that the split in the churches was not only the first break between the sections, but the chief cause of the final break'. Churchmen played leading roles in the moral revolutions that swept the North and South in opposite directions between 1830 and 1860. Churchmen converted the antislavery movement into a massive juggernaut and dedicated the South to preserving a biblically supported social order. To both causes they transmitted the overcharged intensity of revivalism, carrying it even to the troops when war finally came. 'We are charged with having brought about the present contest', declared northern Methodist Granville Moody in 1861. 'I believe it is true that we did bring it about, and I glory in it, for it is a wreath of glory around our brow.' Ministers on both sides of the Mason–Dixon Line shared Moody's sentiment.[46]

The Churches amid Civil War

'When the cannons roared in Charleston Harbor . . . two divinely authorized crusades were set in motion, each of them absolutizing a given social and political order. The pulpits resounded with a vehemence and absence of restraint never equaled in American history.' So wrote Sydney Ahlstrom in his assessment of the churches' role in the American Civil War. Once disunion was a reality politically, so too it became an ecclesiastical reality. Even those churches that had not formally divided, professed their patriotism in unquestionable terms.

Northern clergy who believed slavery was an institutional evil, but were reluctant to resort to war for its destruction, now saw no alternative. Southern clergy who accepted slavery as a necessary evil, and opposed secession in its defence, no longer had any choice.[47]

At its meeting in 1862, the General Synod of the Lutheran Church, now without its Southern members, appointed a special committee to apprise President Abraham Lincoln of its whole-hearted support, characterizing the 'rebellion' as most wicked, unjustifiable, unnatural, inhuman, oppressive and 'destructive in its results to the highest interests of morality and religion'. Southern Presbyterians, who had with equal vigour insisted on neutrality on the issue of slavery, also shifted their position. In the same year, they expressed their deep conviction 'that this struggle is not alone for civil rights and property and home, but also for religion, for the church, for the gospel, for existence itself'.[48]

Not only did the churches attest to their respective governments and armies through sermon and prayer, but also they actively participated in the war effort by bringing a Christian ministry to the soldiers and by organizing noncombatant support among their constituencies. A remarkably large number of chaplains volunteered, and they carried on their ministries with astounding success, actually precipitating revivals among the rank and file. Estimates of conversions vary between 100,000 and 200,000, but regardless of the exact number many agreed with J. William Jones, a chaplain in Lee's Army of Northern Virginia, that

> any history of that army which omits an account of the wonderful influence of religion upon it – which fails to tell how the courage, discipline, and morale of the whole was influenced by the humble piety and evangelical zeal of many of its officers and men – would be incomplete and unsatisfactory.

As Ahlstrom found: 'A fervently pious nation was at war, and amid the carnage and slaughter, amid the heroism and weariness, men on both sides hungered for inspiration and peace with God'. Dedicated ministers on both sides responded, and on both sides 'the soldier's sense of duty was deepened, his morale improved, his loyalty intensified'. Perhaps the war itself was lengthened, as well, and its carnage made worse.[49]

More complicated is the various ways in which the churches interpreted the Civil War. Historians have argued that the crisis significantly modified Americans' theological understanding of history. Such interpretations did not surface, however, until the war was at an end and more patriotic stances were neither no longer needed nor viable. In some ways post-war assessments reflected earlier positions; in other cases they were quite different. Ministers on both sides, however, asked themselves why they had fought and why so many of their number had died.[50]

At the war's end, in both the North and South, there were feelings of relief, dejection and smouldering rage. In the South, Father Abram Ryan, Confederate chaplain, gave voice to what many surely continued to believe when he wrote that the South would 'keep watch over the Stars and Bars until the morning of the Resurrection'. Their hearts would remain with the Lost Cause even after they had been defeated on the battlefield.[51]

Similarly, Southern Presbyterian theologian Robert Lewis Dabney, who had served as adjutant under Stonewall Jackson, continued to insist that the war had been caused deliberately by abolitionists who 'with calculated malice' goaded the South to violence in order to revolutionize the government and 'gratify their spite'. 'I do not forgive', he declared. 'What! Forgive those people, who have invaded our country, burned our cities, destroyed our homes, slain our young men, and spread desolation and ruin over our land! No, I do not forgive them.' He continued to yearn for a 'retributive Providence' that would demolish the North and abolish the Union.[52]

Henry Ward Beecher took a page from Lincoln's Second Inaugural Address and counselled compassion for the South, but he, like most in the North, mourned the war dead and the loss of his leader, nearly deified by an assassin's bullet. His indictment of the South was no less direct and only slightly more temperate than Dabney's condemnation of the North:

> I charge the whole guilt of this war upon the ambitious, educated, plotting political leaders of the South . . . A day will come when God will reveal judgment and arraign these mighty miscreants . . . and every maimed and wounded sufferer, and every bereaved heart in all the wide regions of this land, will rise up and come before the Lord to lay upon these chief culprits of modern history their awful witness . . . And then these guiltiest and most remorseless traitors, these high and cultured men with might and wisdom . . . shall be whirled aloft and plunged downward forever and ever in an endless retribution.[53]

Some Northern clergy made note of the wrath God had already unleashed on the South – as promised in her battle hymn by Julia Ward How – but saw the resultant desolation as deserved. Theodore Munger, a pastor-theologian in New Haven, Connecticut, was representative of this group when he explained in his essay on 'Providence and the War' – two decades after Appomattox – the divine logic by which the South had been punished for its sins, with the North as the 'sacrificing instrument'. Not only had a deathblow been dealt to a diabolical slave state so that America could realize its destiny, but also justice had been done in a most devastating manner, appropriate to the nature and severity of the crime or sin.[54]

Yet another group of theologians was less confident of God's intentions in the war. Some Southern evangelicals found the answer to their questions about defeat in the individual vices and sins of their own people, rather than in the shape and fabric of their empire. Otherwise, they could only make reference to God's will. God, wrote a Georgia Baptist editor in 1866, 'has done what He thought best'. He may have 'laid His hand heavily upon us; certainly we are deeply smitten, but in the midst of it all, we rely on His goodness, and would not, if we could, interfere with the workings of His providence'.[55]

A Virginia editor could not believe that God had designed the Civil War to overthrow slavery, an institution which God himself 'ordained, established and sanctioned' forever. He could not have intended that an 'inferior race might be released from a nominal bondage and endowed with a freedom which, to them, is but another name for licentiousness, and which must end in complete extermination'. He concluded: 'It was Satan that ruled the hour of emancipation.' For this editor and others in the South the war settled the problem of power, not of morality.[56]

Northern views of historical events could be ambiguous as well, and less than certain of their own or their region's moral purity. Agents of both the North and South, they occasionally alleged, shared complicity in the institution of slavery to which God was so opposed that he plunged the nation into war. These clergy searched for a way of seeing the entire tragedy – its triumphs and defeats, on both sides – as meaningful to the nation as a whole. Though perhaps no less certain of the nation's destiny, they saw the need to bring all Americans, not just Southerners, to penitence, reformation and reconciliation with God as His chosen people.[57]

Horace Bushnell of Massachusetts was a spokesman for this position, as was Philip Schaff of Pennsylvania. So too was Abraham Lincoln, perhaps no less a student of the Bible, in his own way. Bushnell and Schaff held the special view that suffering was the instrument by which the nation would be purged of the sins that had brought about the conflict and experience a new birth. Both used the symbol 'baptism by blood'. According to Schaff: 'This very baptism of blood entitles us also to hope for a glorious regeneration.' By references to the Crucifixion and vicarious sacrifice, Bushnell sought to explain the suffering and sacrifice of the war as an act of expiation of corporate sin, thereby opening the way for the atonement of the nation.[58]

Bushnell said that the great sin for which the nation was suffering was the failure in the founding of the nation to recognize that God must be the author of a true and lasting community. He believed that the war would result in a new national consciousness which would rest on a deeper foundation than the illusion of a man-made compact. So too Schaff saw the possibility of a new and redeemed sense of nationhood rising out of the death and carnage. What he added was a more pronounced sense that the war had ultimately readied America for its great role in the cause of human freedom, thereby identifying the war as an event of world-historical significance.[59]

And then there were Lincoln's Gettysburg and Second Inaugural Addresses. In those, his supreme statements on the war, Lincoln too expounded on the significance of the war for an 'almost chosen people'. He never lost hold of the proposition that nations and men are instruments of Almighty God. As he explained in his Second Inaugural, referred to by Ronald White as 'Lincoln's Sermon on the Mount', while the war was still being waged: 'Both parties deprecated war; but one of them would make war rather than let the nation survive; and the other would accept war rather than let it perish'. 'Both read the same Bible', he continued, 'and pray to the same God; and each invokes His aid against the other . . . [But] the prayers of both could not be answered'; and indeed even the North's had not been answered fully.[60]

Turning directly to that matter over which the war had been fought, Lincoln reasoned: 'If we shall suppose that American slavery is one of those offenses which, in the providence of God', had to be, it had 'continued through its appointed time', and God now willed that it be removed. Toward that end God had given both the North and South this terrible war, as the woe due to those by whom the offence came. 'Fondly do we hope – fervently do we pray', he continued, 'that this mighty scourge of war may speedily pass away. Yet, if God will that it continue . . . so still it must be said the judgments of the Lord are true and righteous altogether.' Lincoln concluded his inaugural by confirming his belief in the Union, one nation under God with a moral purpose, which had undergone a great and tragic test of its central proposition, but could be born again by way of charity toward the vanquished:

> With malice toward none; with charity for all; with firmness in the right, as God gives us to see the right, let us strive on to finish the work we are in; to bind up the nation's wounds; to care for him who shall have borne the battle, and for his widow, and his orphan – to do all which may achieve and cherish a just, and a lasting peace, among ourselves, and with all nations.[61]

It would take decades for most Americans to see their way to Lincoln's call for charity.

Reconstruction and the Churches

For most Southerners reconstruction meant one thing: to put back the pieces so far as possible in the way they were in 1860. When the old social and economic structure fell, the South began erecting a new structure, a bi-racial social and economic order, on the foundation of its old philosophy. The South's new philosophy was in part a yearning for a simpler, lost civilization, but it also bolstered Southern resistance to federal control of the region under radical Republican reconstruction and, ultimately, the New South that resulted.[62]

Few Southern whites advocated re-enslavement, but most continued to envision blacks as slavelike inferiors. They remained determined to keep blacks entrenched as a subordinate labouring class. They clutched dearly to every remaining shred of racial control, and added some new methods. They resurrected virtually all of the old rationales for en-slaving blacks. As one historian put it: 'Though many of the more obscure and theoretical aspects' of the proslavery argument 'became moot points after 1865, death of slavery failed to destroy the institu-tion's intellectual foundation'. The Lost Cause became the central religious myth of the time. As Phillip Paludan has put it, the Lost Cause

> anointed not just a status quo but also a status pre-quo – a world of the past that the future celebrated. Little reform was possible when the most Christian of acts was to try to live up to the standards of a slave society in the name and memory of the pure white soldiers who had died. The white southerner's conviction was that 'his regional values and cultural symbols were holy'.[63]

Northerners, by and large, believed that God had vindicated their cause, and they presumed God would stand with them in support of repressive policies against the defeated South. To justify the killing, in often strident, self-righteous terms, they clamoured for change, for the rebuilding of the South in such manner as the ideals for which they believed the war had been fought would not be lost. 'The Devil is in the people of the South', one preacher proclaimed, and he needed to be exorcised. The result was an unprecedented time of testing of resolve that had mixed results. In time Republican reconstruction would give way to political reality, or compromise, and after 1877, which marked the end of Southern occupation, the 'solid South' would rise again. The South would embark on its own course, remaining profoundly separate in its own mind and memory and in its own distinctive religious history.[64]

Northern churches provided the major institutional context in which the antislavery impulse could thrive during the Civil War, and they provided a place for its survival during Reconstruction, even when much of the rest of the nation lost interest. During Reconstruction, Union armies made substantial inroads on Confederate territory, and the Northern Protestant churches were a mainstay of the Radical programme. They regarded themselves as the custodians of the moral factor in the entire sectional crisis, and with the coming of peace they remained the chief popular support for the political leaders who wished to prevent any compromise. This involved them inescapably in the Republican strategies which were designed to prevent or delay the rise of the politically potent South. Yet the needs of the freedman and a grim determination to reform the South best explain why the churches made Reconstruction an extension of the antislavery crusade and why they won such powerful support.[65]

Exalted principles were more easily formulated than implemented. Republicans learned that social structures, tradition and the legacy of slavery could not be transformed by governmental fiat. Yet recovery and even advances were made. The Bureau of Refugees, Freedmen, and Abandoned Lands, established in 1865, never did fulfill the freedman's hope for a place on lands abandoned during the war, but it did ease his transition from bondage to freedom. The cause of civil rights, then and later, was advanced by the Civil Rights Act of 1866, as it was by the Thirteenth Amendment (1865), which abolished slavery, the Fourteenth Amendment (1868), which incorporated the principles of the Civil Rights Act and forbade the abridgement of any citizen's privileges or immunities, and the Fifteenth Amendment (1870), which guaranteed to all citizens the right to vote.[66]

Though not all men acted with pure motives, it is unfair and misleading to deny the reality of most Radical Republican leaders' moral fervour and humanitarian idealism. The efforts of Northern churchmen in this regard can be seen in the hundreds of relief associations they organized throughout the South, even while the war continued to be fought. To coordinate this work the United States Commission for the Relief of the National Freedman was formed in 1863 followed by the American Freedman's Union Commission (AFUC), organized in 1866 to embrace a still larger range of such societies. After 1869 Congress took increasing control of Reconstruction and freedman's aid, and the activities of the AFUC declined. Nevertheless, several denominational societies continued to act independently. The Northern Presbyterians organized their freedmen's commission in 1864, the Methodists their much more vigourous Freedman's Aid Society in 1866. By far the most effective of these church-oriented agencies, however, was the American Missionary Association, founded in 1846 by the merger of several small societies of Congregational origin who shared a missionary commitment to nonwhite peoples and a strong antislavery bent. By the end of the war it had 528 missionaries and teachers at work in the South.[67]

Church efforts in the South were not limited to humanitarian efforts. They also pursued ecclesiastical changes – described by Martin Marty as 'spiritual imperialism' – with similarly mixed results. The three large denominations that had divided over slavery projected plans for displacing the Southern branches of their denominations. Because the Southern schismatics had proclaimed slavery as God's will, they were now considered disqualified from church membership. As one church organ put it: 'The apostate church is buried beneath a flood of divine wrath; its hideous dogmas shine on its brow like flaming fiends; the whole world stands aghast at its wickedness and ruin. The northern church beholds its mission.'[68]

The mission, however, was not easily achieved. Although some large churches did at one time or another use the opportunities provided by military occupation to occupy Southern churches, their efforts at converting the membership to their ways ultimately failed. Presbyterians, Methodists and Baptists remained divided. The only successful reunion efforts among the larger churches were carried out by the Episcopal and

Roman Catholic churches. In those churches, as we have seen, a diocesan polity and a record of ambivalent moderation on the central issues allowed for reunion.[69]

When Southern Episcopalians organized the Protestant Episcopal Church, Confederate States of America, in 1861, they did so with no changes of doctrine, polity or liturgy. The Northern church merely noted the absence of Southern representatives at the 1862 meeting of its General Convention. Three years later unity was restored with a minimum of bitterness. The Roman Catholic Church could not formally divide, inasmuch as the Holy See was outside and above the conflict. When hostilities ceased, the hierarchy resumed its normal functioning, and in the Plenary Council of 1866 all of the country's dioceses were represented. Neither the Episcopal nor the Catholic church sought to press reconstructionist policies on their Southern dioceses.[70]

The chief new ecclesiastical development of the era of Reconstruction was neither reconquest nor reunion of the alienated regions, but rather the rise of independent black churches from their Baptist and Methodist origins. These churches played a significant role during Reconstruction when the Federal army, the Freedman's Bureau and the Union Leagues utilized them to strengthen Radical Republican power. But after 1877 they, too, became a part of the 'Southern solution' (segregation, subservience and tenantry), not to emerge as a radical social force again until the 1950s. Nevertheless, these churches grew apace during the late nineteenth century and gradually developed a distinctive religious ethos which traditional denominational allegiances could neither submerge nor alter. Through a long and bitter century they became the chief bearers of the African-American heritage.[71]

Summary

Abolition was no mere political slogan. As Louis Filler has written: 'Certainly, economic and political motives for abolition had operated largely to free the North of slavery, and they would continue to affect northern opinion . . . But divorced from moral considerations, they tended to become impotent.' The union of politics and morality was not forged until the 1830s, but once forged it became a force that would not, perhaps could not, be stopped or even curtailed until the issue of slavery was resolved. An important step in that direction would be forcing national institutions – not just local or regional institutions – to repudiate slavery. In some cases, as we have seen, for churches as well as other institutions, and ultimately the nation itself, such pressure would result in disunion.[72]

The Civil War was the turning point in the emergence of the new nation. It meant the establishment of a unified national life and the beginning of the American emergence with growing power in the community of nations. Such unity would take time. The wounds of war needed to be healed and sectional tensions eased, and nowhere was that more apparent than in the nation's major churches.

Civil War and Reconstruction not only led to ecclesiastical divisions but also left decidedly different spiritual stamps on the South and North. In the South the fruits of war and defeat bore a tragic sense of life, that lived on in Southern churches when Northern leaders developed ideas and programmes based on progress and optimism. Southern pastors had to minister to more people who were in abject poverty and for whom this world held little hope. They accented the deferred benefits in the life to come, while Northerners would continue to emphasize the post-millennial line of the antebellum evangelical empire and talk about how America might yet be transformed into the Kingdom of God.[73]

In victory Northern evangelicals saw God's sign that the political and moral positions of the Union had been vindicated. The Reverend Henry Ward Beecher spoke of this righteous empire:

We are to have the charge of this continent. [The South] has been proved, and has been found wanting. She is not worthy to bear rule . . . This continent is to be from this time forth governed by Northern men, with Northern ideas, and with a Northern gospel . . . [because] the North has been true to the cause of Christ.[74]

In 1865 the Reverend C. B. Boynton, chaplain of the House of Representatives, described to members of Congress gathered for a Thanksgiving service his expectations for the future:

The American nation occupies a position never held by any people before. It stands the representative and champion of a true Christian democracy in church and state . . . We stand on the threshold of this new era the mightiest Christian nation on earth . . . mighty through the teaching of war . . . with a national life strong enough to control a continent, and which will brook no dictation from a foreign power.[75]

Notes

1. Sydney E. Ahlstrom (1972), *A Religious History of the American People* (New Haven: Yale University Press), p. 649.

2. John R. McKivigan (1984), *The War against Proslavery Religion: Abolitionism and the Northern Churches, 1830–1865* (Ithaca, NY: Cornell University Press), p. 18; Richard J. Carwardine (1993), *Evangelicals and Politics in Antebellum America* (New Haven: Yale University Press), p. 323.

3. Ahlstrom, *Religious History of the American People*, pp. 649–50.

4. Ahlstrom, *Religious History of the American People*, p. 650; McKivigan, *War against Proslavery Religion*, p. 25; Ronald G. Walters (1978), *American Reformers, 1815–1860* (New York: Hill and Wang), p. 78; Carwardine, *Evangelicals and Politics in Antebellum America*, p. 141.

5. Gerald Sorin (1972), *Abolitionism: A New Perspective* (New York: Praeger Publishers), p. 49.

6. William E. Cain (ed.) (1995), *William Lloyd Garrison and the Fight against Slavery: Selections from the Liberator* (Boston: Bedford Books), p. 72.

7. Walters, *American Reformers*, p. 79.

8. McKivigan, *War against Proslavery Religion*, pp. 7, 40–3.

9. McKivigan, *War against Proslavery Religion*, p. 13; Carwardine, *Evangelicals and Politics in Antebellum America*, p. 140; Walters, *American Reformers*, p. 80; Russel B. Nye (1955), *William Lloyd Garrison and the Humanitarian Reformers* (Boston: Little, Brown and Company).

10. David Brion Davis (1984), *Slavery and Human Progress* (New York: Oxford University Press), pp. 150–1.

11. Sorin, *Abolitionism*, pp. 44–5; Davis, *Slavery and Human Progress*, p. 136; Gilbert H. Barnes (1933; 1964), *The Anti-Slavery Impulse, 1830–1844* (New York: Harcourt, Brace and World), pp. 3–16; McKivigan, *War against Proslavery Religion*, p. 19; George M. Fredrickson (1998), 'The coming of the Lord: The Northern Protestant clergy and the Civil War crisis', in Randall M. Miller, Harry S. Stout and Charles Reagan Wilson (eds), *Religion and the American Civil War* (New York: Oxford University Press), p. 115.

12. McKivigan, *War Against Proslavery Religion*, pp. 19, 21; Nye, *William Lloyd Garrison*, pp. 79, 83; Sorin, *Abolitionism*, p. 45; Eugene D. Genovese (1998), 'Religion in the collapse of the American Union', in Miller, Stout and Wilson, *Religion and the American Civil War*, p. 76.

13. Ahlstrom, *Religious History of the American People*, p. 65; Sorin, *Abolitionism*, pp. 49–50.

14. Ahlstrom, *Religious History of the American People*, pp. 650–2.

15. Walters, *American Reformers*, p. 80; McKivigan, *War against Proslavery Religion*, pp. 56–73; Walters, *American Reformers*, pp. 89–90.

16. Drew Gilpin Faust (ed.) (1981), *The Ideology of Slavery: Proslavery Thought in the Antebellum South, 1830–1860* (Baton Rouge: Louisiana University Press), p. 3; McKivigan, *The War against Proslavery Religion*, p. 22; Carwardine, *Evangelicals and Politics in Antebellum America*, pp. 153–4; Phillip Shaw Paludan (1998), 'Religion and the American Civil War', in Miller, Stout and Wilson, *Religion and the American Civil War*, p. 23.

17. Faust, *Ideology of Slavery*, pp. 1–2; Mark A. Noll (1998), 'The Bible and slavery', in Miller, Stout and Wilson, *Religion and the American Civil War*, p. 43.

18. Kenneth S. Greenberg (1996), *Honor and Slavery* (Princeton: Princeton University Press), pp. 110–11; McKivigan, *War against Proslavery Religion*, p. 30; Thomas Virgil Peterson (1978), *Ham and Japeth: The Mythic World of Whites in the Antebellum South* (Metuchen, NJ: Scarecrow Press); Noll, ' Bible and Slavery', pp. 43–4.
19. Carwardine, *Evangelicals and Politics in Antebellum America*, p. 155; Noll, ' Bible and slavery', p. 49; Genovese, 'Religion in the Collapse of the American Union', pp. 74, 77–83.
20. Carwardine, *Evangelicals and Politics in Antebellum America*, pp. 156–8; Bertram Wyatt-Brown (1998), 'Church, honor, and secession', in Miller, Stout and Wilson, *Religion and the American Civil War*, p. 91.
21. See: David D. Chesebrough (1996), *Clergy Dissent in the Old South, 1830–1865* (Carbondale: Southern Illinois University Press); Georgia Lee Tatum (1934), *Disloyalty in the Confederacy* (Chapel Hill: University of North Carolina Press); Carl N. Degler (1974), *The Other South: Southern Dissenters in the Nineteenth Century* (New York: Harper and Row).
22. Ahlstrom, *Religious History of the American People*, p. 657.
23. Carol V. R. George (1997), 'Widening the circle: The Black Church and the Abolitionist Crusade, 1830–1860', in Timothy E. Fulop and Albert J. Raboteau (eds), *African-American Religion: Interpretive Essays in History and Culture* (New York: Routledge), pp. 157–8.
24. Jane H. Pease and William H. Pease (1974), *They Who Would Be Free* (New York: Atheneum), pp. 186–93; George, 'Widening the circle', pp. 159–60.
25. Sorin, *Abolitionism*, pp. 101–2; George, 'Widening the circle', pp. 164–5, 167–9. See also: Benjamin Quarles (1969), *Black Abolitionists* (New York: Oxford University Press).
26. Ahlstrom, *Religious History of the American People*, p. 659.
27. Ibid., p. 659.
28. Davis, *Slavery and Human Progress*, pp. 143–144; McKivigan, *The War Against Proslavery Religion*, p. 13.
29. Louis Filler (1986), *The Crusade against Slavery: Friends, Foes, and Reforms 1820–1860* (Algonac, MI: Reference Publications), p. 154. See also: Bliss Forbush (1956), *Elias Hicks, Quaker Liberal* (New York: Columbia University Press).
30. Filler, *Crusade against Slavery*, p. 158; McKivigan, *War against Proslavery Religion*, pp. 45–6; Carwardine, *Evangelicals and Politics in Antebellum America*, p. 166.
31. Ahlstrom, *Religious History of the American People*, p. 648.
32. Filler, *Crusade against Slavery*, pp. 158–9; Carwardine, *Evangelicals and Politics in Antebellum America*, pp. 167–9.
33. Ahlstrom, *Religious History of the American People*, p. 661.
34. McKivigan, *War against Proslavery Religion*, p. 46; Filler, *Crusade against Slavery*, p. 156.
35. Ahlstrom, *Religious History of the American People*, pp. 161–2; Carwardine, *Evangelicals and Politics in Antebellum America*, pp. 159–60; McKivigan, *War against Proslavery Religion*, pp. 46–7.
36. Carwardine, *Evangelicals and Politics in Antebellum America*, p. 162; Filler, *Crusade against Slavery*, p. 157; McKivigan, *War against Proslavery Religion*, pp. 90–1.
37. Ahlstrom, *Religious History of the American People*, p. 665; Carwardine, *Evangelicals and Politics in Antebellum America*, p.169; Filler, *Crusade against Slavery*, p. 157; McKivigan, *War against Proslavery Religion*, p. 48.

38. Carwardine, *Evangelicals and Politics in Antebellum America*, p. 169.
39. Ahlstrom, *Religious History of the American People*, pp. 664–5; Filler, *Crusade against Slavery*, pp. 157–8; McKivigan, *War against Proslavery Religion*, pp. 87–90.
40. Ahlstrom, *Religious History of the American People*, p. 666; Filler, *Crusade against Slavery*, p. 159; McKivigan, *War against Proslavery Religion*, pp. 48–9.
41. Ahlstrom, *Religious History of the American People*, p. 667.
42. Ibid., p. 667.
43. James Hennesey (1981), *American Catholics: A History of the Roman Catholic Community in the United States* (New York: Oxford University Press), pp. 145–6.
44. Ahlstrom, *Religious History of the American People*, pp. 667–8; Randall M. Miller (1998), 'Catholic Religion, Irish Ethnicity, and the Civil War', in Miller, Stout and Wilson, *Religion and the American Civil War*, p. 263.
45. George, 'Widening the circle', p. 165.
46. William W. Sweet (1950), *The Story of Religion in America* (New York: Harper Ahlstrom, *Religious History of the American People*, p. 673.
47. Ahlstrom, *Religious History of the American People*, p. 672; Sorin, *Abolitionism*, p. 149; McKivigan, *War against Proslavery Religion*, p. 183; Paludan, 'Religion and the American Civil War', p. 28.
48. Henry E. Jacobs (1893), *A History of the Evangelical Lutheran Church in the United States* (New York: Christian Literature Company), p. 452; Thomas C. Johnson (1894), *A History of the Southern Presbyterian Church* (New York: Christian Literature Company), p. 427.
49. Paludan, 'Religion and the American Civil War', p. 24; Ahlstrom, *Religious History of the American People*, p. 677.
50. Daniel D. Williams (1961), 'Tradition and experience in American theology', in James Ward Smith and A. Leland Jamison (eds), *The Shaping of American Religion* (Princeton: Princeton University Press), p. 488.
51. Ahlstrom, *Religious History of the American People*, pp. 682–3.
52. Ibid., p. 684.
53. Ibid., p. 684.
54. Ibid., p. 685.
55. Martin E. Marty (1970), *Righteous Empire: The Protestant Experience in America* (New York: Dial Press), p. 135.
56. Marty, *Righteous Empire*, p. 135.
57. Paludan, 'Religion and the American Civil War', p. 23.
58. Williams, 'Tradition and experience in American theology', pp. 489–90; McKivigan, *War against Proslavery Religion*, p. 115.
59. Williams, 'Tradition and experience in American theology', p. 490; Ahlstrom, *Religious History of the American People*, p. 686.
60. Ronald C. White, Jr (1998), 'Lincoln's Sermon on the Mount: The Second Inaugural', in Miller, Stout and Wilson, *Religion and the American Civil War*, p. 208.
61. Edwin Scott Gaustad (1966), *A Religious History of America* (New York: Harper and Row), pp. 196–7. See Also: William J. Wolf (1959), *The Almost Chosen People: A Study of the Religion of Abraham Lincoln* (Garden City, NY: Doubleday and Co.); White, 'Lincoln's Sermon on the Mount', pp. 208–25.
62. John David Smith (1985), *An Old Creed for the New South: Proslavery Ideology and Historiography, 1865–1918* (Westport, CT: Greenwood Press), p. 7.

63. Smith, *Old Creed for the New South*, pp. 7, 17–99; Paludan, 'Religion and the American Civil War', p. 33.
64. Marty, *Righteous Empire*, pp. 135–6; Paludan, 'Religion and the American Civil War', p. 30.
65. Ahlstrom, *Religious History of the American People*, pp. 691–2.
66. Ibid., pp. 692–3.
67. Marty, *Righteous Empire*, pp. 137–8; McKivigan, *War against Proslavery Religion*, pp. 196–9.
68. Marty, *Righteous Empire*, p. 136; Ahlstrom, *Religious History of the American People*, pp. 695–6; McKivigan, *War against Proslavery Religion*, pp. 198–9.
69. Marty, *Righteous Empire*, pp. 136–7.
70. Ahlstrom, *Religious History of the American People*, p. 696.
71. Ibid., p. 697.
72. Filler, *Crusade against Slavery*, p. 135; McKivigan, *War against Proslavery Religion*, p. 7. See also: C. C. Goen (1985), *Broken Churches, Broken Nation: Denominational Schisms and the American Civil War* (Macon, GA: Mercer University Press).
73. Marty, *Righteous Empire*, pp. 138–9.
74. Ibid., p. 144.
75. Fredrickson, ' Coming of the Lord', p. 124.

Recommended Readings

Barnes, Gilbert H. (1933), *The Anti-Slavery Impulse, 1830–1844*, rpt 1964 New York: Harcourt, Brace and World.
Carwardine, Richard J. (1993), *Evangelicals and Politics in Antebellum America*, New Haven: Yale University Press.
Cash, Wilbur J. (1941), *The Mind of the South*, New York: Alfred Knopf.
Chesebrough, David D. (1996), *Clergy Dissent in the Old South, 1830–1865*, Carbondale: Southern Illinois University Press.
Chesebrough, David D. (ed.) (1991),'*God Ordained This War': Sermons on the Sectional Crisis, 1830–1865.* Columbia: University of South Carolina Press.
Cole, Charles C. Jr. (1954), *The Social Ideas of the Northern Evangelists, 1826–1860*, New York: Columbia University Press.
Davis, David Brion (1973), *The Problem of Slavery in Western Culture*, Ithaca, NY: Cornell University Press.
Davis, David Brion (1984), *Slavery and Human Progress*, New York: Oxford University Press.
Davis, David Brion (1998), *The Problem of Slavery in the Age of Revolution, 1770–1823*, 2nd edn, New York: Oxford University Press.
Degler, Carl N. (1974), *The Other South: Southern Dissenters in the Nineteenth Century*, New York: Harper and Row.
Faust, Drew Gilpin (ed.). (1981), *The Ideology of Slavery: Proslavery Thought in the Antebellum South*, 1830–1860, Baton Rouge: Louisiana University Press.
Filler, Louis. (1986), *The Crusade against Slavery: Friends, Foes, and Reforms 1820–1860*, Algonac, MI: Reference Publications.
Fulop, Timothy E., and Albert J. Raboteau (eds). (1997), *African-American Religion: Interpretive Essays in History and Culture*, New York: Routledge.

Genovese, Eugene D. (1998), *A Consuming Fire: The Fall of the Confederacy in the Mind of the White Christian South*, Athens: University of Georgia Press.

Goen, C. C. (1985), *Broken Churches, Broken Nation: Denominational Schisms and the American Civil War*, Macon, GA: Mercer University Press.

Greenberg, Kenneth S. (1996), *Honor and Slavery*, Princeton: Princeton University Press.

McKittrick, Eric L. (ed.). (1963), *Slavery Defended: The Views of the Old South*, Englewood Cliffs, NJ: Prentice Hall.

McKivigan, John R. (1984), *The War against Proslavery Religion: Abolitionism and the Northern Churches, 1830–1865*, Ithaca, NY: Cornell University Press.

Mathews, Donald G. (1965), *Slavery and Methodism: A Chapter in American Morality, 1780–1845*, Princeton: Princeton University Press.

Mathews, Donald G. (1972), *Religion in the Old South*, Chicago: University of Chicago Press.

Miller, Randall M., Harry S. Stout, and Charles Reagan Wilson (eds). (1998), *Religion and the American Civil War*, New York: Oxford University Press.

Nye, Russel B. William (1955), *Lloyd Garrison and the Humanitarian Reformers*, Boston: Little, Brown and Company.

Peterson, Thomas Virgil. (1978), *Ham and Japeth: The Mythic World of Whites in the Antebellum South*, Metuchen, NJ: Scarecrow Press.

Quarles, Benjamin. (1969), *Black Abolitionists*, New York: Oxford University Press.

Scherer, Lester B. (1975), *Slavery and the Churches in Early America, 1619–1819*, Grand Rapids, MI: Eerdmans.

Smith, John David. (1985), *An Old Creed for the New South: Proslavery Ideology and Historiography, 1865–1918*, Westport, CT: Greenwood Press.

Smith, Timothy L. (1957), *Revivalism and Social Reform: American Protestantism on the Eve of the Civil War*, rpt 1965, New York: Harper and Row.

Soderlund, Jean R. (1985), *Quakers and Slavery: A Divided Spirit*, Princeton: Princeton University Press.

Sorin, Gerald, (1972), *Abolitionism: A New Perspective*, New York: Praeger Publishers.

Staudenraus, Philip J. (1961), *The African Colonization Movement, 1816–1865*, New York: Columbia University Press.

Stewart, James Brewer. (1996), *Holy Warriors: The Abolitionists and American Slavery*, New York: Hill and Wang.

Swift, David. (1989), *Black Prophets of Justice: Activist Clergy before the Civil War*, Baton Rouge: Louisiana State University Press.

Tatum, Georgia Lee. (1934), *Disloyalty in the Confederacy*, Chapel Hill: University of North Carolina Press.

Walters, Ronald G. (1976), *The Antislavery Appeal: American Abolitionism after 1830*. Baltimore, MD: Johns Hopkins University Press.

Walters, Ronald G. (1978), *American Reformers, 1815–1860*, New York: Hill and Wang.

Wolf, William J. (1959), *The Almost Chosen People: A Study of the Religion of Abraham Lincoln*, Garden City, NY: Doubleday and Company.

Epilogue

The most significant trends in the history of religion in America have been growth, diversity and adaptation – the continued increase in the percentage of Americans who take part in organized religion, a similarly dramatic increase in the number and variety of denominations they choose to join, and the adaptation of those denominations to the ever-changing circumstances in which they find themselves. This was especially true in the period ending with the Civil War. As that period drew to a close, however, religion in America entered into another important phase of its development; it followed the nation in its transition from an agrarian society into a market-driven society. Many believed then, as they do now, that the nation lost its soul in the process, and there is some evidence for this. But, not coincidentally, membership in churches grew at an unprecedented rate – from 17 per cent of Americans in 1776 to 37 per cent in 1860. The result was a second establishment, the first having been destroyed by the First Amendment and subsequent state legislation. It was an informal establishment, to be sure, marked by the rise of new denominations – Methodists and Baptists, most notably – at the expense of a few of the older ones, but the effect was the same: a kind of pan-Protestant hegemony over American society and culture.[1]

Commercial culture, also referred to as the market place of culture, is problematic as it relates to religion. Religion is inseparably tied to mystery, miracle and mysticism. Nonetheless, when examined in terms of human actions and human organization, it is a valid concept. As R. Laurence Moore has written:

> I do not think it perverse to suggest that contemporary religion operates in the marketplace of culture under the purest rules of *laissez-faire* left extant in our 'modern' state. Government regulators and tax people put it in a separate category and try to ignore it. No

one dares suggest that neon signs blinking the message that 'Jesus Saves' may be false advertising.[2]

The British economist Adam Smith, often cited as the father of modern capitalism, made the point in 1776. But Roger Finke and Rodney Stark put it most directly when they argued more recently that 'religious economies are like commercial economies in that they consist of a market made up of a set of current and potential customers and a set of firms seeking to serve that market'. In the commercial world success depends on factors related to organizational structures, sales representatives, the product and marketing. The religious equivalents are polity, clergy, doctrine and evangelization techniques.[3]

It might be argued that in the most measurably objective terms, the great age of religion in the United States was not the seventeenth century, however remarkable the theological inventiveness of the Puritans, but the nineteenth century. Christianity was carried in all of its forms, including some newly invented ones, across an expanding nation. The people in the South, both black and white, went from being the least religious folk in the nation to arguably the most religious. Everywhere, church membership rose from a small plurality of people to a majority. At the same time a number of cultural commodities were marketed, many of which were promoted as being helpful, or even essential, to people wishing to be seen as cultured. The obvious items on this list included art, literature and theatre; not so obvious was religion.[4]

Religion's role in the market place of culture began in the nineteenth century as an effort to influence and in some cases to ban the commodities being offered for sale in the market place. Protestant censorship efforts were intended to exert an independent control over the types of cultural items and activities that became available for consumption. In those endeavours they extended the hand of cooperation to all lay people – other elites, middle- and upper-class reformers and even the state – who shared their values.[5]

Rather than merely playing the role of censor, however, religious leaders made their own contributions to the market place of culture. They looked for ways to appeal to all consumers using the techniques of advertising and publicity employed by other merchants. They even created interdenominational non-profit organizations with moral and reform goals that competed with other forms of popular entertainment, and by degrees, as Moore has shown, religion itself took on the shape of

EPILOGUE   193

a commodity. Religious leaders, in order to 'make religion popular',
understood that they had 'to compete in a morally neutral and volun-
taristic marketplace environment alongside all the goods and services of
this world'.[6]

The environment of competition among denominations created by
the separation of church and state accelerated the market rationale.
Religious institutions became consumer commodities, and much of their
activity – otherwise labelled religious activity – became dominated by
the logic of market economies. When religion could no longer be
defined by legal privilege, it had to sell itself not only in the competitive
church market but also in a general market of other cultural commodities that were trying in many cases to break free of religious control.
The wonder, then, is not that under the circumstances religion entered
the cultural market place, but the skill with which religious leaders
negotiated their new environment, indeed the aggressively leading role
that religion played in shaping society and culture.[7] In the few pages
that remain, we will take a look at one major example, literature, and
note a few others in passing.

The Antebellum Book Market

The social and political position of the American clergy changed
dramatically from the seventeenth to the nineteenth century, especially
in New England which led the nation into the cultural market place. As
late as 1740 clergymen constituted 70 per cent of all learned profes-
sionals in Massachusetts. By 1800 that figure had been cut to 45 per cent.
Lacking the apparatus of an established church, this diminished cultural
elite could no longer control public opinion as they once had; neither
could they control the burgeoning commercial publishing houses capi-
talizing on the significantly increased rate of literacy among Americans.
Accurate information on literacy rates in antebellum America is difficult
to find, but, according to the census of 1840, literacy was widespread. In
Connecticut, for example, only 1 in 574 were unable to read or write.
The result was an explosion of newspapers, magazines and books of
fiction and nonfiction for the mass market.[8]

The clergy responded by first trying to limit, on moral grounds, and
then to enter, the market place of reading culture. Religious societies
founded specifically to spread the message of Christianity demonstrated
the possibilities of the new print technology, showing the way for profit-
making applications. Ministers became authors, not only of devotional

material with greater popular appeal but also of books that competed directly with other forms of fiction. In time they even wrote fiction, doing their best to give a religious and moral tone even to print material that did not emanate from the clerical camp or have its approval.[9]

Nathan Hatch has identified the transformation of the religious press as a central theme in the growth of popular literature in the Early Republic, to wit he discusses the millions of tracts, pamphlets, hymn books and devotional books, and religious journals, magazines and newspapers that resulted. The first major effort to distribute attractive devotional literature came from the American Tract Society, which resulted from the merger in 1825 of some forty smaller societies. Another was the American Bible Society, founded in 1816. By 1828 the American Tract Society printed over 5 million items for distribution. The American Bible Society by the end of the 1820s was producing 300,000 editions each year, making it quite likely the largest publisher in the United States in terms of number of volumes published annually, and among the top two or three in annual cash receipts.[10]

The mass production of relatively cheap material held out great promise for turning daily newspapers, magazines and serial fiction into major growth industries. *Godey's Lady's Book* was among the most successful of those ventures, but religious publishers pioneered in innovative ways to use this medium to their ends. As early as 1830 the Methodist weekly *Christian Advocate and Journal* claimed a circulation of 25,000, a figure much larger than that of any other American serial. The *Christian Advocate* aimed at being 'a good, virtuous well-conducted newspaper', but it succeeded because it was livelier than most of the competition. In the years between 1800 and 1820 the number of subscribers to all religious periodicals grew from 5000 to around 400,000.[11]

Formats and content were adjusted to appeal to large numbers of Americans with diverse interests. The American Tract Society advertised its material as short, interesting, striking, clear, plain, pungent and entertaining, which was the way secular publishers of popular literature described what they had to offer. They published titles specifically for young people and hired some of the nation's best artists and engravers to add illustrations.[12]

The American Tract Society may have drawn the line at publishing fiction – which they feared would give readers pleasure by appealing to the free play of their imagination – but others would cross that line and quite successfully. An increasing number of religious leaders found some novels acceptable and even wrote novels themselves. Avoiding whatever they thought might appeal to the prurient imagination, they copied the narrative style of the truthful tale, leaving in some of the adventure but deleting the sensationalism. They were so moral, one critic wrote, that it is difficult to distinguish the appeal of novels written by these authors and that of the 'authentic' stories written by others. Samuel Goodrich, author of the 'Peter Parley' books, was particularly adept and successful. Goodrich sold some 7 million volumes from the mid-1820s until the mid-1850s.[13]

Particularly successful in the second quarter of the nineteenth century was fiction aimed at, and often written by, women. Women constituted a growing consumer group of popular literature, as well as other forms of popular culture, largely because of the moral force such works assigned to women and their newfound alliance with clergy as moral arbiters of the cultural market place. Bad men either stood outside the story or worked their will on peripheral characters. Good men were included to effect a marriage but were largely irrelevant to the moral development of the heroines. Warning their flock about 'trashy, infidel, licentious romances', clergy seized upon and supported this sort of fiction, thereby enhancing its success in the literary market place. By far the most successful minister of the period to try his hand at this type of fiction was Joseph Holt Ingraham. Throughout the 1840s, Ingraham – an Episcopal minister – produced between ten and twenty-five novels annually, accounting for 10 percent of the fiction titles published in the United States in that decade.[14]

Some Other Examples of Religion in the Market place of Culture

Other products resulting from the entrance of religion into the market place of culture were the theatre and the lyceum, as well as programmes for the organized use of leisure time. The effective and entertaining use of the spoken word was demonstrated in the religious revivals of the eighteenth and nineteenth centuries. George Whitefield attracted large crowds through the dramatic power of his words, as did Peter Cartwright a half-century later. The revivals and camp meetings of the nineteenth century, however, became social, as well as spiritual, events. People attended meetings not just to be saved, but also for camaraderie, diversion from routine and relaxation from their daily labours – making revivalism a major force in American religion, and a segue to the increased popularity and acceptability of theatre in America.

During the early years of the nineteenth century, the theatre attracted what has been termed the lowminded, including labourers and prostitutes as well as the wellborn and highminded. The former often responded to the actors and characters on stage by shouting obscenities, catcalling and throwing objects. The latter, joined by religious leaders, deemed the former dangerous. At first religious leaders urged good people to stay away, but when that proved ineffective they worked with theatre owners to guarantee them a 'respectable' audience. Religious leaders and other like-minded elites became patrons of the theatre, and they 'pacified' theatrical audiences by encouraging owners to offer serious, moral, didactic drama. In return they pledged to forego preaching that going to the theatre was a sin, and even promoted it as a useful and wholesome practice, thereby increasing, or at least 'improving', theatre audiences. Audiences of the 'common sort' abandoned such theatres for their own playhouses, which cultural elites continued to condemn, or avoided the theatre altogether.[15]

The lyceum became a prominent cultural institution in the first half of the nineteenth century, especially in New England. In effect, it was another area of oral performance in which religion and commercialization both played important roles. Lyceums were organized to promote the spread of practical information. Because their sponsors wished to avoid controversy, lyceums banished from the podium any form of religious proselytizing that favoured one denomination over another. Such a consciously imposed rule of non-sectarianism, however, was difficult to clearly define and enforce, especially when speakers proposed to address moral issues that transcended denominational boundaries.[16]

Although the institution began in Britain, the American lyceum was a derivative cultural institution that encouraged lectures rooted stylistically in the colonial sermon, buttressed by revivalism. By the 1840s, however, lyceum performances were becoming more commercialized and more dependent on advertising. A network of individuals offered talks on a variety of subjects and commanded high fees. They had to be entertaining, by nineteenth century standards, but morality or virtue remained a staple in their repertoire. The lyceum became a perfect meeting ground for religion and commercial culture, and lyceum lectures the most common venue for religious expression outside the church. Overt references to religion, much like politics, were shunned, but what passed for non-sectarian under its sponsorship actually included a good bit of Protestant creed. Speakers referred to God, Jesus, Christian redemption, an afterlife where good and evil were punished and the authority of the Bible, though always being sure to reflect non-controversial, consensus ideas related to each and to avoid reference to any particular denomination, save as a point of comparison, usually negative, to Roman Catholicism, for example. In so doing, lyceum speakers gave Americans a sense of shared ideals.[17]

Finally, nineteenth-century Americans were learning to play, and, by the middle of the century, religious leaders recognized the need to pay more attention to the way people amused themselves. Colonial clergy more often denounced, or frowned upon, leisure, insisting that all uses of time had to serve the purpose of religious devotion and self-improvement. Nineteenth-century clergy continued to stress the theme of redemptive work and to denounce licentious leisure-time activities such as gambling and consumption of alcohol, but they also abandoned their antipathy to all forms of leisure and, as they did in each of the areas noted above, offered their suggestions as to how leisure might in fact be not only enjoyable but beneficial.[18]

In 1846 the Reverend Henry Ward Beecher made a list of amusements proscribed by Protestants in his popular *Lectures to Young Men*: no shooting matches; no taverns; no reading of novels, newspapers and almanacs; no drinking, gambling, smoking or swearing; no theatre-going; no card-playing or dancing; no attendance at balls, race tracks or circuses. Beecher's list was already dated, however, as each pastime became part of a growing market in leisure activities and play gained a new prominence among all social ranks.[19]

For religious leaders the important point was to combine amusement with education and 'moral uplift'. And, not surprisingly, much like literature and the theatre, rather than remaining a philanthropic enterprise, their efforts became a business venture that competed in the market place of culture. p. T. Barnum is a case in point. At first a sales agent for *Sears' Pictorial Illustration of the Bible*, he went on to become one of the most successful entrepreneurs in the entertainment industry. Purchasing Charles Willson Peale's New York branch of his Philadelphia Museum and John Scudder's American Museum in New York City, Barnum transformed these earlier decidedly educational, and therefore respectable, ventures into commercial successes. While on the one hand, especially early on, criticizing Protestant clergy who condemned popular forms of entertainment in general, on the other he established as his formula for success that which he openly espoused and more or less strove to meet, family entertainment, whereby he would provide men, women and children with morally wholesome entertainment in a morally safe environment. It was an approach with which religious leaders could not quarrel.[20]

Another response to the leisure-time issue of play was what would be called in the late nineteenth century 'muscular Christianity' – drawing its name from the belief that Protestantism was coming under the control of women and effete ministers and therefore losing its effectiveness among the men and boys of the nation. It got its start in the antebellum period, especially with the Young Men's Christian Association (YMCA). Proponents of the YMCA strove to legitimate leisure at the same time that it tried to maintain an equal distance from the lures of commercial entertainments and from denominational religious worship. Started in England, the YMCA organized its first American branches in Boston and New York City in the early 1850s. The controlling or voting members of the YMCA chapters were men who belonged to evangelical Protestant churches. Nonetheless, they wanted to serve all young men, regardless of their denominational affiliation. Sponsors – lay civic leaders tied to mainstream Protestant denominations – reflected the values of that religious tradition, but they also tried to limit any formal expression of those values to non-sectarian terms.[21]

YMCA locals sought indirect ways to exert moral influence, ways that paid less attention to dramatic conversion experiences and more attention to a gradually acquired set of associations that Horace Bushnell, a major liberalizing influence in the Protestant clergy, said were essential to successful 'Christian Nurture'.[22]

Summary

Antebellum entrepreneurs of commercial culture promised a product that would raise the quality of life in the United States. Clerics were sceptical, but when breast-beating over the decline of the power and effectiveness of their sermons became ineffective they entered the market place as well. As such they contributed to commercial culture and enjoyed considerable success in the process. Even though many religious leaders continued to criticize the culture industry and sought to regulate it, religion joined other commodities on the shelves of culture.[23]

Religion is much more than a commodity, but in the nineteenth century in many respects that is exactly what it became. Then, and now, Americans wondered whether religion was rendered less effective by the process of commercialization. Increased numbers of churched Americans, meaning those with actual church affiliations, suggest that Adam Smith was right when he argued that to the degree that religion is left unregulated it will thrive – or, to put it another way, that religious monopolies, or establishments, are counter productive.[24] But were such increases exclusively the result of the success of religion in the commercial market place? Did those numbers reflect a comparable increase in religiosity or spirituality, or did they mark a decline in acceptance of traditional religious doctrine and the onset of secularization? Such questions would become even more urgent in years to come.

Notes

1. Phillip Shaw Paludan (1998), 'Religion and the American Civil War', in Randall M. Miller, Harry S. Stout and Charles Reagan Wilson (eds), *Religion and the American Civil War* (New York: Oxford University Press), p. 21; Roger Finke and Rodney Stark (1994), *The Churching of America 1776–1990: Winners and Losers in Our Religious Economy* (New Brunswick, NJ: Rutgers University Press), pp. 1–2, 15.

2. R. Laurence Moore (1994), *Selling God: American Religion in the Marketplace of Culture* (New York: Oxford University Press), p. 7; Finke and Stark, *Churching of America*, p. 5.

3. Adam Smith (1976), *An Inquiry into the Nature and Causes of the Wealth of Nations*, ed. W.B. Todd , 2 vols (Oxford: Clarendon Press), 2: pp. 788–814; Finke and Stark, *Churching of America*, p. 17.

4. Moore, *Selling God*, pp. 5, 10.

5. Moore, *Selling God*, p. 6; Richard Butsch (1990), 'Introduction: Leisure and hegemony in America', in Richard Butsch (ed.), *For Fun and Profit: The Transformation of Leisure into Consumption* (Philadelphia: Temple University Press), pp. 12–13.

6. Moore, *Selling God*, pp. 6–7; Finke and Stark, *Churching of America*, p. 4; Harry S. Stout (1991), *The Divine Dramatist: George Whitefield and the Rise of Modern Evangelicalism* (Grand Rapids, MI: W. B. Eerdmans), p. xvii; Catherine A. Brekus (1998), *Strangers and Pilgrims: Female Preaching in America, 1740–1845* (Chapel Hill: University of North Carolina Press), p. 12.

7. Peter Berger (1967), *The Sacred Canopy: Elements of a Sociological Theory of Religion* (Garden City, NY: Doubleday), p. 138; Moore, *Selling God*, pp. 7, 11.

8. James H. Dormon (1967), *Theater in the Antebellum South, 1815–1861* (Chapel Hill: University of North Carolina Press), pp. 33–5; Nathan O. Hatch (1989), *The Democratization of American Christianity* (New Haven: Yale University Press), p. 125; Ann Douglas (1988), *The Feminization of American Culture* (New York: Anchor Press), p. 17.

9. Moore, *Selling God*, p. 17.

10. Hatch, *Democratization of American Christianity*, p. 141; Lawrance Thompson (1941), 'Printing and publishing activities of the American Tract Society from 1825 to 1850', *Papers of the Bibliographical Society of America*, 35 (Second Quarter): 81–114.

11. Hatch, *Democratization of American Christianity*, p. 141; Moore, *Selling God*, p. 19.

12. Moore, *Selling God*, p. 20.

13. Douglas, *Feminization of American Culture*, pp. 31, 113–14; Moore, *Selling God*, pp. 20, 25. See also: Joan J. Brumberg (1980), *Mission for Life: The Story of the Family of Adoniram Judson, the Dramatic Events of the First American Foreign Mission, and the Course of Evangelical Religion in the Nineteenth Century* (New York: Free Press); Anne Scott MacLeod (1975), *A Moral Tale: Children's Fiction and American Culture, 1820–1860* (New York: Anchor Books).

14. Douglas, *Feminization of American Culture*, chap. 2, pp. 113–114; Kathy Peiss (1990), 'Commercial leisure and the Woman Question,' in Butsch, *For Fun and Profit*, pp. 105–17; James p. Hart (1950), *The Popular Book: A History of America's Literary Taste* (Berkeley: University of California Press), pp. 98–9. See also: David S. Reynolds (1981), *Faith in Fiction: The Emergence of Religious Literature in America* (Cambridge, MA: Harvard University Press); Robert W. Weathersby (1980), *Joseph Scott Ingraham* (Boston: Twayne Publishers).

15. Moore, *Selling God*, pp. 53, 55, 56; Dorman, *Theater in the Antebellum South*, p. 270; Neil Harris (1981), *Humbug: The Art of P. T. Barnum* (Chicago: University of Chicago Press), p. 107; Bruce A. McConachie (1990), 'Pacifying American theatrical audiences, 1820–1900', in Butsch, *For Fun and Profit*, pp. 47, 49–51.

16. Moore, *Selling God*, p. 56.

17. Carl Bode (1968), *The American Lyceum: Town Meeting of the Mind* (Carbondale: Southern Illinois University Press), chaps. 1–3; Donald M. Scott (1980), 'The public lecture and the creation of a public in mid-nineteenth century America', *Journal of American History*, 66 (March): 808–9. See also: Donald M. Scott (1986), 'Itinerant lecturers and lecturing in New England, 1800–1850', in Peter Benes (ed.), *Itinerancy in New England and New York* (Boston: Boston University Press), pp. 65–75.

18. Moore, *Selling God*, p. 93.

19. Ibid., pp. 95–6, 99.

20. Harris, *Humbug*, pp. 29, 36–41, 79, 107–8, 210. See also: Charles Coleman Sellers (1980), *Mr. Peale's Museum: Charles Willson Peale and the First Popular Museum of Natural Science* (New York: Norton); P. T. Barnum (1927; 1981), *Struggles and Triumphs or, Forty Years' Recollections*, ed. Carl Bode (New York: Alfred A. Knopf); Bluford Adams (1977), *E. Pluribus Barnum: The Great Showman and the Making of U.S. Popular Culture* (Minneapolis: University of Minnesota Press).

21. See: George Sherwood Eddy (1944), *A Century with Youth: A History of the YMCA from 1844 to 1944* (New York: Association Press); C. Howard Hopkins (1951), *History of the YMCA in North America* (New York: Association Press); Paul Boyer (1978), *Urban Masses and Moral Order in America, 1820–1920* (Cambridge, MA: Harvard University Press); Samuel Wirt Wiley (1944), *History of the YMCA–Church Relations in the United States* (New York: Association Press); Mayer H. Zald (1970), *Organizational Change: The Political Economy of the YMCA* (Chicago: University of Chicago Press).

22. Moore, *Selling God*, pp. 113–14.

23. Ibid., p. 268.

24. Smith, *Inquiry into the Nature and Causes of the Wealth of Nations*, 2: pp. 788–814.

Recommended Readings

Adams, Bluford. E. (1977), *Pluribus Barnum: The Great Showman and the Making of U.S. Popular Culture*, Minneapolis: University of Minnesota Press.

Bode, Carl (1960), *The Anatomy of American Popular Culture*, 1840–1861, Berkeley: University of California Press.

Bode, Carl (1968), *The American Lyceum: Town Meeting of the Mind*, Carbondale: Southern Illinois University Press.

Boyer, Paul (1978), *Urban Masses and Moral Order in America, 1820–1920*, Cambridge, MA: Harvard University Press.

Brekus, Catherine A. (1998), *Strangers and Pilgrims: Female Preaching in America, 1740–1845*, Chapel Hill: University of North Carolina Press.

Butsch, Richard (1990), *For Fun and Profit: The Transformation of Leisure into Consumption*, Philadelphia: Temple University Press.

Denney, Reuel (1957), *The Astonished Muse*, Chicago: University of Chicago Press.

Dorman, James H. (1967), *Theater in the Antebellum South, 1815–1861*, Chapel Hill: University of North Carolina Press.

Douglas, Ann (1988), *The Feminization of American Culture*, New York: Anchor Press.

Dulles, Foster Rhea (1965), *A History of Recreation: America Learns to Play*, Englewood Cliffs, NJ: Prentice Hall.

Eddy, George Sherwood (1944), *A Century with Youth: A History of the YMCA from 1844 to 1944*, New York: Association Press.

Finke, Roger and Rodney Stark (1994), *The Churching of America 1776–1990: Winners and Losers in Our Religious Economy*, New Brunswick, NJ: Rutgers University Press.

Gilmore, Michael T. (1985), *American Romanticism and the Marketplace*, Chicago: University of Chicago Press.

Grimsted, David (1968), *Melodrama Unveiled: American Theater and Culture, 1800–1850*, Chicago: University of Chicago Press.

Halttunen, Karen (1982), *Confidence Men and Painted Women: A Study of Middle-Class Culture in America, 1830–1870*, New Haven: Yale University Press.

Harris, Neil (1981), *Humbug: The Art of P. T. Barnum*, Chicago: University of Chicago Press.

Hart, James p. (1950), *The Popular Book: A History of America's Literary Taste*, Berkeley: University of California Press.

Hatch, Nathan O. (1989), *The Democratization of American Christianity*, New Haven: Yale University Press.

Hopkins. C. Howard (1951), *History of the YMCA in North America*, New York: Association Press.

Levine, Lawrence (1988), *Highbrow/Lowbrow: The Emergence of Cultural Heritage in America*, Cambridge, MA: Harvard University Press.

MacLeod, Anne Scott (1975), *A Moral Tale: Children's Fiction and American Culture, 1820–1860*, New York: Anchor Books.

Moore, R. Laurence (1994), *Selling God: American Religion in the Marketplace of Culture*, New York: Oxford University Press.

Nye, Russel B. (1970), *The Unembarrassed Muse: The Popular Arts in America*, New York: Dial Press.

Reynolds, David S. (1981), *Faith in Fiction: The Emergence of Religious Literature in America*, Cambridge, MA: Harvard University Press.

Rodgers, Daniel T. (1978), *The Work Ethic in Industrial America, 1850–1920*, Chicago: University of Chicago Press.

Rosenzweig, Roy (1983), *Eight Hours for What We Will: Workers and Leisure in an Industrial City*, 1870–1920, New York: Cambridge University Press.

Index